A DOG,

A CAT,

AND

A CROW!

The very real and heart-catching story about a boy and his truly amazing, real-life, feathered and furry friends

BY
EDWIN K. DANOWSKI

PublishAmerica
Baltimore

Softcover 1-60563-352-6
PAperback 978-1-4512-5616-1
PUBLISHED BY PUBLISHAMERICA, LLLP
www.publishamerica.com
Baltimore

Printed in the United States of America

A DOG,

A CAT,

AND

A CROW!

The very real and heart-catching story about a boy and his truly amazing, real-life, feathered and furry friends

BY
EDWIN K. DANOWSKI

DEDICATION

This story is first dedicated to the God who made all of us and His Son who taught us what love really is.

It is dedicated to Mother Theresa. She walked the walk in her daily living—a recent example of what human love is and can be. She never asked, "What about me?" Her's was a legacy of finding Christ in the poor and caring for them with all of her heart.

Mother Theresa's life and work are very meaningful to me because the story you are about to read happened when my family was emerging from a period when we had few material things and struggled daily for life's necessities. Yet, it was also a period of our lives where we learned to appreciate the little things and the joy and love they can bring and we can give to each other.

It was a time of sharing and caring—the value of which will always leave their message in my heart.

It was a time when I also learned the value of rising again and again—to push forward each time you stumbled and fell—and that the value was in rising again, starting again and never ever quitting. All one needs to do is make the effort, what ever it takes, and reach out to God. Recognize His willingness to help. He is always there. One needs to totally trust in Him because the roads you travel and the stops along the way may or may not be the ones you hoped for or planed. He is the master at helping you from where you are to where He wants you to be—if you accept Him and let Him!

Trust in Him—is the most solid foundation from which to seek— and the surest path to find—true Hope!

If God adds what He wills and we add what we can—there is no telling where this combination can go.

It is dedicated to my entire family—my wife Mardell, each of our children who have enjoyed elements of this story over the years, their spouses, our grandchildren and the generations to come. It is dedicated to our Godchildren and friends.

This is a true story from a special time back 1950's. It is particularly special to me because I shared it with my brothers Jim and Jerry and my sisters Judy and Jan and our mom, Eleanor, and dad, Eddie. It is dedicated to them and their families.

I dedicate this story to all who take the time to know God's creatures and pray they may all experience and get to know the special joy and meaning that God's special creatures can add to their lives.

It is also dedicated to four of God's unique and wonderful living characters, both furry and feathered who each enhanced the memories of our family and for what they taught us, shared with us and added to our lives.

I do not think that God limited the potential to love to humans alone. I believe He is far more generous than that. There is a very important quote in scriptures about how God felt about the birds in the sky and, therefore, how He feels about each of us!

I hope everyone will take some time to encounter and experience the unique and special traits and personalities that each of God's creatures truly have. It can be special if you take the time to know them and to help some of them to get to know you. May those who try—find the ways to translate this into what it means in terms of relationships, at a higher level, with each and every member of the human race.

The next time you see a crow fly or sit in a tree, think about the one you are about to meet here—how he played and strutted or teased. Wonder at the personality of this unique bird, or other creatures you chance to meet everyday. Marvel at what may be going on in their heads—and what they could share with you if only you could invest enough time and enough effort to get to really know them. Think of how each is matchless—so very different. Reflect on how, despite their differences, they allowed beautiful relationships to form.

The personalities of the creatures you are about to meet were each truly unique. Even more so, then, are we. God doesn't lump us all together. He knows each of us—our each and every nuance, our strengths, our nicks and scratches and where and how we shine. Even when others don't notice the value in us—God does.

The beauty is—God never stops forgiving and never stops loving us under any conditions—never! God loves us all—for all time—with no conditions—each and every one! If we see Jesus daily in the face of every one we meet—man, woman and child—black, brown, yellow, white—healthy or disabled, young or old and we find the goodness of His love in all creatures—then we may know and experience more of who He is and what He is like.

If we search Him out—then we have more of a chance to be like Him. We are made in His image. The more we take the time to understand who He is, the more we can truly follow Him!

I dedicate my book also to John Paul II who lived what he talked— a great example to all of us with what we say and then pray for the help so that we make it match with what we do! He reached out to all peoples as we too should do by loving others as we love ourselves!

LOOK UP

Soft, black velvet wings unfurled in the breeze—as serenely, effortlessly, the crow circled with specific intent and cautiously started his decent.

Gently, purposefully he slowed his approach as he gracefully landed with the softness of a kitten on a pillow.

His feet delicately sidestepped from the edge of the youngster's shoulder closer to the nape of the young man's neck.

There he paused and leaned forward positioning his beak near the boy's ear. He made strange guttural sounds as if he was trying to whisper something in the human's own language.

The boy listened and the crow continued his efforts at conversation.

Over and over again the young bird majestically soared and peacefully, evenly glided over the fields of Oak Creek, Wisconsin near the winding Root River.

That is where this story began—in a very rustic, sprawling country setting. Here it was possible for four creatures, so unique and so varied in heritage, to meet for the first time.

Their rendezvous was the prelude to some very intriguing and unusual things.

OAK CREEK

What if you are too young to drive a car and there's no one to take you where you want to go?

What if it's a long way to walk or to pedal your bike just to get to the home of any of your friends?

Heck, what if your best friend lived 5 miles away?

What if you can't just hop on a bus to go see your best pal or go to the movies, or the shopping centers or the playgrounds?

Buses do not run in the country!

That's the way I discovered Oak Creek at age nine. We had just moved a half hours drive by car from my old home in South Milwaukee.

If you're starting to feel sorry for me—don't! Life wasn't even slightly dull!

Five kids in our family kept any of us from feeling alone. From oldest to youngest my brothers and sisters are Jim, Judy, Jerry, Jan. I'm the first born of the lot.

Most folks call me Ed. Yet, some of my dad's family called me Sonny. Confusing? Probably so! Yet most of dad's family didn't want both of us to come running whenever they called our name. His name was Ed too.

We found so much to do. We weren't magicians! We just used our imaginations!

Doggone it; most backyards were bigger than a whole city block.

Think about what that means!

We could run out the back door and hit a baseball as far as we wanted. We even had our own baseball diamond and backstop in the backyard. Hey, we had our own football field too.

A basketball hoop towered high above the back of a chicken coop challenging those who dared! There were lots of battles with game after game of H O R S E. Dad would drive us crazy with his old two handed set shot!

Special! You bet!

Wide open spaces and I do mean wide open!

Large wooded areas dotted the landscape near the back of the property lines. They were loaded with wild flowers and mushrooms in the spring!

Abundant wildlife of all kinds, with their young, roamed those fields and woods early in the year.

That's not to mention the hidden ponds and trickling streams.

Great places—yes they were perfect for exploring, imaginary games and hide and seek.

A winding river coursed nearby cloaking an interesting array of fish from view. They swam under the dark waters in all sizes. Imaginations raced! Wild speculation readily generated exciting images in your mind every time something potentially awesome suddenly tugged hard on the end of your line. Runaway hopeful expectations magnified while the struggling fish yanked with all its might and was still submerged under the surface hidden from view.

Hours of anticipation were there anytime you wanted. Unbelievable fun poised waiting for anyone who hooked one of these gems on their fishing pole. Shady trees, along the water's banks concealed you and your thoughts from view like a hideaway.

Nobody—that's right; no one knew your secret spots except you!

Clear skies teased the night's abounding aggregate of flickering, shimmering stars to glisten brighter on a special stage—free from the glare of city lights! Plus you saw so many more of them out there— multiplying and enhancing nightfall's special splendor!

Quiet solitude beckoned the harmonizing of millions of crickets and other nocturnal creatures!

Sensational!

It's a great place at eventide to have nice bright, warm, sparkling, glowing bonfires complete with roasting, sizzling hot dogs and crispy, melting, gooey marshmallows at the end of a singed, freshly cleaned stick.

Good tasty smells emanated from scrumptious popping popcorn snapping over the flames.

The evening air carried their sounds like the crackling of so many tiny fire crackers! Neighbors never complained. They were too far away!

Fresh air for the lungs!

Hey, you could have as many friends over as you wanted—there was enough room.

You used your bike a lot to get to their place too!

They also had lots of room.

All of this was there not to mention each other—family that is!

We also had pets we wouldn't dream of trying to raise in the city. However, more about that later!

There was a lot to do indoors too!

One of my hobbies as a young person was to invent games for my brothers and sisters to play during the winter months.

I continued inventing them as an adult including several games I sold—one about dinosaurs and another "Fling" you played in the dark. There was also a golf game that appeared in a magazine and another glow in the dark activity that is still my favorite.

After chores, country living provided an endless number of things to do—if one took the time and used their imagination—even a little.

Creative and new ways to have fun—living in the country fostered all of that.

There was more.

Much more!

1953

The year 1953 escorted in a squishy, spongy spring. Heavy precipitation dominated the past few days muddying already soggy fields.

Melting snow forged untamed patterns pouring into an impatient, raging Root River causing the giant to swell to high levels—rolling far over the banks. Its flooded currents raced dramatically stronger than they had for a few years. Earth stained waters discharged so far north of where they usually ran—lapping, rippling and splashing against the trunks of the trees in Vollmer's apple orchard immediately across the road from where I lived.

This meant the river overflowed its near bank by substantially more than a city block to get that far.

We did not have to watch the floods on TV.

We could see it every spring from our own front porch. This year was the worst!

Our side of the street got by considerably easier because our home sat on a small hill. Ground level was much higher on our side of Highway 38. Lucky for us because when the river powerfully overran its confines—its brackish waters only came as far as our South property line. Yet, it totally filled the lower lands and the orchard just a hundred feet or so directly across the street.

Mom never wanted us anywhere near the river when it got this high.

She warned us repeatedly!

Yet, we pushed the limits and she relented with an OK to get within a good stone's throw of the water—"no closer".

She also made sure we knew what "no closer" meant!

It always amazed us just how much the furious river could swell.

So much water massed for miles and miles teeming over its Wisconsin banks until it finally spilled into another moist, mammoth, misty monster—Lake Michigan.

Wow!

It's the kind of thing that astonishes you while trying to contemplate the infinite magnitude of its primitive uncivilized splendor!

ONE SPECIAL SATURDAY MORNING

I always got up early in the morning. I was ever an early riser—even at sixteen years of age.

This particular Saturday morning offered nothing better to do.

Intrigued by the view, I wandered along the gravel coated shoulder of Highway 38 occasionally kicking at a stone or two along the side the road.

This slender young lad, with dark hair and brown eyes, moved along casually following its curve as it wound slowly southward toward the Root River. As I got closer to the water's edge, one thought occupied my mind. The main body of the river this spring was awesome—absolutely awesome!

The water from the overflow started to recede just a little.

You did not have to look hard to notice the totally immersed farm fields.

It was easy to spot some fairly large heavy scaled carp, good sized bullheads or even pickerel trapped in the furrows from last fall's plowing. Low spots formed natural small sized ponds holding others hostage.

Extra large fish leaping up, flipping over gracefully and splashing like erupting volcanoes made the walk extraordinary!

Curiosity is a strange driving force. I wanted to study some of the denizen of the river and then sketch them later as my friend Wiley Miller did.

I loved to draw ever since the day my dad held me on his knee and put a pencil in my hand.

I treasured drawing wild creatures of all kinds from nature and do to this day. Fish were no exception.

The finned creatures seemed to vary in their approach to the situation just as people do in their approaches to life.

Many of the trapped fish just gave up and lazed around. You could see their fins and the tops of their backs and an occasional flip of their tails.

More fascinating were the ones that tried to jump to safety totally unaware that the next hole could still be a long way from the deeper and safer water of the river. Their symmetrical scales made them sparkle in the early morning sun and made them seem even bigger. Their splash, when they landed, sounded like claps of thunder plunging into the water.

A number of them just did not make it when the water eventually receded and ended up as fertilizer for the coming year's crops.

Some tried over and over again.

Most of them survived.

Those really big ones generated exciting, strong, inviting visual imprints. I hungered for and could just imagine one of them pulling on my fishing line when the waters receded in a few weeks.

We never ate the ones we caught because mom worried about how safe it was since cows often wadded out and cooled in the river proper during the summer time.

We usually just hooked them and let them go again. It was more of a game to my brothers and sisters and me. Most of the fun was in the anticipation.

We had even more fun throwing them back and watching the mighty ones splash on reentry and see their tails flick and their fins disappear like the conning towers on submerging submarines and then fade away into the mystery of the waters.

Thoughts like these swam through my head as I jogged until I was just about even with the long row of young scrub trees that shaded and marked our southern boundary.

That's where I heard it!

It wasn't loud.

It was just a quiet sound—a whimper!

Looking around, I didn't see anything at first.

I moved closer to the row of scrub trees and bushes separating our property from the neighbors.

Then—near the base of a large outdoor advertising sign, just before the water's edge, I spotted her. Miserable, wet and totally all alone shivered a puny little deep chocolate colored puppy.

Small white and pale ochre patches patterned her face and a huge white star on her chest made her irresistible. I reached down through the brush. There, at the base of the huge sign, hid this small fragile living thing. I picked her up—slowly—gently.

She was trembling—maybe from fear, or cold, or hunger—or—maybe all three.

The natural instinct of wanting to comfort her took over.

It was easy to stroke her fur gently—she was so soft. In return, she settled against me and seemed to snuggle closer and closer for more and more comfort.

Her breath felt so warm against my skin.

Apparently she liked the sound of a human voice because a tiny pink appendage slowly made its way out from under her tiny cool black nose and began to lick at my hand. Each warm moist lap of its little tongue said a lot.

It was love at first sight!

Still cradling her, I searched around the wild shrubs, the nearby ditches and the fields to see if there were any of her siblings wandering around. Unfortunately, there were none.

We lived in the last house north of the river—somewhat more than a city block away.

The next farm house was my Aunt Bernice's about three blocks to the South and at the top of a big steep hill.

The river area appeared so deserted in some ways—particularly at night. Because of that, some people seemed to think it was OK to somehow abandon a litter of unwanted of puppies or kittens there.

I'm not sure if they thought they were being more humane or if they assumed that nature would do the rest for them in some way.

Thinking about what must have been going through their minds always upset me.

Occasionally one, like this little heart rustler, managed to find its way to a friendly hand. By now, my brothers, sisters and I should have grown accustomed to this. Yet, inevitably we wondered about the fate of the ones we didn't find.

Now for the hard part!

Heading back home, I had to think about the next step—how to ask mom if we could keep her!

She managed to grow accustomed to this drill by now. We wanted to keep every stray we found. She would always say, "Our two story house only has so much room for new pets—unless they can survive out of doors." However, we always got our way and managed to keep them indoors—if she Okayed our keeping them.

This time, was it going to be, "Yes—keep her?" Was she going to say no?

Lucky?

Guess so!

This happened to be a rare time at our place. The pet supply indicator showed a zero balance on hand!

I didn't know for sure what her answer would be. Yet, I could venture a pretty good guess.

This was such a loving little puppy and mom nurtured a very special soft spot in her heart for dogs. We were all familiar with part of the story.

Fire broke out in her home when she was a girl almost destroying it.

She told us over and over how the piano fell through two floors and into the basement.

She stressed, with some emotion every time she told us, how her dad's little black Scotty dog raced from room to room waking the family members with his bark saving their lives—there were eight children. He roused them all to safety, but raced back into the fire before anyone could stop him apparently thinking more were in the house. Her eyes always moistened when she got to the part about how smoke overcame the small hero who paid the ultimate sacrifice.

Yup—she sure loved dogs! It did not take mom long to say yes.

Jim, Judy, Jerry, Jan and I didn't waste much time naming her. I don't even remember who came up with it. All I remember is we somehow ignored all the large areas of the most beautiful, rich, deep brown fur that covered most of her tiny body. Instead, we focused in on the small sandy areas of ochre here and there in her soft coat. Sandy! Stubby, fine featured nose, twinkling eyes—a real heart stealer—Sandy!

CARDBOARD BOXES

Jan, my youngest sister, found a cushy sized cardboard box.

Judy willingly gathered enough comfortable, soft old rags for a bed.

With Jerry caressing Sandy, each of us scrambled down the basement stairs.

Jan found a cozy spot near the bottom of the steps. We promised mom we would keep her down there until we had her housebroken.

Excited about our new pet—you bet!

Spoil her?

Every one of us certainly did those first few days.

Young Sandy didn't mind—not at all!

She just did what all charming delicate little puppies do to communicate.

She licked our hands and our faces. Undoubtedly she was by far the cutest little living thing ever found in our farm field.

What's not to love about any youngster?

Her precocious, precious, warm little face, tiny wagging tail and four wiggly stubby legs became a major distraction at Route 13 Box 362 A.

Now Sandy could have cared less about our address! Notwithstanding, I thought it was a bit strange that the post office changed our address to 10971 South Howell Avenue shortly after we found her. After all, we still lived in the same house.

Somehow the new address did not seem as country sounding.

There was always lots to do around home.

We no longer had the weeding of times past, the hoeing or picking vegetables and strawberries in our very large truck garden.

We no longer took our produce to the Racine or Milwaukee markets or the pickles to the Splinter Pickle Company.

We no longer had a roadside vegetable stand except for a few weeks in the Fall when we sold pumpkins from our garden.

I no longer peddled ten miles one way on my old Ace bike to work for Carl Robran, a farmer on Rawson Avenue in South Milwaukee.

I worked as a painter with my dad, a painting contractor at the time, during the summers now.

In addition, we always had enough chores to do.

Even so, it was busier than normal around our place the next few days.

That's just how things were.

Jerry, my youngest brother made it even more so.

Years before, we helped dad plant a row of fruit trees about a hundred yards or so from the house.

Jerry was meandering around near there late one afternoon. I remember Jerry saying, he was looking for an arrow we lost a few days earlier.

We would shoot at an imitation pheasant that we made from straw. It was suspended from a tree branch by a lengthy piece of binder twine. Someone would crouch down behind a large, very wide, old Elm tree, next to the orchard. They were safely shielded by a small wooden enclosure.

Then, when the would be archer yelled "ready", the person hiding behind the tree would huddle even lower.

He or she would pull on a second, but extra long, slender piece of binder twine through a tiny slot in the wooden shield.

Next, they would let the stuffed target go swinging—about twenty feet or more from the tree's trunk.

It made the practice sessions more realistic—a lot like skeet shooting. A lot of fun!

One could not have scripted it any better.

De ja vu!

Not unlike what happened to me a few days before, it was now Jerry's turn.

He wasn't having much luck finding the lost arrow.

In contrast, when he searched around—he found something else. Something better!

It was another little, furry, inescapably captivating surprise.

This time it wasn't an irresistible little puppy!

An enchanting dwarf-like little kitten just stood there looking up at him with his blue eyes and meowing softly in a charismatic, melodic, captivating sort of way.

Then slowly, steadily, it wandered up to him.

There—not too far from the road—Jerry stumbled upon this beautiful, wonderful, magnificent little stray. A totally different kind of creature, it was a different species than the new pet I lucked upon a few days before.

I don't know exactly how Jerry reacted.

Yet, I can still imagine his excitement.

Eight years old and finding a treasure like this—yes!

Again, mom answered yes.

Our stable of family pets suddenly grew from none to two!

He really was a dandy! Curious, cuddly, cute all somehow described the infant cat. A very soft yellow orange—almost gold basic color graced its little body. Stripes, an almost burnt orange series of them, provided excellent accents.

It was a no brainer—Tiger! Tiger was the name we gave him!

Someone found a box for our playful diminutive new bundle of activity.

We set up another little bed and put it right next to Sandy's.

A morning sun slowly crawled warmly across my pillow very early the next day.

I scurried down stairs dressing in my T-shirt and jeans on the way.

There was Sandy sleeping in her bed, but—surprise!

There was Tiger curled up against her like a fragile fuzzy ball! Little paws, white whiskers, a very soft purring—golden striped kitten slept. Well so much for separate beds!

Several of my siblings made every effort to have Tiger sleep in his own place.

However, he had a mind of his own!

He continued to sneak quietly over to Sandy's place during the night—as only kittens do.

Tiger did not like sleeping alone.

Even a night light did not help!

From that day forward, I swear that miniature cat thought he was a dog and, as far as we knew, never learned the truth the rest of his life!

HOLD THE PHONE

Both puppy and the kitten continued to grow during the next three weeks.

Without a doubt, we continued to give them both megatons of attention!

Some of us would sit on the floor straddling the tiny gold creature and the slightly bigger brown one.

Of course, we couldn't resist hugging and cuddling the little creatures. After all—that's what they are made for!—Aren't they?

That is exactly what we were doing one day.

The phone rang.

It was my longtime friend, Russ Oelke.

It was a great call.

I will never forget it!

I could hardly believe what he asked!

"Ed," he began, "I climbed this tree to check out a crow's nest."

"Guess what?" he added. "It had three young ones in it and the mother is missing!"

I could just picture him climbing this tall tree peering into a nest!

Russ was always adventuresome and a real out of doors and wildlife enthusiast. He is to this day.

Like his father before him, he continued catching and raising wild creatures—raccoons, fox, rabbits and all kinds of wildlife. He could even follow ring-necked pheasant tracks in the snow to their hiding place and capture them with a burlap sack.

Russ reminded me a of a fictitious outdoor naturalist featured in the Milwaukee Journal newspaper named Mark Trail.

He just knew a lot about outdoor creatures.

"Would you want one?"

"Want one?" The words seem to linger on for a long while. I would give everything I had for an abandoned baby crow! A real crow!

"When can I get it?" I answered and not bothering to hide my excitement!

"I'll be right over," he said.

"Wait till I call you back," I cautioned. "I need to check with my mom first."

I knew that I would be pushing all kinds of limits this time.

Despite some serious challenges from mom—like maybe it might not grow too well in captivity or how would we feed it or were would we keep it—reluctantly she gave in.

Somehow I managed to convince her that the young crow was better off with us than fending for itself with no mom of its own. I emphasized how it could starve to death or, worse yet, be subject to wild predators and become an easy meal with no one to protect it. I probably overdid the graphic images I conjured up of the perils faced by such a young little feathered thing.

Holy cow! A pet crow!

I had never heard of anything like that.

I called Russ back right away! I wanted to be sure he did not give it to anyone else.

This was to be our crow!

Some families may have skeletons in their closet, but we were going to have our own crow! "The family crow!"

Somehow it had a nice sound to it!

It was really exciting around the place when Russ came over with this raven black beauty.

He truly was a beauty!

Spindly legs, a tiny pointed black beak accented flashing dark eyes. They sparkled so much they were like two black emeralds in sunlight. Even then, he had what looked like a joker's smile on his face.

27

This was the third case of love at first sight, within a few short weeks. It really was a multi-sided case of love—five of us kids on one side of the equation and these three tiny creatures twisting us around their tiny paws and claws. They were clearly outnumbered!

We couldn't thank Russ enough! He was like one of the family! Years later he actually joined my family when he married Judy—the cousin of my future bride Mardell.

Needless to say, there was a lot of fussing over the newest of our new pets.

Hours later, when the excitement finally settled down a little, we used Tiger's abandoned box since Tiger now shared Sandy's.

I placed our new feathered friend ever so gently into the second comfortable cardboard box.

We had never had a pet crow before and neither Russ nor any of us knew quite how to handle him much less feed our most recent living wonder.

Dad helped with that.

When food was rationed to families and meat was hard to get during World War II, he used to raise chicks and ducklings hatching them from eggs in an incubator up in the attic. Initially, we took some of the grain mix we feed our current chickens and ground it up so it was really fine. Then we gave the young bird some milk for further nourishment and plenty of water.

These three young creatures—a dog, a cat and a crow seemed ever so different to be companions.

We were not sure how well it would work.

Sandy and Tiger seemed to be getting along just fine. They kept their single bed to themselves. There was just no way you were going to separate them.

And the crow, well he seemed to respect their wishes and kept to his own box—that is, until the third night.

Judy was the first one to discover just how inseparable this threesome could and truly would grow to become. Surprise is not quite the appropriate word when she wandered downstairs.

There was Tiger curled up inside of Sandy's legs.

The body of this young crow, supported by two spindly little black legs, sat on Sandy's back, just like royalty sitting on his throne. The crow sat there just like a cherry on top of an ice cream sundae.

All three seemed comfortable as could be. What is more, they continued this routine night after night for what seemed a long, long time.

WHAT'S IN A NAME?

Naming Sandy and Tiger was easy. Naming this black beauty was something else because he was not your ordinary pet.

No mam! No sir! No way!

Russ called one afternoon. "What did you call your new crow?"

"Nothing yet," I responded.

"Let me know when you decide," he requested.

We talked about so many other things too. We laughed about a certain morning on the school bus. Russ was one of the last students to be picked up.

My unfortunate friend was clearing the traps that morning—as he had done so many times before. This time was different!

When he got to one particular trap, whew—he got a full blast from an edgy, odiferous skunk.

He showered!

He bathed!

Nothing got rid of the wild fragrance.

When the bus stopped and opened the door for Russ, everyone stopped whatever they were doing or saying! It wasn't how he looked! It was the unpleasant bouquet! Poor Russ! I really felt sorry for him— he's such a good guy!

"No," said the driver. "You can't get on."

We all thought he had an original excuse for missing school. Of course he took no end of ribbing about it! He was always a good sport!

Late evening followed a pattern around our place for a quite a while. Dad loved playing chess.

We didn't have a chess set, but we had a checker board. So, I made chess pieces out of cardboard.

A hunk of modeling clay served the base for each piece so they would stand without toppling.

Dad usually got the urge to start playing around ten or so—taking turns with Jim and me. We usually played until somewhere between midnight and one A. M.—with the T. V. on at the same time.

We did this even during the school year despite the fact that the bus came very early.

Sometimes we stayed up later.

We had a lot of fun!

If we didn't do that, I read. I loved to read—still do.

The past few nights we engaged in chess and discussed a name for our bird—no luck!

This particular night, Liberace, a well-known piano player performed on television.

George, the entertainer's brother, stood next to the candle holder on Liberace's piano and played the violin.

Something struck dad's funny bone and he suddenly started chuckling.

"There's your name for you. When the crow grows up he can star on television."

"Call him George!"

Jim and I were not too sure about it at first.

However, when dad made up his mind about something, you had a hard time changing it.

Therefore, George it was from that day on—George the Crow!

The idea of him as an entertainer would fit him well!

At the time, none of us had the wildest clue as to just how appropriate the thought of George the celebrity performer would prove to be!

THREE IS COMPANY,
FOUR IS A CROWD!

Dad not only named George for us, he stirred up the mix even more.

One day he visited Aunt Bernice who lived up the road from us along with our cousins Lois and Alice. Later, their property would be known as Jelly Stone Park.

When television first came out, not too many years before, we'd go to Aunt Bernice's to watch it! That continued for several years—prior to affording a black and white set of our own.

Anyway, he came home from his sojourn with a small box and brought it into the house.

"Eleanor (that was mom)! Kids!" He called.

"Come here. See what I've got!"

We all gathered around a small shoe box on the kitchen table. Holes riddled the cardboard cover.

When we were all packed around about as tight as we could get, he popped the lid open and reached inside.

Out came the surprise.

There in his hand was a young gosling.

Baby chicks and ducklings are cute, but so is an infant goose!

Well, you can guess what's coming.

Our family entourage toted this young gander down to the basement.

Since Tiger's original home still remained unused with Sandy, Tiger and George sharing the same single box, it became home for our new bird.

32

Unlike the other three guests, he kept his own turf for sleeping.

So, our two motels were now fully occupied.

With all the creativity in our family, one had every right to expect an innovative name for this new wonder resident. However, we did not.

As long as we knew him—we called him just plain, not so fancy, Goose!

Oh, and one more important note, mom made dad promise to raise goose outside when he matured.

I think dad originally had other ideas about keeping it in the basement, but he quietly agreed.

MOTHER'S MUDDERS

Aunt Gertrude, mom's sister came to live with us. She had spinal meningitis as a teenager and had serious physical limitations.

When she needed a place to stay, Mom and dad made our home her home.

She could make the most beautiful crafts that a social worker would then take and sell for her. In this way she was able to earn a little spend money.

Aunt Gertrude had a good deal of difficulty walking and usually dragged her right leg behind her.

She also had serious problems with her kidneys.

I remember that she had numerous bottles of medication on her dresser.

Every now and then she had to go to County General Hospital in Milwaukee for a check up. Dad would take her to a bus in Milwaukee on the way to work. Then, usually me or sometimes Jim or Judy would travel with her.

The day usually included a lunch stop at one of the Woolworth stores, some shopping and a visit with, her sister and my mom's, Aunt Ruth Kozlowski.

This gave us many opportunities to dialogue. She had a significant influence on me.

One of the things I remember most was that she tried very hard to live her life so that her physical limitations didn't dominate her—real as they were.

She used to say you can't let it control you—even when we knew it was not easy for her.

Much later, I would learn more fully just what she meant.

She added, you have to maximize the strengths you have, know your limits honestly and work with the combination of the two.

She would say over and over, "If I give it my best effort and do my part, God will always be there for me—maybe not always at the time, the place and the way I think He should be—but, He will be there!"

Aunt Gertrude also would point out that God didn't create difficult situations for us, but was—instead—there to help us through these times if we looked to Him and trusted, really trusted, Him!

It is too easy to get caught up with the pointing of the finger at Him in difficult and testing times when, instead, we could be asking him for help.

There would be many times in my life later on when I would draw on the strength of her example. She lived what she shared verbally with us. There was no pretense here.

Aunt Gertrude would stay single until she moved back in with mom and dad years later in life—long after I married and left home.

At mom and dad's she met a really kind and loving person named Roy, who seemed to come out of no where. Roy married her and took care of her in her most difficult years. This happened at a stage in her life when she spent most of her time confined to a wheel chair. "Maybe not in the time and the place and the way", but He did take care of her!

Aunt Gertrude was also very prayerful and shared her love for prayer with us all.

She also loved ice cream! Drumsticks were her favorites—all covered with chocolate and nuts!

She would often ask Jim or I to travel the three miles one way to Elighter's grocery store in Racine County or two miles to Hoppe's meat market, in Oak Creek, to get them for her. Of course, we always got one for our efforts.

Speaking of country stores—I pulled a really good one time—a real classic!

I'm jumping a bit ahead to next spring to share this one, but trips to the store were a regular part of our routine!

Mom sent Jim and I to Hoppe's meat market on foot one day for the equivalent of three paper bags full of groceries. It was just like walking to the country school because it was about the same distance.

Because it was a spring day and the snow was melting, mom made us wear boots.

I really don't remember what was on the list, but it seemed longer than usual!

I really have to admit to being the one who came up with the bright idea. Because there was so much to carry, I suggested—no—insisted, that we go cross country to save some of the walking time.

What I didn't know was just how muddy it was in those farm fields under some of that melting snow.

The first couple of fields that we crossed weren't too bad because they were on higher ground and had been used as hay fields.

As we got to lower ground, it became muddier and muddier.

Eventually the mud would cling to our boots. Sometimes a sucking pocket of mud would hold our feet fast—boots and all!

I never experienced that before, but clay gets quite a grip on something that sinks into it when the soil is wet and soggy.

Our hands were too full of bags to help with the problem. A few times we fell trying to fight our way loose. When that happened, the paper bags got wet!

There was no turning back!

At that point it was shorter to try to make it home than to go back!

Well, to make a long story short, we finally got home!

However, the wet bags ripped and try as hard as we could, we couldn't keep the contents from falling along the way—one by one and later two by two and so on.

The final tally was that I lost both of my boots.

Jim lost one of his.

We lost a fair amount of groceries scattered across the fields.

And, for as much patience as mom had, we were both still afraid she would loose her temper!

I told mom it was my idea and waited for the worst!

Instead, she never raised her voice.

She asked if we were ok.

So now we knew—we were a higher priority!

We were told never to try that again!

Dad later quipped, "That's what mom means when she says try—try again." Only he added that if there is a next time he would find a way for us to pay for it!

Not all creatively conceived ideas are successful in real life applications!

GROWING UP
AND
CLIMBING UP

One thing you can bet on, little creatures do not stay little very long. Funny thing is they grow so much faster than humans.

The fuzzy little, busy little, stripped little kitten was the first to figure out how to climb the stairs. It did not surprise us since felines often seem a bit more independent than other animals that share a domestic arrangement with humans.

Since the arrival of the fur and feathered fearsome foursome, this forced the first real moment of truth in our household.

Although not yet, Sandy would eventually be welcomed into the upstairs living area, but not the others. Mom maintained that—from the first day—that this whole episode began to unravel in our home.

Well, you know how it goes. Tiger started climbing the stairs and purring and meowing at the door. We all begged mom to please change her mind – just for this poor, tiny, cute as blazes, lonesome kitten.

"No," came the answer!

"Country cats don't belong in the same areas where we sleep and eat. They catch field mice!" Well, that all seemed pretty final.

Either mom did not communicate that to our young Tiger, or he just did not seem to understand. The silly little kitten just continued to climb the stairs and parked outside the door to the kitchen sitting there and letting us know he wanted in with the rest of us.

Mom was the boss in this matter.

Born, April 28, 1916, Esther Eleanor, she was a bit shorter at five foot three inches and very slender with brown hair and blue eyes.

Her maiden name of Czerwinski tied back to Czerwinski on the Vistula River in Poland.

Truly a family person, she knew no other way than to give her family everything she had and then even more if that's what it took. Meanwhile, she never asked for anything for herself in return.

Her ever present smile ranged from impish to soothing depending upon the circumstances and clearly became her legacy. She implored us to smile at those times when she knew that we least felt like it. She would often say, "It is the instant cure for anything—particularly if you smile hard enough and try your best to mean it."

Mom seemed to always sense when those around her needed a hug or a boost of some kind. Her very special gift was somehow making you feel better about yourself and your struggles and knew just what to say to inspire you and keep you going.

She had the unique ability to be your best friend when you needed it most and yet managed to get you to stand up on your own. She was so sensitive to how others felt. This is the same lady who said no to kitty coming upstairs.

Mom could also be firm when she felt it was needed.

Kitty kept the pressure on—crawling up the stairs and meow, meowing at the door.

This went on for several days.

None of us dared say another word about it.

Mom didn't say anymore about it. Yet, we sure put loads of pressure on her with our facial expressions and the doleful look in our eyes.

Even dad did not dare get into it.

Then, one morning, the impossible happened! There was Tiger curled up in front of the doorway to the master bedroom. Each of us looked at the other wondering who let her in.

Mom suffered through an entire round of denials by the rest of us. Then, with a sheepish grin that deviated somewhat from her usual smile, she said, "I Did."

From that day forward, Tiger was truly one of the family. In fact, he got to sleep upstairs whenever he wanted—often at the foot of mom's bed!

It was quite understandable that Sandy did not like this too well. Hey, Tiger was her sleeping buddy and Sandy did not like sleeping without her fluffy pal. So, she tried to rectify things.

She tried hard to pull herself up onto the first step with her front paws. They just did not have enough strength to help her realize the miracle of climbing yet. It bothered her though.

Whenever Tiger made his way upstairs, Sandy would bark that funny little bark that only puppies have.

Sounds of frustration echoed up from the bottom of the steps at this unconquerable challenge—one she had not mastered yet. Moreover, she sure could whine and squeal without end to make her point.

I guess it was not all that strange.

We didn't even have to ask about bringing her upstairs.

One day after washing clothes with the old Speed Queen wringer wash machine in the basement, mom carried our puppy up stairs. The two of them, Sandy and Tiger, curled up in front of the bedroom door.

And mom, well she was a mom. She put a dish of milk out for each of them.

You did not have to tell us twice. From that day on, the dynamic duo lived on the main floor with us, played with us and lavished in all the attention five kids could shower upon them—sometimes individually and sometimes collectively.

Now that left George and Goose! Neither could transcend those darned stairs. However, neither of them could bark nor meow either. Nor, did either of those birds fly—at least not yet.

I wanted George to join the rest of us and our upstairs crowd in the worst way. Finally, I persuaded mom to let Jim and I take our black feathered friend up to our bedroom provided we kept him there during the day and cleaned up after him. Yup! That's just what we did even though potty training a crow was not easy. A shoe box was a start.

Some of my fondest memories where the times we got to visit with young George up in our room.

He was so responsive when you talked to him or played with him.

It wasn't long before he would skip across the top of my desk and jump onto my finger. Then he'd look at you with the most inquisitive expression on his face.

When you talked to him, he would cant his head one way or another to let you know he was really listening. As we learned later on—he truly was lending an ear.

He seemed to understand far more than we realized at the time.

George was no longer just a young crow. He was truly a special, lovable and wonderful friend! A very special friend!

Jim was a talented musician who played the guitar. Eventually, he would do an excellent Elvis interpretation.

George loved to listen to Jim play and sing. He would just sit on my desk intently listening as long as Jim strummed the guitar and/or sang.

Music ran in the family.

Mom's uncle had an accordion band in Milwaukee.

Her brother Ray played the accordion with a famous musician named Frankie Yankovich who known throughout the country as the Polka King.

My cousins Bobby and Jimmy both played in trumpet and sax in bands that performed all over the area. In fact, Jim played with the Booze Brothers Review, a famous band that was featured at major events throughout the Midwest. Some members of that band performed in Vegas.

My nephew Scott, Jan's son, played in a marching band at The University of Arizona and Jim's son Michael plays guitar very, very well.

Our crow really liked music!

Sometimes dad played the harmonica or the guitar. Whenever that happened, George would stop whatever he was doing and just perch and listen.

Dad and mom both played the piano.

Dad took an instant liking to the crow and while mom was the one to break the rule for Tiger, dad was the culprit who fostered a soft spot for George.

41

One night, after work, dad went upstairs to our bedroom, brought our bird down and put him on the mantel of the fireplace in our living room in a large shoe box. That turned out to be George's favorite spot.

He could not fly yet, but he loved to prance—almost like a strut—and look at himself in the long narrow mirror that hung just above the mantel piece.

First he would walk to one end and look at himself and then to the other—back and forth, back and forth.

At first we believed he thought that the image in the mirror was another crow.

Every time he would stop and look, he would cock his head one way and stare and then tilt his head to the other side and observe the image looking back at him.

More often than not, he would pay attention to what we were doing or saying when we were in the room. It was just as though he was part of the discussion or activity—just like one of the family.

Sometimes, it seemed he would just doze off and take a short snooze. He would just perch there with his eyes closed tight like a living statue—a very humorous sight.

I don't think mom was too happy about this at first.

Then, it just became a matter of routine.

She now relented to let us keep George on the main floor. There was one stipulation! He could stay as long as he was in a box on the kitchen floor when we were not in the living room.

He wasn't alone very often.

If we were not giving him attention or feeding him—Sandy and Tiger spent a lot of time lying in front of his box as a matter of ritual.

Sometimes though, we would wake in the morning and find George perched on Sandy's back with Tiger curled up between Sandy's legs.

They seemed to like that arrangement a lot.

Goose was another question. He never did make the main floor.

Somehow the four of them maintained their relationship. A key reason is probably the fact that we would take the other three down to see him every day.

The timing couldn't have been better for Judy, Jerry and Jan.

They were just about done with the school year and would have a long summer to spend a lot of time with our four new additions. It was double fun for them because they didn't have to walk the three miles one way to get to the country school during summer.

Lucky for me, I only got to do that during the seventh and eighth grades.

It was kind of ironical that we walked to grade school, but got to take a school bus to high school.

I do have a few memories from my two years at the Oakwood Road country school.

There were only two kids in my class.

There was only one teacher for eight grades. She needed help so I got to use an hour or two a day to help teach first and second graders how to read and occasionally the third graders. I enjoyed that and it probably carried over to later in life when I taught college courses, conducted seminars around the world and guest lectured on many subjects.

Also, later, I would lecture and give demonstrations in the classroom to grade school children over a ten year period on art including serigraphs, cartooning, drawing and painting.

Another memory of the school involves a kid named Dale. When I was in eighth grade, he transferred into the seventh grade after moving from Michigan. He lived just down the road from us. One day while walking home from school, we took a short cut across the fields. Some of the kids in the group were trying to tell Dale about things which required some caution—like electric fences. They also pointed out what a poison ivy patch looked like.

I don't know why, but Dale took issue with them and said, "It's not poison ivy." The argument reached a crescendo.

Dale, to prove his point, tore up some of the green vegetation and rubbed the stuff all over his chest. "See," he said emphatically! And see he did—when it actually turned out to be poison ivy!

He was in terrible agony for a few days. He may not have known what poison ivy was, but he sure could play football.

We didn't have pads or helmets or enough kids to field a team for each grade. So, the fifth, sixth, seventh and eighth grades pooled their talents and formed a team. So did the other country schools we played against.

We played our baseball games the same way.

That's where I met a lot of my future friends—kids I played football and baseball against from the other schools. There were kids like Jerry Ashbaugh, Eddie Lentz, Elhart Kadilec (who would later marry one of my cousins, Lois), George Abenshein (who would also marry a cousin of mine, Alice), Russ Mathis and others. We had something in common. We all loved sports.

That is also where I met Russ Oelke. He played for the Scanlon School. We've been friends ever since. Without him there would have been no George.

HAY, WHAT IS THIS?!

Summer of 1953 was the one in-between my junior and senior years at South Milwaukee High School. This meant working with dad as a house painter.

I had been doing this since I was ten or twelve years old. I started out slowly.

First, it was the boring job of wiping up paint spots and dad was fussy about getting them all.

Next I mastered the art of scraping peeling paint.

Then came the apprentice skill—apply putty to touch up windows.

Finally, I got to do something that was more like a true apprentice's work. Dad taught me how to hold a sash brush near the very end of the handle to keep it steady. This skilled transferred to painting windows.

If I didn't know better, it was almost as if they were hiding me.

I got to work in confined areas working on things that were usually the least fun. Those with junior seniority often do. Usually I got to tackle the stacks of storm and screen windows in the home owner's basement or garage.

Although I did not know it at the time, this skill with handling a paint brush and holding it steady and movement with the wrist had some application to painting with oils and watercolors. Later, I learned to paint with a watercolor brush uniquely designed by a world famous watercolorist and, later, a very close and dear friend—Zoltan Szabo.

I also got to refine the skill under the tutelage of some other wonderful artists and friends like Berta Sherwood, Bob Johansen and

Larry Rathsack. You never know how learning something you do not particularly like will translate into something that gives you a great deal of satisfaction.

There were definitely some things I disliked about painting.

High on the list were the seemingly endless spindles and railings on porches. Because there were so many that I covered with paint over the early times, in a way, I imagined that I got to paint most of them in the Milwaukee area over the years. Certainly it seemed like every one of them on every main floor and on every second floor porch. It also seemed like I got a good shot at most of them on the third floor porches too.

It felt as if my big opportunity came when I worked my way up to enameling bathrooms and painting closets and the insides of cupboards.

Yet—it seemed consistent with the other tasks I learned earlier as a painter's apprentice the times when I seemed hidden away.

Finally, I got to do the whole show and paint everything dad did. I even learned to hang wallpaper including the murals that were so popular back then.

I guess the thing I enjoyed most was the fact that I got to spend quite a bit of time with my dad this way. We had a lot of time to talk and to know each other.

I also had a good chance to learn things I never would have learned so young any other way. I learned how to talk to people the way my dad had to with his customers.

I experienced how to tolerate some of the idiosyncrasies people can have at times because you have to as a business person.

I also got to learn how much dad genuinely cared about people and the pride he took in what he did.

We got to talk quite a bit when we would go fishing too, but this was different—I got a chance to observe dad doing his thing in the real world.

He never finished grade school even though, twice, the teachers skipped him ahead a grade. Nonetheless, he sure had a knack for relating to people, listening and satisfying his customers.

I also had an early preview of how the world might react to the march of technology such as the later advent of the computer.

On a far lesser but vivid scale, I remember when someone invented the paint roller and the first latex paints.

Dad thought these advances would put the professional house painters out of work because these two advances eliminated brush marks most amateurs used to leave when using oil based paints.

Latex was also easier to clean.

This was a particular blessing for the novice who would normally struggle when they tried to use traditional enamel or semi-gloss paints. When using the real thing, oil based paints, the professional painters really got to show their skills—particularly enameling. It was a real art to apply the enamels without leaving brush marks or having the enamel run.

Dad's reputation started to grow as an independent contractor and he started getting schools to paint like Hillside and Oakwood Road Schools in Oak Creek and Saint John's School and Church in South Milwaukee. He hired more painters and, about once a month, he gave me a weekday off.

I always enjoyed them because it often gave me a chance to play baseball with my brothers and sometimes my sisters would join in too.

Dad was quite a ballplayer and did a good job of passing it on to his sons. Later, we all played for my dad's team at one time or another when he sponsored one. I also played with a bunch of my friends from the country. We had a good team then too with a lot of heavy hitters. All of us could hit for average and the long ball as well.

One such day in late summer Jim, Jerry and I were hitting a few. One pitched. One hit. The other chased. We tried to place our hits so the fielder didn't have to run too far.

Our neighbors, the Dittmars, were harvesting their hay.

This harvest was later than normal.

Because it was so late, the farmers were in a hurry to get it off the fields.

The hay was already cut and the rush was intensified in order to get it into the barns before it rained. Among other things, wet hay is very combustible and a fire hazard.

Dittmar's home and barn stood on the property directly to the North of our land.

Glen Dittmar, his cousin Gilbert and Glen's dad towed the wagon they were loading behind their red Massey Harris tractor. Load after load went from the field to their barn.

Inside the old wooden walls, a huge hay fork with long sharp blades, rode on a rail that went from one end of the barn to the other.

The farmer maneuvered the fork along the rail until it was in position directly over the hay wagon. Then he triggered it by releasing it with a pull rope.

The immense fork would swing down by way of pulley from the ceiling.

It traveled downward with a lot of force. It was like a giant dinner utensil attacking spaghetti and meatballs.

The fork sank deep into the hay—driven from the weight of its fall.

It grabbed a load of hay from the wagon and lifted it up high upwards towards that same ceiling.

Then, guided by the farmer, it rode along the rail again to transport it to the spot they wanted it. The farmer then stopped and tripped the fork again. Just like an engineer, he would drop the hay into the exact spot in the hay loft he wanted it.

Dittmar's had another big field. It stretched from the southern boundary of our property, about where I first found Sandy, even further south. It went up to the very edge of old Root River.

When Glen learned I was home for a day, he asked me if I would drive their team of horses that afternoon, as I had done every now and then over the years. That way they could use two wagons to haul hay and get done sooner.

Another driver meant one more person available to pitch the hay up onto the wagons.

One of the things about the country in those days—almost everyone dropped everything they were doing and pitched in if someone needed help. So I did.

I walked north, from our home, across their field to get there.

The horses lathered up from the heat of day and working hard. I got here just as they were resting and being watered. A part load of hay still sat on the wagon.

Glen's brother and sister, Ray and Inez, were sitting there eating lunch. They were a good six to eight years older than me.

Shortly after, their dad, Walter, had me climb up on the wagon and handed me the reins.

Ray and Inez climbed up on top of the half load and found a comfortable place to sit.

Fastened to the front of the wagon was an old wooded ladder. I leaned against it, grabbed the reins and started the horses down their long driveway.

We turned right, onto highway 38 and headed South past our rural mail box.

Just before the team of horses reached our driveway, a car came up behind us. The driver got as close to the wagon as he could. He tailed us for a few seconds. Then he must have lost patience with the slow pace of the horses.

The horn's blare resounded with tenacity.

It was like standing directly in front of an air raid siren or a big old factory whistle at noon hour.

The loud blast startled the tar out of me!

Even worse, it raised total havoc with the horses!

The old brown horse on the right side of the team bolted without warning. Then they both lurched forward jolting the wagon with a sudden force and burst of energy. It was like a large bomb going off underneath.

The whole wagon shuddered as though it was coming apart!

The intensity of their power surge tore at the reins nearly wrenching them from my hands.

I held on all the tighter!

Their pull wedged me so firmly against the ladder in front of me I thought my arms would rip right out of their sockets!

There I was with a runaway team!

My friends were ridding somewhere on the wagon—holding on! I didn't have time to even look and see! Later Ray and Inez just said they sank the pitch forks, they normally used for loading the wagon, as deep into the hay as possible for survival.

I never knew that four legged old-timers could streak so fast.

The elderly pair of farm horses stormed downhill and around the curve in front of our house.

Somehow they managed to stay on the road and not tip the wagon. And boy, oh boy—they sure hauled us on a real hair raiser—for about a block and a half before I was able to bring the whole show to a halt!

Luckily no one got injured!

However, the horses lathered heavily and were frothing extensively at the mouth.

After about an hour's rest for the horses and for us too, we got back to it and hauled hay until just before sundown.

Because of the predicament the Ditmars were in, dad gave me the next day off so that I could help finish the field.

Those horses virtually took me for the ride of my life! Hey, nothing like it at the amusement park or a computer game! This was the real thing!

I really enjoyed working with horses.

Working with a team was something special.

It taught a lot about patience and learning and understanding the strengths and limitations of the creatures with whom you worked.

It also somehow made you feel the power and the gifts of the natural order of things. Somehow it made me feel more of a part of the earth.

That night I sat on the porch with Jim, Judy, Jerry, Jan, mom dad, Sandy, Tiger, George and Goose.

We just enjoyed sitting there talking with each other and watching the stars.

They seemed so much brighter that night and the sky looked so clear and comforting and safe.

WOOD-BURNING FURNACES

Reds, oranges, golds and browns lined our North East and West boundaries as the trees and the brush on mom and dad's small farm clearly told everyone that autumn was here.

The brisk, clear breezes in the air caught each leaf as they fell from their branches—guiding and gliding each and every one of them.

They drifted as if something or someone predestined each one to some particular spot on the ground.

Thank goodness kids living on farms do not have to rake the leaves that land in the fields.

Our four house guests were changing more rapidly too, but not in colors!

Goose was getting more than a mite large for the basement and dad brought him up and introduced him to our yard. This was his new home.

He took ownership of that turf from the very first day and never relinquished it.

Although not fully grown yet, this gander was beginning to show signs of what would become his trademark. Whenever a stranger would enter the yard, he would spread his powerful wings and lean his head forward almost like a prize fighter going into a crouch.

Then he would spring forward hissing as he darted straight at the trespasser.

When Goose got older he was awesome. You did not need a watchdog with a full grown gander protecting the place.

Sometimes I muse about whether those nights in the basement convinced this rather large bird that it was every bit a dog just as Tiger seemed to think he was.

Just like the others, he too was special!

Speaking of Tiger, he also picked up his trademark—although his was a rather dubious one.

As fall turned to winter, it got intensely cold in the country with the winds blowing across the open fields.

Almost hiding in the basement like a huge ogre was a gigantic industrial wood burning furnace that dad salvaged.

Its metal walls curved and had deep grooves almost like the slats of a monstrous corroded barrel.

As it burned, it devoured the split logs with ease.

Bright red ashes would filter through the grates as though the metal giant was spewing them from its mouth.

Hot and glowing, embers and heated sparks would shoot through the grating—then settle in the ash trap in the bottom of the furnace.

The ash trap did not have a door that closed. It was always open.

Well, with Goose staying outside full-time, now just the troublesome threesome stayed in the house. Even here the pattern began to change.

As it got colder, Tiger wanted to sleep down the basement again. It must have been the heat from the furnace that attracted him.

He slept closer and closer to the wood burning rust-colored ogre.

In fact, close just was not enough.

Sometimes he would virtually fall asleep—stretched out and with the front part of his body sprawled into the ash trap.

I know!

One of my chores was to get up early each morn and make sure I filled the wood furnace appropriately to heat the house by the time the rest of the family woke up.

One night tiger went too far.

Hot ash or embers slipped through the rather large grates and singed off the tips of Tigers ears.

This episode truly branded him for life.

A unique cat, this one!

It had ears that stood at about two thirds the length that they used to extend.

We still loved him just as much anyway—maybe even more!

He was definitely a one of a kind now!

It was almost as if someone branded him!

He was also very independent in some ways—yet very affectionate—and definitely with a strong attachment to Sandy, George and Goose.

Another trademark was that Tiger loved attention.

He would let you know he wanted some tender loving care from time to time.

Tiger had this way of semi arching his back, lifting his tail while swishing the tip of it from side to side to some unhearable syncopated rhythm. Then he would softly rub up against your leg with his head and his body.

When you'd stroke him between the ears or rub the smooth fur on his back, he would purr and just sit there for more.

Sometimes, when you were seated, he would just hop up on your lap as if to say I am here! Treat me nice!

Sandy, Tiger and George continued to spend time on the main floor with us during the day.

Sandy was a typical growing pup.

She loved to chew anything and everything she should not. It seemed she wanted to prove to us that her teeth really worked.

She was also showing signs of becoming a very loving family dog.

She certainly succeeded.

George, I am convinced, spent the next number of months studying us and casing the joint. He walked around with a deliberate self styled strut and a half measured grin that seemed to say I know something that you don't know.

He was starting to show some of his own very special trademarks in very little ways.

He was becoming a tease—a class a major league tease!

He was also learning to fly!

Tiger

CHRISTMAS

While these furry and feathered creatures grew and developed, our lives continued too.

Maybe because I was a teenager they began to grow a little faster for me.

Christmas was approaching.

I was in for an experience that I remember clearly to this day as though it just happened.

It was about two days before Christmas.

I was working after school and weekends at Ray Bussler's Restaurant on highway 41 and Oakwood Road—about three miles from home.

My duties were dishwasher, a cleaner upper, general handy person and anything else the owners needed done.

I even helped a retired carpenter build a major addition on to the restaurant.

It was quite a place for my family.

My sister Judy worked here as a baby sitter. My mom was a waitress at the restaurant for many years.

My brother Jim would later work here doing many of the same things that I did.

Ray Bussler was a former All-American football player at Marquette University and later played for the Chicago Cardinals in the NFL.

He and his spouse Ann ran a four star restaurant that was a major stop for many athletic teams that traveled between Chicago and Milwaukee on the main roadway in those days—Highway 41.

These included the Chicago Cubs, the White Sox, the Bears, the Green Bay Packers, the Milwaukee Braves, pro wrestlers like Billy Goelz and Gypsy Joe and lots of other celebrities that traveled between the two cities.

I have still got some of the autographs somewhere.

Ray and Ann wanted something a little special for their friends and family this particular Yule season.

As a result, when I came to work that night, I found someone else at the dishwasher.

At first I thought I goofed up in terms of remembering which night I was scheduled to work. However—no—Ann called me upstairs. Their living quarters was above the restaurant.

Spread out on the couch was a beautifully exquisite red velvety suit with abundant white soft fur trimming, a silky, curly white false beard, a red hat with gold glistening bells for a tassel and a big—and I do mean big pillow.

It must have been very expensive!

She looked at me and said, "A bit thin but you will do." I was pretty slim as a young man.

Ann smiled at me. "Santa is very busy this year," she began. "He needs a helper Ed. Instead of having you work at the dishwasher tonight, I volunteered you as his number one assistant!"

Ann was the boss's wife. So, she got no argument from me. Besides, I loved Christmas—always have.

After tying the pillow around my waist, I changed into the fancy new attire. After turning around two or three times to check things out in the mirror—I called to Ann, "I'm ready!"

She led me into another room and pointed to a large white bulky sack with sides bulging to the breaking point.

It was loaded with bright wonderfully colored packages wrapped in silvery ribbons.

Each one contained special gifts for their family and friends.

Ann handed me a list with names and addresses and the keys for their brand new Oldsmobile. Driving a brand new snazzy car was enough of a thrill for someone my age.

I started out with a rather conspicuous smile.

It was my one and only venture dressed as that jolly old soul from the North Pole. Every adult knows that Santa needs help from time to time. He recruits from some of the humans scattered around the world.

This was my turn to step up—even though I was still a teenager.

It started snowing shortly after I left the restaurant and was accumulating quickly. Several hours slipped away before making all the stops on the list.

When I finished, the snow was drifting and the roads were slippery. There already was a fair amount on the ground from previous snow falls.

It was also dusk and the velvety violet shadows ventured gracefully across the soft silky snow and began to play games with the last gasps of daylight.

My youthful hands guided the hardly used Oldsmobile south on 13th Street to Oakwood Road. There I turned right to travel the last mile or so back to the restaurant.

About halfway there I saw a car partially off to the right side of the road. Its back tires were spinning desperately trying to get traction.

So I did something you should not do these days because it is not safe to trust people you don't know today. But, trust was the natural thing to do back then with most folks.

I pulled over to the side of the road a little behind the spot where the stranded vehicle stood.

It was like a caged creature mired firmly in the snow with its wheels spinning and spitting snow every where. No matter how much it spun, it just couldn't get traction!

It was definitely trapped and going no where!

Getting out of the Olds, I trudged through snow well over my Santa boots.

The young mother rolled her car window down. Tears were working their way down her cheeks. She looked totally frustrated when the window finally came down.

Then she got this really unusual look on her face.

Peering through the open window, the scene in the back seat was equally sad. There were the heavy sobs of her two young children crying.

As I leaned over to ask if I could give her a push, I realized that I was still in full costume. It was about the same time that the children noticed too.

Suddenly they stopped crying and stared—extremely excited disbelief.

One peak told me it was a standard shift!

"Put it in low gear," I told the mom. "Wait until you hear me tap on the trunk and then accelerate slowly."

I trudged around to the rear of the car. After a lot of shoving and sliding, the car moved forward! The car was out of the rut.

The second to last thing I remember about that night was the mom poking her head out the window and yelling, "Thanks Santa. There will be cookies and coffee for you at our house Christmas Eve!"

The last thing I remember was the two little tots with big wide smiles waving at me through the rear window with wonder highlighting their faces. Of course, I waved back! I will never forget it.

Every now and then, on December the twenty fourth, I think about a man and a woman somewhere telling their kids about the time Santa stopped to push them out of the snow drift.

ANOTHER CHRISTMAS
EIGHT YEARS EARLIER

As I drove home from Bussler's that night, I could not help but think back to another Christmas eight years earlier. It turned out to be a very hard winter—for my family. It was our first one in Oak Creek.

Money was at a very low ebb for mom and dad that year. Dad tried to farm most of the thirty-seven acres that summer, build the house we had to move into by autumn and work a full time job besides.

Getting started in farming took much more time and money than dad anticipated. The basement and the frame of the house were completed.

It was truly winter in a very small place. None of us were prepared for it or had experienced anything like it before.

Only the two rooms were semi completed with no wall between them. The rest of the rooms were nothing more than two by four frames. Our house in South Milwaukee was sold and we had no choice, but to move.

The house was very cold. Because there was no siding, the only insulation from the wind came from the tar paper covering the siding boards.

The only heat we had came from a brown colored pot bellied stove with a dark black pipe sticking through the wall to the outside. As the winter got colder, so did the two rooms we called home.

Dad had sealed off the master bedroom and the living room. All seven of us slept, ate and lived in the kitchen/dinning area with the beds, kitchen table, electric range, refrigerator and the stove taking up most of the room.

We transported the water we used every day in two milk cans—purchased at an auction. There was no well yet. We used that water for cooking, drinking, bathing, washing dishes and what ever else. It did not take long to learn just how precious water was.

There were days when the meals were meager at best—often eating soup.

I also remember walking with cardboard stuffed in the shoes so we could wear them a while longer to compensate for holes in the soles.

Mom was sewing our clothes from remnants.

It must have been this kind of existence that made mom go to work as a waitress as soon as I was old enough to baby sit.

On really cold nights, heat from the oven often supplemented the pot bellied stove. Mom or dad took turns staying awake to make sure we were safe.

Even then, we sometimes sat bundled with heavy coats around that old stove. When it was time to sleep, we piled the coats on top of our blankets for extra warmth. Sometimes we went to bed early just to stay warm.

It was eerie how the howl of a wind of any velocity could scare the Dickens out of you in living quarters of that size. It's surprising how spooky it can seem at night when you would hear wind gusts echo through the entire floor above you.

The feelings amplified when you looked up at the ceiling at night and saw the muted orange and yellow shadows from the window of the pot bellied stove dancing in the night on the ceiling above you.

More than once I woke during the night and would hear a Westerly or a Northern wind screech. This was particularly true when there was so much unfinished structure. It could be very scary to say the least!

It seemed at times that every board would creak, groan and scream under the force of the wind. Some nights, you would swear the house would blow apart, but it didn't.

The adjustments for each of us were dramatic!

In this small physical space we experienced a lot—and we learned a lot.

Much of it was about sharing, caring, priorities and selflessness.

As long as we had each other nothing seemed to matter.

Mom was the glue and dad was the strength. The toll on him was tremendous. The heavier the challenge got—the harder he tried.

I think at times it wore him down and was almost overwhelming. Yet, he always fought back with all he had and tried to keep from showing his strain to the rest of us. Yet, there were days you couldn't miss seeing it.

I remember him saying one night, "That his dream, when he started this venture, was to make it so much better for his family." That was as close as I remember him coming to letting us know he never dreamed it would be this way that winter.

Most of the time though, despite how he might have been feeling inside, he tried to make the load seem lighter to the rest of us. His teasing and his joking hit higher planes and he always tried to find ways to make us feel better somehow.

In some ways the Great Depression might have prepared him somewhat for this.

Being one of the eldest at home, he left so there would be food on the table for his younger brothers and sisters.

I wish that I could remember all the stories he would tell on those few occasions he talked about it.

I do remember him telling of twice jumping a freight train and going to Washington to make a few dollars picking apples. He was a young man then but stayed in the hobo camps along with many young unemployed men at that time.

He told of how tough it could get at times. It was certainly a quick growing up process for him!

He talked about the Western states and cities and the Western sea coast. Every now and then he gave enough clues to know that it was not easy.

Yet, there were some very interesting places and people that he encountered.

One of the jobs he had along the way was in a lumber camp where he would top trees.

Even though he had this exposure to tough times, I know from watching him that he was not comfortable at all with watching his family go through this winter—or, for that matter, the next few years while he did everything he could to make it better.

Mom added a different dimension to our family experience at this time.

I remember her saying, "God is so different from people. At the end of each day He doesn't ask for an accounting of your successes, but only of your efforts." These words have guided me all my life.

She would say, "If you can go to bed at night and honestly say God, I gave it my best effort—it does not matter to Him whether or not you succeeded or missed the mark by a mile. You could be at peace because you used the tools he gave you to the best of your ability.

Just never quit.

Never stop trying."

I believe this is what both of our parents did in that fledgling town of Oak Creek.

Despite the hardships, they worked extremely hard at it to build the feeling of family through love, togetherness and fun. We learned you do not have to have a lot to have fun—or to love each other.

We played Monopoly on a small sized kitchen table. Even though the table was small, we sometimes played ping pong. It certainly tested your reflexes.

Some nights, we sat around the pot bellied stove wrapped in blankets to keep warm, singing songs and telling stories. Many of them were original. It was a good spawning ground for creativity.

Sometimes we played a card game that used two decks, called Canasta. Mom liked that game a lot.

In that little space, we learned to love even that much more. We learned to totally discount petty things that really didn't matter.—A roof over your head, heat, water and food were important. Most important of all were two things—that we had each other and that everyone stayed healthy.

We learned that God is good! He surely takes care of the least of his creatures as we found out, those first few years in Oak Creek, in so many ways. He fills the voids—when you do not have a lot. It seems we gained a lot of things including a special sensitivity and deep appreciation of the little things and of each other.

Mom stressed the need to search for and focus on the positives and to overlook the obvious negatives one experiences and finds in one another.

We learned to make the most of just being there with each other and to be happy and thankful for that wonderful gift.

We learned never to give up—never to quit. We experienced the value of sacrifice. These things also served as a good foundation throughout my life.

The first Christmas in this small place was what I thought about as I drove home from Bussler's that night.

Jan was just a baby. Thinking about her and our circumstances at that time reminded me of another Child born in a small place a long time before.

A few nights before that Christmas in Oak Creek, I woke from my sleep and overheard mom and dad talking. Dad whispered, "But Eleanor, we don't have anything for the kids for Christmas."

There was a pause and mom whispered back," But Eddie, you gave us all that you have." I will never forget those words either.

Christmas could have been very quiet that year. It wasn't! In fact, to this day, when I think back about Christmas, it was one of my favorite ones.

We each got new caps for our heads. Jim and I each got one that looked just like the World War II U.S. pilots wore complete with a wool lining and a pair of goggles that we could pull down over our eyes. Dad said they were just like the ones a radio program hero, Captain Midnight, wore on his radio show.

Judy and Jan got fur lined hats that covered their ears with matching muffs and Jerry got a stocking cap and a scarf.

Dad also made a bean bag board, for the five of us, out of a scrap piece of masonite. Mom made the bean bags from things she had—one of my all time favorite gifts as a child—probably because of the fun we had playing it.

It was also the only time I remember dad reading Dickens's Christmas Carol to us.

Then, true to form, he had us singing Christmas carols, laughing, playing the bean bag game, eating peanuts and drinking ginger ale.

We sat around that pot bellied stove later that night with our tree, and the flickering flame from the old stove, providing the only light. It was a beautiful sight.

Mom always had something special to say for special events. That night she said, "It's not the things you do or the gifts you give but the thought behind it that counts. God counts, more than anything, the thoughts behind your actions!" There were a lot of thoughts that year for which we had reason to be thankful.

The rest of the way home, I thought about all the wonderful things that happened that Christmas seven years ago. I thought again about the smiling children in the car I just helped get out of the snow.

AHEAD OF THE SCORE

When I got home, I talked with my parents about my adventure on Oakwood Road.

Mom said maybe it was your chance to repay an earlier kindness.

She was thinking back to a time when I was in about the 5th grade. Jim, Judy and I went to a parochial grade school in South Milwaukee at the time—Saint Adalbert's. Dad was taking us to school in the morning and picking us up at my grandmother's at night on his way home from work at Buscyrus Erie.

The particular night mom was referring to; Dad picked us up at Grandma's later than usual.

It was snowing fairly hard.

He headed the black model A Ford West on Rawson and turned South onto highway 38.

His head lights had trouble searching out very far into the distance.

All of a sudden the wind kicked up and the snow turned into a blizzard. It blew so hard that each flake looked a white dart racing at the windshield.

The wind was so rugged you could feel it jolt the car with each gust. The snow began to drift. It wasn't that far to home in real miles.

Yet, we crawled ahead slowly. The old Ford seldom reached speeds of more than five to ten miles an hour.

So what does dad do? He sings to ease our fears. However, each mile became harder. Soon, dad was stopping to clear the windshield of the heavy snow.

The stops came more often!

Then dad stopped singing!

A large flash of lightning went off without warning.

It reflected against the millions of tiny particles of snow flakes.

It was like a zillion high powered flashes going off in your eyes!

It was so dazzling, you could not see anything!

It was all brilliant white!

It's called a white out!

Everything was one bright, glowing, startling blaze of white!

The old Model A continued fighting to get through drifts. Sometimes it seemed as if we wouldn't make it.

All at once, another flash of lightning—another white out!

We hit a giant sized wall of blowing snowy flurry that would not let us move any more. We were stuck in a huge drift and the storm outside was merciless.

Dad was frightened and it showed. He had faced a lot of scary situations over the years, as we learned little by little. But, this was different!

He was scared for us!

Dad opened the car door into a tenacious wind that wanted to pull it off its hinges.

Then, he reached in and picked up my sister Judy. He held her close to protect her from the savage fury of the snow.

It seemed to be cutting holes, deep into your skin with each piercing flake.

Dad told me to hold onto his coat tightly and to hold on to Jim's hand the same way.

After all these years I still don't know how he had the sense of direction to lead us from the stalled car.

Somehow he managed to get us to that house on the Southeast corner of Oakwood Road and Highway 38 in that blizzard.

It was nearly three quarters of a city block away. A golf course is there now.

I couldn't see the house lights from there. I don't know how he did! Maybe it was just strong instinct!

The family living there gladly let us in. They and gave us shelter for the night from the ferocious storm.

I saw my first chess set during our stay there. I still remember fingering the dark shinny red and the pale white pieces wondering what they did and how they moved across the checker board.

The hospitality was great! They had each of us take a warm bath and gave us hot chocolate and then something to eat. Our wet clothes were spread around the kitchen to dry.

Dad telephoned mom to let her know what happened and to make sure she was OK.

It was calm in the morning, but the snow piled like small mountains across the highway in drifts bigger than I can ever recall.

Dad headed out alone for home.

Somewhere around noon he returned with shovels and the Ditmars' two sons.

Snow drifts completely buried dad's car. The heavy white stuff buried it deep.

It made it that much harder for dad's crew of volunteers to dig out our Model A. First they had to find it as was the case for many other stranded cars and trucks that day.

The snow plows could not even begin to do their job until all the owners found and liberated their vehicles.

I can still remember looking out the window as the individuals used their shovel handles to probe down through the snow to locate the cars. Wisconsin recorded it as one of its worst known snowstorms.

"If it was returning a good deed someone else did for you", mom went on to say, "That's fine. But, I believe—in life, you shouldn't keep score. Instead, in terms of good deeds done for others, you should be way ahead of the game on the delivery end."

Evenings in the country were particularly great for families talking with each other and sometimes, like this night—memories.

CHRISTMAS DAY

This Christmas Day was a special one for mom. One of her brother's had been missing for a number of years.

Dad went searching for him and found him, brought him home and invited him to stay while he reestablished himself.

He had been on tough times.

While mom had more of a quiet humor, Uncle Eddie's bubbled over!

It is amazing what you learn from someone.

I learned about his collection of old pulp Western magazines.

He used to like to listen to a lot of the same old time radio that I liked including The Lone Ranger, WLS Barn Dance, The Whistler, Bulldog Drummond, The Fat Man, Boston Blackie, Red Skelton, Baby Snooks, Inner Sanctum, Lights Out, Henry Aldrich, Blondie, Gene Autry, Bob Hope, The Shadow, Jack Benny, Gang busters, Mr. and Mrs. North and Lux presents Hollywood.

We had an instant base for dialogue that went in so many different directions. He stressed going to school to me.

He also kidded mom about the daytime soaps to which she would listen.

The unusual thing was that, every Saturday morning, he would turn on one of my favorite radio shows, from when I was much younger, for my sister Jan—Let's Pretend. And when he did, some of us older ones would sit right down with him and enjoy my little sister enjoying them.

He loved to sing! The Missouri Waltz was his favorite by Patti Page.

It was a delightful Christmas because it was so special to mom having her brother home after a long absence.

On a lesser scale, this was the Christmas I got my first flash camera from mom and dad. It was a Kodak! It replaced the big old Kodak box camera I got for my birthday years before.

I took numerous photos with my new toy much to the chagrin of the other members of my family. You'd think I was a photographer for Life Magazine.

Although I didn't shoot as many rolls of film as I did before the advent of digital cameras, I shot way more than anyone wanted to pose for.

First, Jan and Jerry got to pose like outlaws coming down the stairs with their six guns drawn.

I would shoot photos of them sleeping and in their bathrobes.

Jim got to pose with a bird we were nursing back to health from a broken wing.

First I had him pose with the bird sitting on his guitar and then Jim looking at the same spot with the bird off! I have to admit to inheriting my dad's crazy sense of humor.

It got much more creative after that—and much more fun for me and that much more of a pain for my free models!

They had to love me or they wouldn't have tried some of the crazy poses I asked them to try.

A STORY I HADN'T HEARD BEFORE

That evening, Sandy and Tiger both sprawled out contentedly in front of the fire place.

George, a little pesky, flit from one to another wanting his feathers stroked. He liked that!

Finally, he settled down on his favorite perch—Sandy's back.

It never ceased to amaze me how Sandy at no time moved or seemed to mind when he landed there.

After a while it all seemed so gentle and natural.

While we chatted with my parents about things from the past, I posed a question that had been channeling through my mind for quite a while. "What gave you the determination to make it through the really tough years—our first ones in Oak Creek?"

"It shouldn't have been that way to begin with," dad said slowly—somewhat surprised at my question!

"Before we moved out here, town officials told me I could build a combination service station and small grocery store on the curve in the road. After buying the land, I applied for a permit to build them and even negotiated with Texico for a franchise. The town officials then turned me down saying they were going to zone our new land so it couldn't be used commercially. I was stuck and had to try farming instead! I didn't know much about it and that made it difficult!"

Although he didn't know it at the time, dad was giving me my first real lesson in what local politicians can do to affect the lives of people with simple tools like new zoning! As I looked back some years ago, it

70

became clear to me that dad's new business ventures could have posed a competitive threat to other existing businesses that were a several miles away. Although I am not positive, that could well have been one of the reasons for new zoning.

"As tough as that was, other people have it tougher," dad said without hesitation. "You learn from that if you have to live through it. The irony of it is you hope that your children don't have to go through the same learning experiences you did. You somehow hope the can learn the same lessons some easier way—like from talking with you or others."

That triggered another old timers' discussion about the past and the Great Depression.

Mom opened with her recollections about pulling us in a red coaster wagon to the A & P for groceries when they could afford it and other times going to the food lines.

Then she told a story about dad that I had never heard before. I have to admit it surprised me.

She began…When the Depression was at its worst and lots of folks were without jobs, it severely limited the food supply for everyone's families. Dad's parents, brothers and sisters held a meeting. The result—a plan of action.

Pooling their money, they pitched in to buy gas so someone could drive to Winnecone, a small town on the Wolf River in Wisconsin.

The pool also had enough cash to pay for minnows. Whoever went would hopefully catch lots of fish and come back in a few days with more than enough to share. They decided to send dad.

So, he went. Fishing was excellent! He was having tremendous luck. Nice sized Walleyes and a few Northern Pike more than filled his stringer.

Suddenly loud scuffling sounds and a threatening noisy commotion drew dad's attention to something happening just a few fishing spots away from him on the bridge.

Looking down the elevated structure, he saw three tough looking guys giving a fisherman a hard time.

First they shoved him.

Then, they roughed him up.

Next, the hoodlums took the beaten fisherman's stringer full of fish and, cursing, threw the struggling guy's fishing gear over the bridge splashing it into the river.

Three hoods skipped the next couple of fishermen.

Now they started straight for where dad was standing!

Dad thought back to when he lifted his stringers bulging full out of game fish out of the water.

He hypothesized maybe they caught sight of him checking his full tally.

He just witnessed what they did to the other guy.

The sight of three big bruisers really terrified him—particularly the thought of losing what he worked so hard to get.

All of a sudden—things happened with the tenacity and explosiveness of an avalanche!

All he could think about was not losing the family fish.

The biggest guy came directly toward dad and started trying to intimidate and threaten him.

He then took a full swing at my father.

Dad blocked it and hauled off with a severe counter punch.

The thug fell with a hard resounding thud. The guy dad decked must have been the leader because the other two guys turned and ran.

What the guys didn't know ahead of time is that dad learned to box in the CCC camps sponsored by the federal government before they were married. He even had an exhibition bout with a world boxing champ and knocked him out. That little piece of information is still a family legend.

Dad worried, even though he didn't start the violent confrontation, that he might have seriously injured the guy because the bully was not moving at all and dad's hand hurt a lot. Moreover, dad was so concerned that he followed his first reaction and fled with the fish.

It was about two weeks later and lots of anxiety before dad learned what actually happened.

He thought he should call and check on the thief's condition. So he called the bait shop near the bridge at Winnecone.

The owner told dad he was a hero.

These guys had been harassing the fisherman in the area for a week or so—stealing their fish and sometimes their tackle and then selling it at high prices. They even hurt some people. The bait shop owner told dad, "The thug you decked was out for a long period of time. Nobody came to his aid—not even his buddies."

When the villain came to—he left, but—not in very good condition. No one called the police because they were glad somebody stopped what was going on. Yet, dad called the Police and thought he should report it. It seems they knew all about it and were trying to locate him. They wanted to say thanks!

Dad brought lots of fish home, but went through immeasurable anguish. Even after learning the culprit was OK he remained troubled that he was forced to defend the food for his family. It bothered him that some people would steal food from others during a depression. Every one knew that if you took it from someone their families would go hungry. It took him a long time to get over it.

Mom said they were lots of examples of how families had to sacrifice and neighbors help each other. You learned to make do with what you had. And—never give up.

We would go fishing to the famous bridge a few more times before I left home to marry and start my own family.

However, the next March, when the Walleyes started running, we stood at the same railing he did years before.

We held our fishing poles, as we had so many times before, and looked out over the water below.

I asked dad about taking up boxing and about the incident again.

He really did't say much about it.

Although, he did take the time to give me a dissertation—on not fighting.

Dad told me to never engage in a physical altercation. "Always walk away!" He stressed. "Avoid arguments that could lead to heated tempers. You could unintentionally hurt someone or, even worse, inadvertently take their life. "I grew up in different times," he said. "It's not worth the risk! Just walk away!"

"Boxing isn't street fighting. There are no rules in the streets! If you ever learn to box, don't use it anywhere but in the ring!

Walk away!

Don't be the cause of heating a situation up. Don't stick around if someone else starts to get pushy." He asked me to promise that I would "always walk away!" "You almost always have everything to lose and relatively little to gain unless it is truly a situation where you are in grave danger."

"When I think about hurting someone, I'm not sure how many things are worth that price?" The authority in his voice and the sincerity of the experience that echoed in his tone gave me a message for life.

After all the years I knew him, I was just beginning to learn some of what he had been through.

WHAT A DIFFERENCE
A YEAR MAKES

We really celebrated New Years Day on January 1, 1954. A lot of good things happened during 1953—a lot for which to be thankful.

Actually—it really did not start out very well at all. In truth, the very first day, January 1, 1953, could have been one of the worst days in our lives.

It did not start out like all other January ones. Yet, January 1 1953 had the feeling of being special.

Excitement filled the air because the University of Wisconsin football team was going to play Southern California in the Rose Bowl.

The term avid sports fans describes our family well. Not only that, but the Rose Bowl Parade was a big spectacular.

Everyone eagerly intended on watching it on television.

The day was a chilling cold, not unlike many others for this time of year.

A warm comfortable fire roared in the fire place. A mesh screen, in front of it, was in place intended to keep the sparks from escaping.

Dad had just put a few fresh logs on the grate and the flames were dancing high.

Our long living room covered the whole width of the house and was about sixteen feet wide. Standing in front of the fireplace screen offered the warmest spot—particularly when you first woke up.

I sat on the floor in front of the TV, this particular morning, intently watching the preliminary coverage that preceded the parade.

Dad and mom were in the kitchen fixing something to eat. Judy just woke up.

She was wearing a new bathrobe she received as a gift from her aunt. She took the prime spot for warming up—directly in front of the fireplace.

Nobody was aware of a terribly tragic secret. The manufacturers made the robe from a synthetic material that turned out to be highly flammable.

Judy and I said our morning greetings and we talked about the parade.

Then I turned my eyes back to the TV again to watch the floats that were getting their final finishing touches.

Suddenly I heard this terrible scream.

I jerked around and looked up to see Judy. She was running! A spark somehow managed to squeeze through the screen landing at the base of her robe. It started to blaze at the bottom as she ran toward the kitchen.

All that came to my head was something a nun had said to our third grade health class years before. "If someone's clothing catches fire, throw them to the ground and roll the flames out. Don't let them run!"

I tackled Judy just before she got to the kitchen and started to roll her on the floor. Dad was there no more than an instant behind. He used his hands to extinguish the robe—burning them in the process. He grabbed a throw rug using it to completely smother any remaining flames.

Judy was in tremendous pain. Her legs needed a lot of medical care. Mom and dad took her to Milwaukee County's General Hospital.

We all worried about her. She's always been a special part of our family. We all loved her and wanted her home. It was touch and go for a while. We almost lost her those first few weeks. None of us realized just how serious it was. She spent about three and a half months recovering while going through extensive skin grafts from her back to her legs.

Judy always had a lot of positive resolve. She always did! She needed all she had of it this time. Then, step by step, she started to recover and edged her way back. Her determination has always had a significant impact on me.

Mom did not drive, but she also did not miss a day. Oak Creek is as far south in Milwaukee County as you can get. Dad would take her to the bus in the early morning and she would take the long ride to the far northwest side of Milwaukee.

Then, she would take the bus back as far as it came and usually got someone to pick up her up at the bus stop and drive her the remaining four miles home.

I know the days had to be challenging some times, yet she always came home with a smile. That was her. Mom was like a candle. She always glowed brightest when someone needed her most.

Next, she would go to work. Occasionally she would just walk the distance to the bus. That daily routine told me a lot about a mother's love!

Dad went up a lot after work in the evenings and usually stayed very late sometimes falling asleep at her bedside. Sometimes we got to go along and see Judy.

The good news is that despite the difficult challenges she faced, Judy recovered and came home to be with us again just in time for spring. That was a truly big cause for thanksgiving and celebration!

As if her return home in 1953 wasn't enough cause for celebration,—it also gifted us with the extra added bonuses of finding Sandy, Tiger, George and Goose.

WHAT ARE FRIENDS FOR?

Big, yellow and slow—but really a good place to form friendships—that was our school bus!

Russ Oelke and I grew in our friendship with our mutual love for the out of doors, baseball, basketball and football. However, almost nothing surpassed wildlife as a key interest that we shared and both loved talking about.

Russ and his father spent much of their free time trapping wild animals including raccoons and pheasants. Russ's vivid descriptions of tracking wild game fascinated me. He particularly hooked my interest when he described how he would track pheasants, creep up on where they burrowed into the snow and then catch them by throwing a coat or a burlap sack over them. We would talk about this for hours.

Wiley Miller, who later became well known as the artist who painted the covers for and illustrated the insides of Fishing Facts Magazine also took part in these discussions and was in my art classes. He also took part in these discussions and was a friend.

There was one time though when no one wanted to talk to Russ. It was the time he probably most proved to us that he really did all of that trapping that he always talked about!

This particular morning the bus pulled up to the stop for Russ. He was one of the last students to get on the bus each day. This time when Russ got on the bus, everyone stopped whatever they were doing or saying and looked up!

It wasn't how he looked!

It was how he smelled!

Russ was clearing traps that morning. When he got close to one particular box trap, a skunk let him have it full blast! Odiferous—you bet! Poor Russ! The bus driver refused to let him on. It certainly was an original excuse for missing school!

Kids being kids, you can imagine the ribbing he took for some time.

But Russ was good natured and was able to handle it well—except that some of his old friends still bring it up!

SPRING TAKES FLIGHT

Our two furry and two feathered creatures all grew during the winter months.

Sandy, Tiger and George spent much of it indoors.

Meanwhile, Goose continued to do very nicely out of the house.

The bonding continued for the three house bound Musketeers.

The amazing thing is that I never saw them fight in any way. Birds, cats, dogs—natural adversaries right? Not this group! They were truly close.

As spring approached, dad had a few talks with me about George. "It will not be good for him if he stays tame," dad would say. "Think about leaving him out more. Maybe he'll take up with other crows and learn from them." He wasn't trying to get rid of my pet! The two of them were now close buddies.

That was very hard to handle. The thought of turning him loose had never even entered my mind before.

Dad explained, "It's a lot like your children growing up. The hardest part of loving, sometimes, is letting go—so they can take wing and become independent when the time's appropriate."

That did not make the thought any easier.

I talked with Russ about it too. He agreed, with dad, that it might be better long term to try to let him free as much as possible. We all talked. It was a family decision!

We started spending more time out of doors with George.

Next, we started to leave him outside when we'd go in.

At first he didn't seem to understand.

He would caw loudly and fly up to the sill outside the kitchen window. There he would perch for the longest time. If he was having anywhere near the feelings that we were, then this new pattern of events must have confused him terribly.

Every day we would let him back in for varied periods of time. He still got to spend evenings in our home. I worried about his safety out of doors at night. I did not know where crows slept in the wild or how protected they were.

Eventually he started to disappear for short periods of time. He was flying very well by now and he would just take off for who knows where.

Sometimes we'd be in the woods sawing trees for fire wood and he'd soar overhead or land near by for a visit. Other times we'd be in the field or the yard doing the things we did and he'd show up.

Jan loved to go down to the river. There was an old stump near the foot of the bridge. We'd go there with Sandy and sit, watch the river flow by and talk about lots of things. George would sometimes drop in to visit and take part in the conversation.

He journeyed all over the place.

Yet, he always came back and wanted attention from all of us including Sandy, Tiger and Goose. He always got to come into the house and George usually stayed overnight to leave again sometime the next day again.

He had some favorite things when he was home.

Top of the list seemed to be to strut across the mantel on the fireplace and thoroughly examine that look a like character reflecting back from the mirror. He looked like an old vaudeville dancer the way he moved with a swagger that was all his own.

Sometimes he'd fly over to the couch or a chair and hop up on someone's shoulder. He loved to get his beak close to your ear and would make sounds almost like he was conversing with you. His smooth hard beak would press against your ear and these soft, funny sounds would come out like whispers.

He also liked to sit on your knee or wrist or forearm. Yet he was ever so gentle with his claws.

It wasn't unusual for him to hop up on one of us and sit there for the duration of a T.V. show.

He also seemed to enjoy perching on the back of an empty chair while we played chess with dad.

We just treated him like one of the family.

He was!

UPSTAIRS TO THE BEDROOM

George loved the bedroom Jim and I shared. He loved to join in the activities.

Jim played guitar. He also sang all kinds of ballads, pop music and country western. His Elvis interpretations were pretty darned good too. He was really talented.

Sometimes some of us would try to sing along with Jim.

I swear that some of Judy's girlfriends came over just to hear him croon and play guitar.

Most in my family had fairly good voices. But they all carried me when I joined in. My voice was in the sub minor leagues, but I never let that stop me from trying.

George liked to watch and to listen.

Sometimes he would just sit for hours on end. Sometimes he would make sounds as if he was trying to join in.

In the beginning, his trips back home were almost like family reunions. Then the excitement became less pronounced, but to all of us it was a relief, each time he returned,—just to know that he was OK. I was always a bit of a worrywart anyway.

As time progressed, his patterns changed. Sometimes he would be there every day and just hang around the house. Other times he would be gone for a while—sometimes two and occasionally even three days at a time. I worried every time he didn't come home at night.

Then, one day a startling thing happened!

Some of us were playing catch in the backyard with a hardball we picked up during pre game practice at a Milwaukee Braves game. Stan

Musial of the St. Louis Cardinals came up to the outfield fence and gave it to us—a nice guy!

George was gone about three days.

None of us had seen him.

I don't know who noticed first.

A large flock of ebony garbed crows flew overhead.

They landed in unison as if a huge black cape instantly enveloped our small orchard.

They filled the huge elm tree that shadowed part of it and the smaller fruit trees.

The unexpected dark sooty colored visitors also lined the row of bushes and trees that formed our northern boundary line.

This was a whole lot closer than so many crows had ever come to us before. Yet, they maintained their distance indicating a wariness.

Initially, we tried to make sense of it all. After a short while, we did something that we felt foolish and self-conscious about at first.

We started calling. "George! George!" He had to be the answer!

We did this several times. "George! George!"

Suddenly a single crow broke from the flock and lifted off a tree branch. It circled over us once or twice.

I will never forget how his descent seemed almost slow motion as he lowered himself slowly, deliberately, gently onto my shoulder. The touch down was something else!

What a thrill!

He stayed for the longest time.

George flew from one to the other almost as if he was introducing us.

His chatting and interaction was such that, after a while, we barely noticed the other crows seemingly taking in all that was going on. Maybe they had difficulty believing it too!

Then, suddenly, George flew straight up. The other crows took off directly after and seemed to follow him to some destination unknown to us. Colossal! Stupendous!! Phenomenal!!!!!

Early that evening, there was a pecking at our upstairs bedroom window—like someone tapping with a small coin! I opened it. There was George! This was the very first time he had ever done that!

He sat there wistfully at first, with the light from our bedroom reflecting off his jet black feathers framing him against the dark sky. Our coal colored vagabond just hopped casually from the sill directly onto my desk.

The crow was just like one of the boys coming home from a night at the bowling alley.

He uttered a group of guttural sounds almost as if to ask how we liked the show that afternoon.

He made those throaty sounds for the longest time.

He turned his head one way and then canted it another.

Sometimes he strutted back and forth across the desktop as though it was a stage.

After a while, he spread his wings and hopped to the floor and waddled over to the door.

It was obvious he wanted to go down stairs.

He did not hop down the stairs this time. Instead, he spread his wings and glided down over the staircase, maneuvered gently to the right through the hallway and landed on the living room mantle.

He visited with everyone—jawing and jabbering about one thing or another.

When he finished with us, he glided gracefully over to where Sandy was lying flitting gently onto her back—just as he did when they where much younger. Sandy never moved a muscle. She never even flinched until George settled comfortably. Then, Sandy lifted her head acknowledging her guest. Again George made a series of guttural sounds—she seemed to understand. We hadn't seen that in a long time. It was just as though George was home sick. Sandy seemed equally happy to see him. Again George chatted!

I do not know where Tiger was, but he apparently did not want to be left out. Suddenly, there he was purring in front of the dog and the crow. The young tom cat continued its soft sounds and slowly twitched his tail back and forth. George made some more vocal sounds. After a while, Tiger curled up between Sandy's legs as he had done so many times before. Eventually they all fell asleep—just like when they were younger.

Despite their continued closeness, our pets became increasingly independent of each other and started to live the more traditional lives of their species. Yet, somehow, on their own schedules, they always managed to spend some time with each other.

In the evenings, it was a common sight to see Sandy curled up somewhere near dad's rocking chair. Tiger often stretched out somewhere very near by—usually immediately in front of the fireplace. We also had a small box we kept in that area for the nights when George would stay over. And, sometimes—but not as often, we would see the three of them in their Ice-cream Sundae mode with George sitting on top.

We never had another mass landing of crows when George would visit. Yet, this diminutive, energetic, real live entertainer carried on part of the phenomenon that he started that day.

Sometimes George would solo flight home.

However, on a fairly frequent basis, a flock of crows would fly overhead and I would call out, "George!"

Almost as if to the amusement of the other crows, and certainly to ours, he would circle down from the flock and land on one of our shoulders.

The other crows would continue their flight.

George, however, usually stayed for the day.

He would have been something in vaudeville even without a hat and a cane. Every grand entrance by him from the sky was always a thrill!

Sometimes we got to see him approach the upstairs bedroom window. Large black wings would open wide as the solitary bird would glide toward the window's ledge.

He would survey the landscape as he searched in all directions.

Then his silver black beak would peck at the glass window pane fully expecting an answer.

These are experiences that are hard to fully explain to anyone who never encountered them first hand. I would not trade them with anyone, but would love to share them with everyone!

They were so special!

RAT-A-TAT-TAT

Living in the country is full of surprises!

Not all of them are the kind that a person appreciates!

There was one totally unbelievable episode just like this that no one in this whole family wants to remember! It probably is still hard to believe because we all love living creatures so much. But, there are some that just aren't welcome in certain places!

It all had to do with keeping the house warm and feeding the chickens! Now—you say—how in the world do those two things get together and cause anything a person wouldn't want to recall?

Hard to believe? You bet! Easy to forget? Not on your life!

It is almost inconceivable to describe an occasion such as this with all of the love our family has for the wonderful living creatures that surround us. But it is true and so it should be told.

That old discolored iron—wood burning—furnace in the basement was every bit a monster of sorts!

It was a big old industrial rusty looking furnace and it devoured a lot of wood and had to be fed much more than once a day. It was not fed intravenous style unlike the gas or oil heat of today where you just set the thermostat!

This ogre ate wood at a steady pace to generate heat. And its appetite was a huge one!

Satisfying this big cast iron beast truly wasn't easy!

It meant that dad and Jim and I and sometimes Jerry would go to the woods in our old model A.

Two of us, at a time, would grab hold of opposing ends of an old sharp buck saw and cut up trees that had were struck by lightening or fallen for some other reason during the course of the year.

We would then tie a large chain with huge links to the logs and put the smaller pieces of tree limbs inside the Model A. Dad would haul them a half-mile or so from the woods to our back yard.

The hard work wasn't over yet!

There we put the logs and limbs on the table portion of a large pulley driven saw where dad would slice them to bite size pieces—large enough to fit through the hungry jaws of the furnace's door.

Oh, yes—next, we also had to split the pieces with steel wedges and a sledgehammer—almost like the old photos they show of Abe Lincoln.

Dad and I had pretty healthy biceps from splitting so many chunks of wood.

Ah, but all of this furnace fuel needed to be stored somewhere!

Winters were long and cold back then. So the pile of split wood needed was indeed a large one!

We also kept a nice big stack all along one wall in the basement so we didn't have to run out into the cold during winter—particularly at night!

But, how does all of this lead up to something we'd rather forget?

Well, let's talk about the chickens!

They had to be fed!

Because the only outside building we had at this time was the chicken coop—we couldn't leave the grain and corn for feeding the chickens outside. Too many of nature's wonderful creatures and some not so desirous would find this a feast to good to pass up—and there would be very little left for the chickens in short order!

So, guess where it got stored? Well, where else? The basement of course!

Now this is all well and good as the backdrop for what happened next! Perhaps this is best told from here on out to relate it just the way it happened!

It all started with the cover for the drain tile under the basement floor was damaged and dad decided to replace it. Sounds simple enough!

He got a new one that was nice and round and full of holes for the water to drain from the basement floor into the sewage system. No big deal—except he didn't have time to seal the drain cover in place. Why? Because he put it in place early in the week after work and wanted it done so my mom could wash clothes in the basement the next day. So he did what he thought was the next best thing. He put a small rock on top of it so it wouldn't get kicked loose, and trip someone, until he could finish the job.

I'd say Tiger was about a year old at the time. Tiger, he was the one that lifted the curtain on the show that would follow! You have to know that Tiger seemed utterly fearless. Nothing chased him that we ever saw! After all, he thought he was a dog and had a fearless goose for a friend!

One autumn afternoon, just after we loaded the basement with freshly split firewood for the upcoming winter; Tiger made a bee line past my mom's legs as she started to descend the cellar stairs. Tiger didn't just whiz by! He streaked by screeching!

It startled mom enough that she wouldn't go down the stairs. Instead she waited for the school bus to drop us off.

Jim and I got the word and headed down the steps—a little cautiously, but not too much so. After all we were teenagers! Teens weren't normally intimidated by something in their home. It was a mystery to us. And—mysteries needed to be solved!

So, down the steps we trod—a little on the loud side—making just enough noise to scare anything down there just in case!

We looked around and saw nothing—absolutely nothing!

Dad laughed about it at the dinner table and thought it was probably a log that fell off of the basement woodpile and startled poor Tiger. Judy was the one that popped up with the reminder that "nothing scares Tiger"! But, dad let it go at that! After all, we saw nothing!

Night went and morning came! As per usual, I turned on the cellar light and headed down the basement steps about five in the morning to re-stoke the embers in the furnace and feed it some more wood for its breakfast to awaken it. I was usually pretty alert when I first woke up in the mornings. I am still a morning person to this day!

The remaining basement lights had to be turned on by pulling on the chain hanging next to the bulb.

Just as I reached for the brass colored chain nearest the woodpile, I saw it! A long—slender—rounded—smooth tail disappeared into the woodpile. It startled me at first as it wiggled while the creature it belonged to crawled quickly and deeper into the woodpile. Then I saw another! That made two!

No doubt in my mind what they were! I didn't reach for any wood!

Instead, I turned and moved back up the stairs much faster than I came down. I made sure I closed the basement door behind me, testing it to assure it was really closed! I don't think I slowed down until I caught dad by his shoulder.

He too was a morning person! We went back down together, but saw nothing. Dad didn't touch the woodpile. He said he didn't know what was in there and would use another means to find out other than moving the pieces of wood. Instead, he searched around.

There, in the center of the floor, was part of the answer! The sewer cover was moved over—rock and all! It exposed a whole big enough for something to crawl through!

Back up the stairs we went—both of us!

He woke mom and told her his theory—rats!

This did not go over well to say the least!

Then he made things worse.

He told mom about an article he read in a magazine—I think it was Popular Science—about how rats often traveled in packs scouring the countryside seeking food during the winter and that they usually had a king rat. He went on to describe in painstaking detail how the king was supposed to be clever and also the biggest and wiliest of the bunch! Usually they invaded corncribs, but they took the food wherever they could find it.

This did nothing at all to ease mom's mind! Talk about misreading what mom needed at the moment! Mom let out a terrible screech that caught everyone's attention.

Dad realized, all too late, that he was much too explicit!

Her plea was quiet but forceful—"Get rid of them! I'm not staying in this house until you do!'

Dad pleaded with her to wait until he came home from work! But, no—the time was clearly now.

As soon as the stores opened up, dad went and got traps and other aids.

The various tools and methods worked. He was sure of it. Altogether, he eliminated twenty-six of these not so inviting creatures from our basement over the next several days!

As the numbers rose, so did mom's disdain for the basement!

She wanted nothing to do with it—even after dad sealed the cover back into place.

Nor did most others in the household!

Mom did her next round of washing clothes at dad's parents' home. Mom wanted the basement thoroughly sanitized first!

When I look back on it now, it was as though we had fully set up a banquet table, established sleeping quarters and added the comfort of a warming fire for our unwanted guests. We didn't plan it that way, or advertise it, but they found it and the figured out a way to access it and made themselves at home.

My job still continued in the mornings. Fire up the furnace!

So, after all was supposedly back to normal, I went down around five again one morning. Tiger usually followed me down and I usually rubbed him behind the ears and spent a few minutes with him while I made sure the new wood in the furnace was burning, as it should.

This time, Tiger wouldn't come! I have to admit to being more than just a little curious! But dad said it was over and that meant to me that it was over. So, down I went.

There it was—plain as could be! This very long tail wiggled back into the woodpile. It was very, very long—much longer than the others I had seen before! Rather than panic mom again, this time I tapped dad on the shoulder and put my finger to my lips and motioned him to come with me. Once in the kitchen, I told hem what I saw! "The king", he said firmly! We didn't get the king!

Dad took mom to Milwaukee on the way to work that day! No way was she staying home.

I don't think that in our wildest imaginations—Jim, dad or I were ready for what would take place that night!

Dad got home early! We already got home by school bus.

So down the stairs we went!

How concerned was dad?

Well, first he took down the basement stairs. They were still toe-nailed in place to the floor joist for the base of the house. It took a nail puller and several good yanks with a crow bar to remove the nails. Jim and I looked at each other a little surprised when he did that.

It also meant, if something couldn't use the stairs to get out of the basement—neither could we. We were all stuck here together—with what ever!

But, somehow that still seemed OK, because we were still here with dad!

Then we watched dad set up. He gave Jim and me our baseball bats and told us to stand back, near the furnace in case he had a problem. Now that made us just a little nervous!

We could see what he had in mind! On the floor to his side was the net attached to a large frame that he used to catch crabs for perch fishing. He held a clothes pole in his left hand while his right had a very tight grip around a large baseball bat of his own. I never thought of a Louisville Slugger being used for something like this.

Once he was set up, he turned to us and told us he had talked to some of the farmers about rats.

They told him that when a pack took over, the king was often the hardest to catch and was dangerous if it felt cornered. He told us that's why we had the bats! He told us he hoped to throw the net over it if he could. That was indeed his preference!

Then he began! One by one, he used the long slender clothes pole to move the logs from the pile. He started from the end closest to where the stairs now lay on the floor and began to work slowly toward the corner of the wall! Log by log! Nothing happened! More log by log! Still nothing happened!

Then there was a loud shrill animal sound that sounded part scream and part warning! Out darted a rat—a fairly good sized one! Dad clobbered it directly, nudged it with the clothes pole, and when it didn't move—shoved it aside.

Then, without warning, a second rat sprinted out like a shot! It ran away from dad and directly toward Jim and me! Talk about not being scared of things smaller than you—and then—suddenly seeing something so comparatively small loom larger than life—it suddenly seemed huge—really huge!

It ran right at me and suddenly swerved. That's when I caught it. I must have swung extra hard because it went sailing and never moved again. I wasn't hurt or bit, but my adrenalin was pumping a lot faster than when this all started!

Maneuvering the baseball bat in my hands didn't seem anything like manipulating the controller for a video game! Oh no! Nothing at all! It seemed like the reflexes with the bat had to be light years faster! Maybe that's what happens when your heart beats really fast!

The question was—did we have them all now?

One by one, he continued to disturb the woodpile—slowly—almost painfully—one log at a time!

The floor was getting to be a shambles with split pieces of log strewn all over as the pile continued to be dismantled moving slowly but surely toward the corner.

Then it happened! With only a few feet to go, suddenly this large ugly rodent broke from behind the few remaining logs and ran with amazing speed and determination toward the stair well!

It must have noticed the stairs no longer in service and made a huge powerful leap. Unbelievable how high it jumped! It seemed to us like it almost flew as it desperately lunged trying so hard to reach the landing to the main floor. It hit the wall with a definite thud and fell—somewhat stunned.

Just as dad dropped the clothes pole and started to stoop to pick up the net, the rat was back on its feet. We all learned quickly what it means to corner a living wild creature!

It looked fierce with its jaws open and teeth showing as it made a straight line racing directly at dad. With a golf like swing he swung the bat! Rat and bat met in mid air as the creature leapt at dad. Scared? You bet! I have never seen anything like it before or since! It wasn't meant to be that dramatic. Yet, there they were—man and creature defending themselves.

The king lost!

I grabbed an empty five-gallon bucket and quickly dropped it over the rat—tossing the mouth of the bucket toward the floor to cover it. Dad took a few startled breaths and slid the cover under the bucket to seal it and then flipped it over and took it outside. Everyone's adrenaline was really pumping! We never did ask what happened to it from that point on.

Oh yes, there was scrubbing after scrubbing of the basement before mom would go down the basement again!

The wood was always piled outside after that—no matter how cold it got! It was not piled close to the house either!

It would be negligent to not tell you why the rodent intimidated Tiger! The rodent was much, much bigger! I didn't know they grew so big!

(There is a side story to this episode. Dad never played golf prior to this, but was one heck of a baseball player. I think his experience and quick reflexes saved him that day. He would later take up golf in his early fifties and became a low handicap golfer. He would later admit, that what happened was nothing like what he had intended. He really thought he could just frighten and then trap the rodent with his net, but the creature had its own ideas about the situation!)

It really bothered us all to have to kill living creatures! To this day we all love God's creatures of all kinds! Some of us would do sketches and paintings of them as would our own children and their children— but not of those rodents with long pointed thin tails!

NO SKILLED HUCK FINNS THIS TIME

It was early May of 1954 and this was my senior year in high school—an exciting time for me.

A ceramic brown glazed bear, about four and a half inches high, that I made free hand just won honorable mention in the Scholastic Art Awards competition for the state of Wisconsin.

A watercolor of a Red Headed Woodpecker perched on the side of a heavy barked tree got an honorable mention in The Milwaukee Journal Art Calendar Contest.

Also, I was aspiring to be a cartoonist or to work as an animator for the late Walt Disney.

I loved creative things even back then.

Graduation was only a year a way.

I was already beginning to think about how much I would miss my friends.

School had been fun.

My favorites were the writing classes and the art classes.

I loved history and studies about different parts of the world.

I also liked speech, geometry and science.

I was particularly fond of English. I loved learning how to write and spent part of my time working for the school newspaper.

I enjoyed chess club.

I had some great teachers too like Audrey Bartlett (my high school art teacher). Say what one will, but perhaps marks of the good teacher are some of the students that move on to success because he or she turned their candle up to burn a brighter flame.

There were a number of really talented students in my classes with her. I think she made them all better.

For example, there was Wiley Miller who would eventually go on to illustrate the cover for Fishing Facts magazine for many years and the insides as well.

There was Ron Osicki, who used to live across the street from me on Manitoba Ave. in South Milwaukee who had fabulous creative skills at a young age and decorated our class year book. (Years later my sons Don and Greg would both decorate the year books for their class at Saint Catherine's High School in Racine.

There was another youngster named Marty who would go on to become an art teacher in Racine—and so many others.

I still remember my first painting in her class. It was of a Red Headed Woodpecker on the barky side of a tree.

There was also Mrs. Bettinger (a very prim, proper and strict teacher for Pan American History whom I feared at first, but who really taught me to take notes and how to study—I owe her the most). I absolutely loved history.

And, there was Doc Hintz—my biology teacher who taught us to study hard and at the same time to have fun studying. I had an interesting experience in Doc's class. Early in the first semester in Biology he asked me to stay after class. I wondered what I might have done. Instead it turned out to be a challenge. A large part of the grade in his class was a project that he expected from each student. Doc took me into a room and showed me a collection of projects he had saved from over the years. One of them he showed me was from my Uncle Leonard when he had been a student there nine years before me. Uncle Len was dad's youngest living brother. Doc first asked me if Leonard Danowski was related to me. I answered yes. Then he said, "Ed, your uncle did this project years ago. It is one of the best ever done in my class. And so I expect you to turn in something of the same caliber." The gauntlet had been set and from a source I would never have expected.

I thoroughly enjoyed doing projects for the various classes where I could use art. These included a poster I did for history class where I

96

drew the heads of all of the presidents of the United States, in ink, from the beginning to that date and mounted them in 3 D relief on the poster board. I had a lot of fun doing two for biology featuring watercolor paintings of a number of birds mounted in 3D relief on one poster board and the various parts of a bird's anatomy (labeled).

I shouldn't admit it here because I would have scolded my own children big time if they did the same, but I also did a number of other for some of my classmates to help them out – particularly the girls. There were three of them that hung on Doc's walls at one time or another, but they had the girls' names on them. Doing these—put me on the spot in more than one way. They all got "A"s. The girls were happy, but I was always worried that maybe I would be detected. Not a good idea! Again, I would have really taken my children to task if I ever found out that they did something like that.

I loved to draw and paint.

I also loved participatory sports and dad encouraged it.

Through the art classes, I got to help decorate the bulletin boards for athletic events and social events.

Usually this meant designing the themes, slogans, titles and sketching the rather large sized caricatures.

It also meant painting them with poster paints and highlighting them with colored chalks plus some time off from classes to set them up.

Actually I got started doing this kind of thing when I was in eighth grade at a one room country school I attended—the Oakwood Road School.

Our teacher gave me the task of filling about ten full chalkboard panels with colored chalk drawings as decorations for the school's Christmas pageant.

Four depicted the nativity, complete with wise men and shepherds.

The others featured Santa riding in his sleigh and led by eight reindeer over the roof tops of Oak Creek's farms.

Initially I was a bit nervous about it because all of the other students in the school, since it was one room, would watch and I had never done anything like that before.

That experience gave me the courage to get up in front of groups after that and not get too nervous.

I found out it was OK.

Besides, the teacher gave me a thank you gift. It became one of my favorite books. I still have it—Robert Lewis Stevenson's Treasure Island.

Getting involved in school activities was a good way to make friends.

Some of my pals from high school, wanted to come out and visit our place. One day, it seemed like a particularly good idea.

I was driving my own car now—an old blue dodge coup. It was my first major purchase with the money I saved while working at Bussler's. Like everyone's first car, you never forget it.

I volunteered to pick everyone up.

None of these guys ever spent much time in the country before. Once they got there, they had more ideas for what they wanted to do than you could imagine. You would think they never saw fields or woods before. They were Dave, Alan and George.

It didn't take long for them to focus in on our woods. It was only about a half mile away.

We just started out in that direction when this rather large flock of crows approached us from the Southeast. Dave was the first to notice them.

Of course, you can probably guess what happened next. But, there is a little twist to it.

I could not resist! I bet Dave a quarter I could get at least one crow to come out of that flock and another quarter that I could get it to land on my shoulder.

There were a lot of doubters. It was unfair, but it was an easy bet to make.

Every magician has to have a line of mumbo jumbo and baloney before performing his all time greatest feat. So, I had to have mine.

I elaborated how I knew all there was to know about crows and how certain inflections in your voice were important. I stressed that by calling to them in a personalized way by using their name could actually coax them to come to you.

"If you are really lucky," I said, "maybe one would even land on your shoulder."

As they approached, I called, "George! George!" My school friend George thought I was calling him, looked at me in an odd sort of way and said, "Ed, I'm right here!"

Just as he did so many times before, my black beauty circled in the cerulean blue of the sky and streaked down from the flock.

His wings sounded almost like helicopter blades as they flapped in a little stiffer mode to both slow him down and to steady his approach.

George's landing on my shoulder, as always, was with his extra gentle touch.

Wow, talk about an impression!

They could not believe what they were witnessing.

I just took it all in.

It was fun to watch the amazement all over their faces.

"How did you do that?" That question came up a number of times and with more than just a little curiosity!

At first they didn't even begin to believe my explanation or that this was my pet crow. It took a lot of explaining before the truth sunk in.

What finally cinched it was when my brother Jerry came out of the house and George flew over to him. They all thoroughly enjoyed the experience.

We spent a fair amount of time visiting with my bird. They particularly enjoyed how he tried to talk into our ear.

George seemed equally curious about them.

Jerry was kind enough to walk off with George back toward the house so that he wouldn't pay attention to where we were going.

Oh, by the way, I didn't accept the two quarters even though Dave tried to pay.

We started for the woods, my city pals and me.

We pushed our way through what remained of the corn fields that dad planted the year before.

We even flushed a pheasant to add to their new experiences.

We had so much fun gabbing about this most unusual crow that it dominated most of the conversation until we got to the edge of the wooded area.

It was a real adventure exploring the woods, visiting the secret pond located near the middle, some strange shaped giant trees and witnessing the abundant varieties of small wild creatures.

I never have tired of seeing animals and birds of all sizes and shapes—no matter how many times I've encountered them before.

After about an hour of that, one of the guys wanted to see the railroad trestle that I told him about from time to time. To get to it we had to continue through our woods, then head south and then wind our way through Dittmar's woods to the point where the trestle crossed the Root River.

It was an old skeletal looking bridge made of steel girders and struts resting on a concrete abutment. Its rust caked frame formed a fascinating silhouette against the sky and underscored the trees around it.

Real appreciation for it came if you were there at the right time and got to watch a locomotive roll across and got to experience the rickety clack of its many cars trailing behind. It often sounded its whistle just after crossing the bridge because the next cross road for the tracks was only a few blocks to the South.

Stepping out from the woods and into the clearing, the panorama exposed everyone to quite a sight!

Flood waters filled the Root River up to the very limits of her banks. She wasn't nearly as bad as she was the year before, but nevertheless, she was flooded.

My three wide eyed guests stared in wonder at the river—adventure written all over their faces.

I think it was George who saw the loose railroad ties. They lay scattered near the base of the trestle's embankment.

Someone yelled, "Let's make a raft."

I started to get really nervous about the direction this conversation was going.

I tried to talk them out of it.

I really did!

No amount of reasoning did any good. It only deepened their growing resolve to try river rafting.

I had a lot of respect for that old river after watching rather large sized branches swept effortlessly downstream by its silent currents. I knew they were there even if you couldn't see them.

At first I stood back as they started to drag the ties to the waters' edge. I remembered mom's cautions all too well and always respected them.

No matter what I said, they harbored little intention of listening to me about this.

Because I was worried about my buddies, I did not intend to let them try something this stupid alone.

A bad choice—breaking a commitment I made to someone whom I respected and loved.

It was the wrong thing—even if it meant not staying with my friends when they did something they really wanted, but I knew it wasn't the right thing to do.

We were about to learn that seventeen and eighteen year olds do not fully understand how everything in the universe works—at least not yet. Nor do they make the smart choices every time.

We hauled seven railroad ties to the river—one at a time. They were very heavy.

We also were missing some things like a rope to lace them together.

These were intelligent guys. Some members of this group were honor students. Moreover—I thought that maybe this crazy idea would end here.

It didn't!

Resourcefully, Dave, found a part roll of barbed wire and we bound the ties together with the rusty old stuff.

About now you begin to get an idea of how much clear thinking went into this. You would never know that some of these guys were actually quite intelligent.

With the raft fully assembled, we pushed it closer to the river's North bank.

Next, we searched for and found some long, slender fallen limbs from nearby trees to use as guide poles. After stripping some dead twigs and lighter branches, we had four.

One more time, I tried talking them out of trying to go down the river.

Nevertheless, they insisted on a tradeoff. Instead they agreed to pole the raft only to the other bank of the river. I warned them about the currents, but they were certain they'd make it.

Two of the guys got on the raft standing with their poles in hand and their jeans rolled up to look like Sawyer and Finn.

Dave and I pushed at the part of the raft that still clung to part of the shore.

Finally, the raft was almost free and floating.

Dave and I both climbed on.

We shoved away with our poles.

The first few pushes were easy as the poles reached bottom.

Suddenly, they didn't any more!

Terrified—that isn't the word for it!

The current was unbelievably powerful. It took our makeshift raft like a paper box swirling it a bit at first and then pulling it faster and faster as though some invisible something was trying to throw a scare into us.

Then the trouble really hit.

Our strong, well-designed makeshift vessel broke in two.

One part, consisting of four ties, carried George and Alan.

The one I shared with Dave was almost non existent. Ours consisted of three ties—not very many. The front stayed fastened together, but the back was coming apart. It resembled riding bareback on a very weak version of the letter of the alphabet—"V". I was on that back part!

Not to panic, but—we were heading down stream at a speed that seemed to be ever increasing. It was just as though the throttle jammed on a race car and an engine was racing out of control.

The brute strength of the current had us firmly in its grip.

That's when I told Dave the good news.

"I didn't know how to swim."

"Can't get more stupid than this," I thought!

We were accelerating downstream. Faster and faster! We were also edging closer to the South bank and quickly approached a sharp bend in the river—so sharp you couldn't see around it.

We were now at least a city block from the launching point.

That's when I saw it!

Stretched across the flooded waters was a single strand of barbed wire used for keeping cattle from wandering. It was hanging about six to eight inches over the water. That means the rafts would pass under it—but we could not!

Railroad ties aren't very long.

Our raft was steadily coming further and further apart! The bard wire was stretched to the max and straining as though it wanted to snap.

Traveling at this high rate of speed, I didn't know how any of us could possibly get over the wire, while our piece of the raft went under.

It didn't seem possible without some of us tumbling into the river's savage current.

This had all the earmarks of a tragedy about to happen!

I thought to myself, "Why didn't I listen to mom! Of all the times to pick not to listen!"

Our rafts were both totally out of control!

George and Alan were ahead of us and rounded the tip of the river's sharp curve first.

George, on the lead raft, was the first to see this big, thick, old tree branch. It stuck out over the water several feet short of the wire.

Both makeshift craft were now headed at top speed for that lonesome but deadly strand of wire.

The branch was our only hope. It was also a one shot deal. "Grab the limb!" George yelled.

Dave and I watched as George and Alan successfully garbed hold of the limb.

George's adrenaline was steaming.

He saw to it that both of them moved quickly.

They edged hand over hand along the thick girth of the branch and toward the bank. They clearly tried to make room for us to attempt the same maneuver.

We were bearing down on them at full speed.

Then, it was our turn.

It was scarier than I can put into words!

Everything was happening so fast. It was grab the limb and hang on—or else!

Dave caught it first and I was right behind.

Our torsos, from the waist on down, were below unbelievably ice cold water and, for the first time, I felt the full force of the current. It pulled our legs straight out in front of us and we had to really struggle to just hang on to this solid extension of a tree.

The perverse trick was to hang on tight and yet edge along the limb, to shore and safety, without being sucked under by the current's force.

We did it! Wet, cold and shivering, all four of us survived what could have been a real disaster!

Our guardian angels clearly pulled us out of that one!

We stood there on shore a while in silence and just stared at the old river.

Each, in their own way, was thinking back over where we had been and where we could have been.

Then someone broke the silence.

We needed it.

Alan laughed and we all joined in.

The longer we laughed the louder it got.

By now, we all noticed the first funny thing to happen on this misadventure. Dave had been wearing hip huggers and when the current shot our legs forward, off came his jeans!

There he stood, sopping wet, shivering in his briefs.

Thoroughly exhausted and so relieved about being safe and on the ground, it seemed even funnier. We nearly rolled in hysterics at the sight of Dave standing there soaked and cold in his skivvies.

At first he looked sheepish.

Then he laughed too—as heartily as any seventeen year old could.

As for the rest of us—well, we continued chuckling almost uncontrollably, as though intoxicated, until we were almost exhausted.

What we all knew is that Someone, graciously, just awarded each of us another chance to laugh.

I did not notice until we stopped laughing that we had company. Someone must have let George the crow out. Suddenly he came from nowhere and landed on my shoulder. It's hard to say how much he saw of what just transpired. He just seemed to take it all in.

That was the second time my friends had seen that patented on the shoulder landing in the same day. It was a good feeling just to be there and to have it happen again.

For Dave, however, the humor lasted only so long. He had a problem that the rest of us did not have.

Even though we couldn't or didn't want to stop kidding him about it, we still felt good buddies should help him out at least a little.

We made our way west along the south bank until we got back to the trestle and crossed to the other side.

One last look at that river!

Then we continued quickly across the clearing and back through the woods.

We were still drenched. Our shoes were water logged and squished with each step.

As we left the last of the tinted trees, scarlet streaks started to stretch slowly searching for something across the early evening sky.

Slender sepia shadows began to slink slowly like so many spiders spinning webs in secret patterns across the ground.

It was a good thing dad planted that corn field the spring before because its leaves and its shadows concealed us fairly well.

We quickly plowed our way through the crackling rows of browned corn stalks.

Dave must have known a little of how Adam felt with the proverbial fig leaf!

We finally made it home. George flew overhead, gliding in circles, following us all the way.

Mom was in the house but didn't see me come in the front door. Dave and the other guys stayed hidden in the seclusion offered by the corn field. I made it up the stairs and changed into dry clothes and slinked back out again with an extra pair of my jeans for Dave.

Lucky so far! I'll say! However, we still had to get Dave past his mom without her catching sight of him with my trousers.

So, we took Dave home first. He tried to sneak up the stairs to his room just as I did about twenty-five minutes before.

Oh, Oh! Moms do notice everything and his observant mom did. She noticed, right away, that the jeans he had on were too long and were not his.

Very quietly, she started the interrogation.

She never raised her voice.

We never openly laughed either, until later, when she finally said, "David, where are your pants?"

She couldn't have said it any plainer than that.

Dave covered up best he could by telling her he tore them on barbed wire—closer to the truth than any of us wanted to think about.

It was quite a day. I know that the four of us are very lucky to have survived.

The hardest part was surviving the guilt I had for breaking mom's trust.

I was very, very careful about that in the future with mom and anyone else to whom I gave my word.

That evening, a tell tale tap echoed off the upstairs window pane. Jim opened it.

In hopped George.

He seemed to fuss a lot.

He swaggered, pranced and chatted.

It was a louder chatter—excited—almost like a scolding.

Eventually he jump-skipped onto my shoulder and put his cool, hard beak next to my ear. He just seems to make soft soothing sounds. He acted as if he wanted to stay there a long time. It was as if he knew something out of the ordinary happened that day and was relieved it was over.

That night, George wanted to stay upstairs. I put an old flannel shirt on top of my desk and he went to sleep. So did I, but not until I laid there for what seemed like a very long while contemplating the day's events. We were sure lucky—more than lucky!

My eyes opened early the next morning. Sitting on my chest, was George, just looking at me—turning his head slowly one way and then another—never taking his eyes off me.

He moved forward slowly and sat on the flat part of the front of my collarbone.

Leaning forward, he moved his beak to my ear and started making soft almost purring intonations.

He did that for a long time.

He definitely was trying to tell me something that was on his mind.

He never made a morning appearance like that, on my bed, before or after!

George stayed around the house for about a week that time—much longer than he had been doing recently. It was good to have him around so much!

There is one more little sidelight to this adventure.

Almost a year after this incident, Dave, some other friends including another buddy, Craddock, who would later become a heart surgeon, and I wrote our Senior Class Day play.

We had a vignette near the middle as part of a little inside joke commemorating the trip my friends made to the country. One of our classmates got to portray Liberace playing at the piano. Dave got to play Liberace's brother George, after our crow of course. He played the violin—which Dave did very well by the way.

There, at a very poignant point in the music, his suspenders let loose and his trousers fell exposing his gym shorts.

There were four of us who laughed louder and harder than anyone else.

We kept the real meaning of it to ourselves for a long, long time.

GRADUATION

Graduation came at an interesting time. It was the Eisenhower recession. Very few of the guys I graduated with were able to get jobs for the summer.

My friend Kaddie and I used his dad's truck for a few days trying to find scrap metal to haul to junk yards and sell for what we could get. However, that didn't pan out as we had hoped and lasted only a week or so.

Any ideas I might have had, about going to California to become an illustrator for Walt Disney, were out of the question because I was a minor—only seventeen when I graduated.

Dad and I talked about me working for him as a painter. However, he said he couldn't afford to pay me what I could get working for another contractor. I was welcome to work for him, but he wanted to me to it on my own try first. He said I was ready for it. So, I tried.

The first few contractors did not want to look at a kid who was seventeen. Yet, I did get a painting contractor to take a look at what I could do. He told me if I could paint as well as my dad thought I could he would hire me. Nevertheless, I would first have to prove I could hold my own by painting as fast as any of the painters he had working for him.

I felt really uncomfortable going to someone looking for a job and unabashedly selling my skills.

I think that is true for most people.

I felt particularly awkward saying I could paint faster than most, but, that was what dad said to do. Though I was uneasy doing it, but I followed his advice. As I learned later, that's what you have to do to get anywhere—not be afraid to really sell yourself and to let the right people know about what you've accomplished. It's unfortunate you have to do that because it feels like you're patting yourself on the back. Except, that's the way it operates in the work place. My friend Jack would later say over and over, "If you don't do it, who will?"

I never expected the trial to be anywhere near the experience it turned out to be. Curiously the contractor's name was also Ed. He instructed me to show up on the site of one of his jobs in Milwaukee.

Ed, a former marine, saw combat in some of the World War II hot spots during the Pacific campaigns and was very soft spoken.

He stood a little stooped at the shoulders and always had a pipe in his mouth. He also walked with a slight limp—a souvenir from his military days. His pointed nose accented his dark brown eyes giving them an almost beady look.

He called me Edward and never did get that straight.

At any rate Ed said, with that soft voice, "I'm going to give you a little test and, if you pass, you've got a job."

There he stood with a stop watch!

Nervous is not the word for how my stomach swizzled. This was much harder than drawing on the chalkboards in eighth grade— although that experience actually helped me.

He had me paint windows for about an hour.

Suddenly he called, "OK, stop!" He walked over to me as I got down from the ladder. He didn't look up at first. He continued to study his notes. It seemed like forever. "OK, you start tomorrow," He said as he handed me the address for the first paint job I would do for him.

I worked for him all summer long. Yet, it got rather curious near the end of August. He told me one day that, since I was young and agile, he bid on painting a barn. It wasn't a very high barn so I didn't mind too much. The next one; however, was something else.

The next barn was so high that Ed had to rent extra long ladders to try to reach the peak. When I showed up for work a 7:30 A.M., he and the farmer were setting the extension ladders on top of a hay wagon to try to reach the tip of the old barn. They didn't make it. I don't mind saying I was just a little anxious about the whole thing. Ed didn't have any safety belts or harnesses.

Next, he tied the paint brush to a broom handle.

His instructions were to let the bucket hang a few rungs lower on the ladder, lock my knees into the sides of the ladder and just do the best that I could with the peak.

It went OK for a few minutes when a sudden breeze came up and shook the wagon.

The ladder started to slide to my right!

It edged slowly at first, but then began to move a little faster!

Luckily, as it slid, I was able to catch the opening at the top of the hay loft that served as a window. That broke the slide or it would have been a long trip down.

This was a far shorter, but even scarier than the Root River ride a few months earlier.

I thought I would lose my job when I told him I wasn't going to paint any more barns. Fortunately he didn't and I finished out the summer working for him.

While heights didn't bother me much before this episode, they do bother me a little now.

MORE SUMMER OF '54

I didn't mean to skip over the rest of summer because there was more going on than going to work—far more!

The older members of our family were beginning to get more involved in things that young people tend to do when growing up. We also worked hard at staying close as a family because that is something we all enjoyed and all wanted very much to continue.

We used to catch a few outdoor theater movies every summer as a family. We did a few more times this summer. Mom loved westerns and dad loved John Wayne so we saw one of his movies. Mom also liked Dean Martin and Jerry Lewis and she loved musicals. One I remember in particular was going to see a doubleheader. We saw a new Martin and Lewis comedy and Showboat the same night.

One thing about the outdoor, even though you stayed up late, it was cheap entertainment on buck night. You could take as many people in as you could squeeze in your car for a dollar. I always did love the soda pop and the special smell of fresh popcorn.

Surprisingly though, probably the best entertainment that year happened right at home.

George started to show us a new trait that he must have perfected on his trips away from home. He mastered the art of becoming a tease. He perfected it so well that he almost became a pest at times except he was just so doggone funny you could not keep yourself from laughing at him.

The first real sign of his new prowess came with the chickens. Along with the usual grains that we fed to them, we also feed any old bread scraps we had, but first broke the slices into crumbs.

One day Jan was out feeding these scraps to the chickens when suddenly George appeared from nowhere! He was good at that by now.

He watched the chickens go after the crumbs for a while and must have noticed how they all tended to rush for the last few scraps.

When there was just one single morsel left, George dove for it and picked it up. He flew about seven or eight feet away. Then, he dropped it from his beak.

All the chickens made a dash for that single crumb.

George also flew at it again.

He captured it with his hard covered snout just before the lead chickens got there. He picked it up once more and flew another seven or eight feet and dropped it again.

The chickens chased after that solitary piece of stale bread once again.

George made this whimsical sound almost as if he was laughing at them and provoking them at the same time.

Then he hurried and repeated this skit over and over again with the same solitary piece of stale bread until the chickens tired of the chase.

When that happened, he tired of it too and just left the piece of old stale bread to lie there by its lonesome.

If he thought that was humorous—he succeeded! We were in stitches! I think he knew we thought it was amusing and that must have encouraged him all that much more.

He played this game repeatedly and never seemed to tire of it and the chickens never seemed to learn. It always ended with that last morsel just sitting there after the chickens finally gave up and George taunting them whimsically.

Then there was Goose.

I was there the only time I know of his trying this on Goose.

Old Goose just raised his old wings and hissed and George just dropped it right there. Neither one of them touched the bread.

They just stood there for a while. George cocked his head a little keeping his gaze directed at the now rather large farmyard fowl.

Goose, waddled a few steps toward him and they just stood there making noises at each other for at least five minutes.

Apparently that was all they had to say to each other.

Goose just turned and waddled away.

George flew over to my shoulder and whispered in my ear. I still did not understand him. Though, finally, he let me know that he wanted to come into the house for a visit.

GEORGE

George was just getting started. Nobody taught him. He just kept inventing new games. I can't even remember them all.

However, another involved dad.

Now that was high risk territory!

Still, George did not seem the least bit concerned.

It was a weekend and an unusually hot summer's day.

Dad was setting the flagstone in place for our chimney and I was mixing the cement for him.

This is the day that I think George got even with dad for the name dad gave him in his infancy. It was the same game George played with the chickens, but with a new twist designed just for humans.

Dad had two wooden carpenter's horses set a short distance apart with a plank stretched across them.

On one end he had the mortar board where the wet cement and gravel mix went conveniently close to his mason's trowel.

On the other end he had a pitcher of green Lime Kool Aide.

Also, he kept a package of Lucky Strike cigarettes and his cigarette lighter nearby.

Dad turned with a trowel full of cement to put it in place for the next piece of flagstone.

There, in a blur, was George coming from nowhere. He was really good at coming from nowhere these days.

He set down slowly on the end of the plank. Then the feathered fiend started trying to make his own brand of conversation. He continued until we both looked up. He wanted to be sure we were paying attention.

Then, quick as a wink, he grabbed dad's pack of cigarettes in his beak and streaked about fifteen feet away.

Apparently, he got it into his cranium that humans could travel faster those chickens. So he made sure he dropped the object of the chase a little farther away.

Dad made about three attempts at retrieving his pack before he let loose with some rather harsh sounding superlatives.

Dad did not think this was funny or entertaining any more. He was now the victim.

George knew it right then and there. It wasn't prudent to continue!

He stopped dead in his tracks and had the gall to fly right at dad and land on his shoulder, cigarette pack and all. He just perched there and waited for dad to take it. Some scientists might call that instinct. I call that something else!

Dad reached up for his cigarettes and laughed as he cussed out the young black thief. George just stayed there awhile and talked into dad's ear until he thought he made sufficient peace.

Then he flew over to me where he knew he was totally safe.

If I told you I didn't laugh to myself while this was going on, I'd be kidding you. I just wished at the time that I could have laughed out loud. However, that also would not have been a judicious application of anyone's judgment. I wanted to live a lot longer.

Dad was always a great tease too. So it was twice as comical to see the teaser being teased by the tease.

Anyone who says that non-human living creatures do not have some form of intellect has to prove it to me.

I think our arrogance as humans may get in our way when scientists declare whether or not living creatures think. It may well be that they haven't yet comprehended how birds and animals think or how quickly the are able to apply what they learn.

Science continually overturns old theories changing long standing positions on subject matter that they once considered to be sacrosanct. This shows just how much we have to learn about so many things.

George just kept doing things that seemed to have some amazing thought pattern to it that were more than simple instinctive responses.

He also seemed to know when enough was enough.

Remember way back to when I mentioned that I thought George spent much time in the house during his youth casing the joint and each of us too.

Well mom was not left out of the loop.

One Monday, mom washed her white sheets and other white things. Unfortunately—it suddenly started to pour without warning before she got them out on the clothes' line!

Mom was pretty patient. She left the wet things sitting in a wash basket out in the back hall. She figured the rain would stop sooner or later and maybe the sun would come out. It was still fairly early and she had hopes of getting the wash to dry. There were no clothes' dryers yet.

I got home just before it stopped raining. Ed, the painting contractor, only had outside work to do and you don't paint to homes when the wood is sopping wet.

Somewhere around noon, the faithful old sun made a midday appearance.

Mom put her goulashes on and, with Judy's help, hung out all of her good white clothes.

If you have ever been in the country and seen it rain heavily on clay soil, you know that means a sea of mud. Nice sticky mud clings tenaciously to your boots or shoes and almost sucks them off your feet.

However, the clothes had to dry.

In addition, mom only had a small window of time because she went to work as a waitress around 3:30 in the afternoon at Bussler's.

She finished hanging the last clothes pin and trudged into the back hallway. She was covered with mud well over the tops of her boots.

All of a sudden—you guessed it.

There was the tell tale sound of George. Caw, cawing, it came through the air. It was unmistakably his call.

It was taunting!

It was deliberate!

It was loud!

Mom shot to the kitchen window.

Then, without putting her boots on, she streaked through the kitchen door, out the back hallway and out the back door.

"Scram!—Scoot!—No!—George,—stop it!—Stop it," her voice cried in agony and in vain!

We raced to the window too late.

There he was.

Old George was picking off clothes' pins with his beak and dropping them, very causally, one at a time.

The white bed sheets were falling to join the other clothing already swimming in the mud.

Mess?

Oh what a mess!

Not happy! No! Not happy at all! Mom was as angry as I remember ever seeing her. She did not get angry easily.

She looked right at me. "It's your crow! You brought him here! You get the mud out of these clothes!" She had tears in her eyes.

Getting the mud, particularly clay out of clothing is not the easiest thing to do!

I didn't know where to begin.

I felt as badly as I ever did—and for something I didn't do!

Yet, George was my crow!

I had to own up to the responsibility I accepted when he came to live with us!

Lucky for me, mom calmed down quickly.

She was amazing!

She took charge and I helped out.

We got it done!

Young George had struck again.

There were lots of other lesser antics too.

For example, when he was in the house, he would move pencils around and other small objects.

Eventually some small items such as coins or safety pins would disappear and we knew that George was starting to collect things that were shinny and then hide them somewhere.

He was also becoming a pack rat.

Regardless of how he loved to tease, he never seemed to try this with Sandy or Tiger.

Instead, his visits with them were more a case of his sitting near to them and twisting his head one way or another and making those conversational sounds he made. It was similar to watching old friends chatting in the park!

I often wondered if somehow he was explaining his newest taunt or his latest conquest to them. Neither Tiger nor Sandy ever smiled—so, I couldn't tell.

George never quite tired of perching on Sandy's back. Every now and then, when he stayed over night, you'd find him resting there in the evenings and Sandy never seemed to mind.

Neither did we!

FALL TERM

It was time for me to learn about college. Much homework—and whether or not it got done was totally dependent on whether or not you wanted to do it. The professors didn't coax you. It was all up to you. Many classmates never made it past their freshman year.

I was just so pleased to have the opportunity to go to college! I knew I was fortunate because dad never had the chance. I watched him struggle with that through the years as he ran his own business and would try his hand at creative writing. The lack of more formal education to polish his skills held him back. I think maybe this is why he so encouraged me to go to college even though it meant such total commitment.

Later, he would go to night school at the University of Wisconsin Parkside so that he could begin to polish his writing skills. He started to rework a novel he had written before going back to school, but he never got finish it.

Between the job, hitchhiking to school both ways and homework—there just wasn't much time available to flexibility in my schedule one way or the other. It was a juggling act to be sure. And, if one or the other took more time, then one of the others took a hit. My days started at 5 in the morning and often didn't end until 1:30 in the morning and sometimes later. This schedule didn't leave much room for catching up if I got behind with homework or to keep up if I had to work extra or unexpected hours. Sometimes that affected my grades if an assignment was late or if I didn't have time to study for an exam. So, I used every minute after catching a ride or riding a bus once I got to Milwaukee. If I had homework, I had to get it done in the time window available.

One particular day though, I was stuck trying to complete a college algebra assignment. I hitchhiked home from Milwaukee and found out that my boss wanted me in to work right away and that I would have to work late.

Oh, Oh! I was in trouble, but I had no choice! I had to turn around and go right to work. Dad drove me there. He asked how it was going and I told him about that blankety blank Algebra assignment and the conflict with going to work unexpectedly.

I still worked at Bussler's thirty-five to forty hours a week to pay for my tuition and other expenses. Sometimes there would be fifty to sixty hour weeks. If I had a long shift I often got home from work a little after midnight or maybe one A.M. The cook, Blanche, drove me home!

This particular night, when I got home, there was dad reading my Algebra book.

I just couldn't stay up that night. It had been several weeks in a row of working late and then doing home work until two or three A. M. Sometimes I just went around the clock and snoozed for short periods. They were never more than quick cat naps in the Student Union between classes. I had too much to do! Plus I had a big exam the in an early class that morning.

I told dad that I planned to get up early in the morning, 5 A.M. or so, to take another crack at it. I usually started thumbing my ride at 6:30 or 7 A.M. I forgot to set the alarm and slept right through.

About 5:30 A.M., there was a tap on my shoulder.

It was dad.

We went downstairs to the kitchen table and he proceeded to explain how to do the problems. What's more, he had them all worked out for me just in case I wouldn't have time.

There was just a slight sign of being pleased with himself. He told me that morning that he always wanted to go to college. That is when he told me that he never got past the seventh grade. I didn't know that. All I remember hearing before is that Grandma Anna, his mom, telling me he skipped two grades in school because he did so well and that the principal put him ahead. That meant only five years of formal education for him in total.

He was the second oldest from a big family and he had to help out. Yet, he always desired to learn. He was always going to the library, taking out books on things he wanted to learn about and studying.

He learned many of the trade skills he needed to build our home from studying about them out of library books including plumbing, electricity and masonry.

He also read a lot of fiction and historical pieces.

Another time, I had a term paper to type out. I had it partially drafted and the rest was in outline form.

Again, it was just like the previous situation. I came straight home from school and had to go to work—this time until about 1:30 A.M. Bussler's' served a large Christmas party.

I fully expected to come home and be up all night typing and finishing the paper like so many papers before. Gratefully, I didn't have to this time!

There, on the kitchen table, was my typewriter. A note was next to it—on top of a paper in draft form.

Dad's note said he did all the research to fill in my outline. He said I should check his notes and state things my own words—and that he didn't want to do the actual writing.

He had a stack of books on the table from the Milwaukee library which was at least an hour and fifteen minute round trip for him. Good thing, because I only had a few reference texts.

It was an easy paper. The only real digging I had to do was the information for the footnotes.

The outcome was a good grade and I knew dad cared.

I was the first one from either my mom or dad's family to go to college. I know it was important to him.

Later, my cousins Bob Kroll from my dad's side and Bob Mankowski from my mom's side would finish college. My second cousins, Bob and Jim Slawny also went. That isn't many from a very big family! College was very special. Not many got to go back then. The other thing that was reinforced for me, even though I had seen it for myself in other ways over the years, was just how brilliant dad was. That however was far overshadowed by the knowledge of just how much he cared!

HITCHHIKING

Getting to school wasn't always easy. The only cars I could afford were old clunkers. Sometimes they ran pretty well. Sometimes they didn't.

Also, I was not a mechanic like my dad. He could fix most anything and was a mechanic for a large trucking company some years back.

When the old Dodge died that fall—I had no other choice. I hitchhiked to school.

I would stand along side the East side of the road on Highway 38 and thumb my way into Milwaukee.

Sometimes I would get lucky and catch a ride all the way downtown.

Sometimes it would take several rides just to get to Milwaukee.

Though, most often, I would get a ride to just north of Mitchell Field. Then I would walk to the end of the bus line and catch one to downtown and transfer to get to Marquette University.

If I missed the connecting bus, I would sometimes jog the fourteen or so blocks to school down Wisconsin Avenue.

Occasionally, I could walk quite a way before someone picked me up.

If I got a ride right away and made good connections, it took about an hour and twenty minutes. The worst ever was probably two and a half hours.

It was particularly difficult when it got cold or the weather was inclement.

But, I wanted to go to school.

Mom did not particularly like it and she worried about me.

Then it wasn't too bad.

Today, you don't dare hitchhike at all. You stand a good chance of being mugged or much worse.

At any rate, it was quite an entourage that watched me leave in the mornings.

Sandy would sit on the hill overlooking the road—almost like my protector.

Sometimes Tiger would join the vigil next to Sandy.

Most times, George would circle overhead. I don't know if George ever followed me part way, yet I often wondered!

Once inside the car, I used to muse about whether or not the driver ever suspected the show that was going on outside.

CHOICES

Periodically I had to go up to school in Milwaukee in the evenings during summers.

My younger brother Jerry was quite the guy. Often times he would offer to come along to keep me company. It gave us some time for some good chats about a lot of things. We were all very close and no one hesitated to do anything for each other.

I still struggled with what I wanted to do after I finished school.

Dad wanted me to be a lawyer.

After learning more about it, I thought I would continue with my Political Science major and head toward law School but maybe use it to go into politics. I gave much thought to maybe trying for the U. S. Senate someday. The closest I would later come would be to offer some advice to First Lady Hillary Clinton about a project she was working on and still have a thank you note from her. I also have a thank you note from George W. Bush—for something else and at this writing am helping a congressman with another issue. But, this is as close as I would come to this dream.

Mom had a relative who a one time was a judge in the 6th Branch Milwaukee Circuit Court. In fact, he was highly respected and recognized through a special honor bestowed by Governor Kohler in 1930. He was also a great guy.

I got to know him when I was about twelve years old.

Somehow, mom arraigned for me to do his lawn and gardening once a week during the summer. Dad would take me to Milwaukee on those days and I would take a bus to his old brick home. He liked hanging flowers and took a lot of time teaching me how to do it just the way he wanted it done. When I finished, I'd take the bus back to my Aunt Ruth's home near 60th and Oklahoma Avenue in Milwaukee and wait for dad to pick me up. Later, dad was contracted to paint the judge's home and I helped with the work.

One souvenir I still have from him is a thin world atlas featuring the picture of Douglas McArthur on the cover.

The other I have is that he talked me out of law school.

Since my real goal at this time was politics, he took me under wing and explained that unless I could afford to pay for all of my own political campaigning and support, I would end up needing to get it from others and that could end up in tremendous pressures from some of the contributors to reciprocate in ways I wouldn't feel comfortable because of my value system.

The message didn't sink in—in terms of what it meant right away. Sometime later, when it did, I still continued with law school as an objective for a while because I began to think about Foreign Service for the government.

Later, I even changed my mind about that because I didn't know how that would affect the family I someday hoped to have. The more that I learned, the more I was sure that it wouldn't fit my idea of family life as I envisioned it then.

I was too committed financially to change my major by that time and continued with the one I had. (Later, after the military, it would mean starting the master's degree program through Johnson Wax and going to school nights for a number of years to pick up my accounting and the other business courses I would need.) If I could have afforded it financially then, I probably would have switched to business or journalism.

By this time in life I had a rough idea of how to be patient, tighten my focus, develop a plan and continue to work directionally toward where I wanted to be.

Dad and mom were both very supportive as I took the time to try to sort all of this out.

GOOSE

One day, when I came home from school, mom could hardly contain her excitement. There was something she wanted to tell.

It seems that, about midmorning, mom heard a series of noises out in the yard. It sounded like metal clanging.

She looked out the window and saw an old pick up truck parked on the north side of the house. A little ways away, two strangers were looking through dad's scrap parts pile. One of them was a fairly big guy and he looked like a real tough to her.

They didn't belong there!

Every farm had its scrap pile. Sometimes they were a real important when you needed a certain nut or a bolt or a metal bar or a piece of metal shaped a certain way or a spare part. It was usually when you were in a hurry to fix something like a tool or piece of equipment that broke down. Otherwise, if you didn't need some pieces after a while, they were worth some money to sell as junk metal.

Mom said she really became frightened because dad was at work. The rest of us were at school. She was all alone.

She certainly knew enough to stay in the house and not go outside. She also called dad at work.

She said the window was open slightly and she was peaking from behind the kitchen curtains.

All of a sudden these two guys started running toward their truck.

Goose came after them in hot pursuit! His wings were fully extended and flapping with a powerful noise. His head was protruding forward like a battering ram. His wide open and intimidating beak looked pretty scary come at you at that speed.

Goose also generated that frightful sounding fearsome hiss of his.

Suddenly, there was George, flying low, circling their heads and squawking loud as he could.

Sandy comes tearing around the front of the house barking, snarling and bearing down on them.

"It was like watching a movie," she exclaimed

"It was as if the three Musketeers had arrived."

The fearsome threesome chased the two intruders right up to the truck. She said they jumped in as fast as they could and slammed the doors shut.

Mom said those guys didn't even bother to turn around.

They backed up so fast and furiously—they tooled right out onto highway 38 and nearly got wiped out by a semi truck.

Their pickup screeched down the road, around the curve and toward the bridge, streaking South in the direction of Racine.

George settled into a tree near the driveway and seemed to watch for a while. Sandy sat alertly in the driveway and Goose just wandered away.

I can still imagine the thoughts that must have gone through the minds of the uninvited intruders.

Mom let us know that she felt much safer knowing that she had guardians protecting our home. So did we!

Goose and me

A FEW OTHER TIMES

There was good reason for mom to have been so concerned about the intruders in the yard.

Most of the time, living in the country offered a lot of serenity, less smog and other advantages to living in the city.

In contrast, however, there were some things that invited the unusual.

Just the fact that there was a lot of space between neighbors left country residents a little isolated. The nearest neighbor to the North of us was about a city block away. You had to travel a long way South, around a big curve, across a river and up a steep hill about a third of a mile before the next residential dwelling in that direction.

The river and all the trees made it seem extra secluded at night!

We had people come to the door with simple things like running out of gas. Conversely, there were other things that happened too!

One such incident occurred shortly after dad left to pick mom up from work—a little after midnight!

Following what must have been a wild party, three car loads of people decided to stop and continue their festivities on our front lawn.

A raucous commotion, from blaring car radio music, laughing and shouting,—startled all of us out of our sleep.

Some party-goers started banging on the front door and windows. Jim hurried all of the kids into an upstairs bedroom and shut the door.

We called the police.

Then, we sat there in the dark with our old twenty gage shotgun and the bow and arrows my Uncle Leonard bought for me a few years before.

They were still pounding on the door when the squad cars pulled into the yard.

The men in blue quickly dispersed the whole boisterous contingent and sent them on their way. "Too much party," the law enforcement officers offered! "It will be OK now!"

Another night, a young lady knocked furiously on the door looking for protective aid. "Help me," she pleaded!

Her boyfriend suddenly turned hostile while they were sitting in his car near the Root River.

Her ex-friend pursued her to the door and dad chased him off. Mom and dad wrapped a blanket around her.

Then mom and dad also drove her home!

We grew up in many ways through living in the country!

More notable perhaps, was early one other particular evening.

Seconds after Jim and I had just gone upstairs, we heard two cars racing at high speed. Wheels strained and tires shrieked as they rounded the curve on highway 38 in front of our house.

Pop!

A loud bang hit the front door.

Pop! Pop!

We heard two more loud bangs as the two cars continued to race.

Dad yelled, "Stay where you are!"

It got very quiet!

A few minutes later, he called to us, "Come on down!"

A large sized hole conspicuously splintered through the front door.

Not absolutely sure what it was at first, we could make a pretty darned good guess!

The same projectile that bored the opening in the door also pierced its way through the wall directly across the hallway.

Dad searched the closet on the other side of the wall. It partially pierced and finally imbedded itself in his long heavy black winter topcoat—a 38 caliber slug.

Just who was in those cars?

We never knew!

They sure didn't act like good guys!

We also never learned what happened to the other two shots or if they hit each other.

Luckily Jim and I didn't get in the way!

Sandy almost went wild when it happened.

She barked and yelped almost uncontrollably at the door for the longest time.

Anytime a car went around the curve a little fast after that she would howl—particularly if its tires squealed!

I have to admit, for a while, to getting a little sensitive to strange noises and to strangers at our door.

The spring after we found our pets, Jim, Jerry and I were at Eddie Lentz's place playing baseball.

Meanwhile, several of Judy's girlfriends stopped at home to visit. Jan was also there.

Unexpectedly, Eddie's mom screamed from their doorway, "Hurry home—someone's upstairs in your house."

We never waited to hear the rest. All of us piled into Eddie's parents car—each carrying a baseball bat—and raced the mile home.

Judy, Jan and Judy's girlfriends huddled in the ditch in front of the house—scrunched together in a state of total fright.

The high embankment between the ditch and the house concealed the girls somewhat!

Nearly hysterical young ladies told how they were sitting in the living room.

Then, without warning, they heard several loud bangs and a crashing noise from upstairs.

Somebody was up there.

They were positive!

Without hesitation, Eddie, his two brother, Jim, Jerry and I went charging into our house! Baseball bats, held at the ready, waited to swing at anyone who might come at us.

We proceeded slowly, tentatively up the stairs.

No one thought to stop and call the police! Foolishly—we just reacted.

There, at the top of the stairs stood the chief culprit—it was Tiger!

"Meow!" A few feet away, in the last room dad was finishing in the house, stood his two accomplices!

A few feet apart—beat up, old carpenter's horses rigidly held their ground! A few two by fours stretched carelessly across their tops.

On the floor lay several more of the nasty villains.

First, an overturned laundry basket cowered above spilled dirty laundry in disarray!

Clearly, Tiger knocked it over when she jumped up on the horses and then into the basket. She must have tipped the balance.

As the basket started to fall, it caused a noisy chain reaction of several boards that were evidently leaning against it.

Obviously, they crashed to the floor in some clangorous, clattery sequence scaring the dickens out of the girls downstairs.

I think the girls were all a little embarrassed; however, we were relieved.

With some of the things that happened from time to time in the country none of us took these things too lightly until we were sure there was no real danger.

However, we did have a good laugh following this one—thanks to our very own Mister Innocent—Tiger.

There was another historical reason why I lead the charge to go rescue my sister and the girls.

The first dates back to our short stay in Chicago the year of Pearl Harbor.

Dad took a job as a supervisor in a manufacturing plant on the South side near Comiskey Park, home of the Chicago White Sox.

I still remember the Pearl Harbor announcement on the radio and mom and dad's shock.

I also remember going to a Polish parochial school to kindergarten where I learned two Polish songs that I still remember in part. Pojdzmy Wszyscy is a Christmas song about hurrying to the stable to see the Christ Child and His family. The second was about our Guardian Angel.

Dad was working second shift and mom ran out of milk for dinner for us young ones—Jim, Judy and I.

She asked our landlord if he would keep an eye on us while she made a quick trip to the store.

Although it was not very late, it was quite dark out because it was early winter.

A telephone call came for our landlord, who lived upstairs and he said he would leave us alone for just a minute.

I sat on the floor of our basement apartment with Jim when I saw a red glow in one of the windows.

I saw the same glow and the same face in another window and then heard the window shatter!

I'll never forget the man coming through the window!

Our landlord somehow picked up on it too and came running with a pistol.

The intruder smashed the window further with a chair and quickly squirmed back out.

He never was caught.

I know the impression it left with me.

Dad quit his job the next day and moved us back to South Milwaukee.

So, when Judy called, we had no idea where in the spectrum of things, her danger might fall. It was really gratifying to find that Tiger was the only cause of her anxiety!

Most of the times it was so peaceful where we lived, but there were times!

TIGER

One night, after school, someone mentioned that they hadn't seen Tiger for several days.

A few more went by and still no Tiger.

I was feeling considerable guilt because I was so busy with my job and school that I didn't have much time for our pets during the week or even notice that Tiger was missing.

Still, my brothers and sisters had time with them. Jan, the youngest, was nine years younger than me.

On Saturday, around noon—because I remember we were sitting at the kitchen table having lunch, we heard George cawing outside.

Then he flew to the sill and started pecking at the glass pane.

That was the very first time he had ever tried to enter the house through a downstairs window.

We opened it and he flew in. George glided to the floor next to Sandy and started squawking.

At first I thought it was George's excitement, but I wasn't sure what was going on.

Sandy moved to the door and barked. As I opened it, she brushed past my legs and scurried out the door like a blaze of fur. George flew after her. They both disappeared heading west through the fields and toward the woods.

I ran after them for a little while, but there was no way I was going to keep up.

They never came home that afternoon or evening.

Sunday morning came and now none of the threesome was around. Sandy, George and Tiger were all missing.

We all felt it and concern definitely took over.

Sometime after church, someone noticed Sandy slowly coming up through the field carrying something. George was sitting in the young fruit tree orchard making lots of unusual noise.

Sandy stopped when she got to the far edge of what we used for our baseball field, about 500 feet or so from the house.

Whatever she was carrying, she set her special package down very gently.

She then laid herself down right there on the spot with her paws outstretched across her treasure.

We tried to, but we just could not make out what it was from inside the house.

Sandy just stayed there moving only her head from time to time— staring away into the distance.

George continued to stay in the orchard and kept up the fuss.

Everyone was quick to leave the table and hurried outside to see what the commotion was all about.

We got to within about fifty feet of Sandy, but really couldn't tell what she had because the field grass had browned wearing its autumn colors. It was also a bit too tall at that spot.

When we reached that point, she gave out a growl—something she had never directed at us before. It was quite clear she didn't want us to come any closer.

Again she growled, but it was mixed with a weird kind of bark— almost as though she was in some sort of pain. It struck home deeply. Obviously something was wrong.

It was at this point that George left his perch and winged in the same direction. He settled slowly to the ground near Sandy and you could hardly see him in the tall grass. He made very odd sounds.

It was an unusual duet, but one thing was perfectly clear. We were not going to be allowed any closer.

Each of us backed off a way and tried calling to both of them. Neither one budged!

We were very puzzled. Moreover, we felt helpless and we just sat there and watched the unusual drama in front of us.

Every now and then, we'd try calling them again. In our hearts, by that time, we all had a secret suspicion about what was happening.

Dad came home from wherever he was around this time. He was quick to join us.

After we explained this unusual scene, he suggested we move up a little at a time and continue calling their names.

We edged a lot closer than before and again Sandy growled in a low guttural sound.

Little by little we were able to continue to creep toward her. This whole process took about two hours. Finally she let us approach.

She didn't move one inch and neither did George.

When we got close enough to see, there was a very precious pelt resting quietly beneath her paws. Its characteristics had the same telltale colors that belonged to Tiger.

Finally, Sandy let dad come closer.

The rest of us stayed back a little way.

Best dad could tell Tiger had been shot by some hunters. It was that season of the year.

Colors of the season somewhat offset the sadness all around us.

Although Sandy would let us really close now, she had no intention of yielding her old friend.

We left her in mourning.

It was several more hours before we could coax her to leave her prize and ours.

When she did, we placed our pet carefully into a large shoe box.

Tiger would rest—in a place away from the hot cinders of the wood furnace.

We moved him over to the orchard so that no future plowing would disturb his resting place.

Sandy and George followed us.

There we left our pet to rest where the blossoms bloomed every spring and the leaves provided a warm carpet every fall.

George and Sandy stayed.

We got them to come into the house at night; however, they would both return and continue mourning the next day.

This went on for three or four days.

Anyone who thinks animals don't have feelings never saw anything like what we saw in the autumn of 1954. The memories are quite vivid.

CHRISTMAS BREAK

That event from a day in autumn left its mark on all of us. Sandy and George seemed affected just as much. George spent far more time home than he had been doing for some time. We all seemed to need something to break the spell.

Mine came from a few days helping dad. Since I was off for Christmas break, I worked mid afternoons and evenings at Bussler's.

However, now and then I had a day or two off.

It was one of those off stretches that dad said he could use my help.

He bid on and signed a contract to paint the second floor of a flat in Milwaukee for a lady I'll call Mrs. X to protect her identity. Speaking of creatures, she turned out to be a really odd duck.

It was extra cold outside.

When dad showed up to start painting he found the temperature in the rooms to be about forty-five degrees—much too cold to paint.

After a lengthy discussion with Mrs. X, she agreed to raise the temperature.

She raised it to sixty degrees but, refused to move one degree higher.

Every now and then she would show up, as customers have a right to do, but she would go around from room turning off light switches she didn't think should be on. We were always careful not to be wasteful. So, we would have to go back, after she left, and turn them on again because we needed them.

She also gave dad fits about the color in one of the bedrooms. She picked out a Dusty Rose, from a paint chip she selected from a Mautz

Paint store. Dad ordered the paint from the store of her choice and painted the room.

Well wouldn't you just know it; Mrs. X thought the paint was too light. Sometimes that happens.

So, dad took it back to the store and had it darkened just a little. He painted the room again. Guess what? The color was too dark and definitely not the color she picked out—or so she said.

Dad was a patient sort with his customers and tried to give good customer service. So he asked her to go to the store from which she selected the paint and have it mixed in front of her until she was satisfied.

So—dad painted it one more time. When she came in to see the room, she accused dad of darkening the paint after she brought it from the store.

His patience was now completely gone.

Dad developed a strategy to deal with and alleviate her confusion.

He wanted to finish that bedroom and one other room to complete the job. He hoped to somehow paint and get out in a single day.

If I painted the dining room, he would concentrate on satisfying her with the bedroom color. He may have said something about painting Mrs. X a dusty rose too or something to that effect!

Anxiously, he put his plan into effect.

He went back to the paint store and ordered more paint the same color as the original chip.

He also brought three empty paint buckets from home. (When finished with paint cans from oil based paints, he would burn out the insides to clean them. Then, he could use them as spare paint cans.)

He took a single gallon of paint, freshly mixed from the store. Then, he poured the paint from it into each of the other three cans. He now had four paint cans, each containing the same color.

Then he took a paint brush full of paint from one of the cans. At that point, he applied the color to each of the four walls with a single stroke each. He stood back and smiled at me and said, "Let's see what happens?"

Next he invited his nemesis to come up and take a look.

Well, the mark on one wall was too dark, on the next wall it was too light, on the third it was almost right and on the fourth wall, it was just right. With her present, he put a lid on each of the cans he brought from home and said, "Well, Mrs. X, we'll use this one." With that she smiled and went back downstairs where it was warmer.

As soon as she left, dad and I both smiled. He opened the three cans he had just closed and poured all the paint into one bucket. Then both of us proceeded to paint the infamous bedroom as fast as we could. Then he helped me finished the dining room.

She was very happy.

Dad got his check.

We left for the bank and cashed it as fast as we could.

Several days later she called dad back.

He just held his breath anxiously.

Much to dad's total amazement, instead of complaining, she offered to have him paint another flat.

Dad said that unfortunately he was far too busy.

She offered to set the thermostat, by contract, to whatever temperature he wanted. She kept insisting.

Still, dad held his ground. "No thank you," was his final answer. Again he smiled.

He saved those four paint cans for quite a while. I am not sure he ever explained why to anyone else. They just sat in the corner for a while gathering dust.

That night we sat in front of the fireplace laughing about the whole situation. We were all enjoying a beverage.

No one noticed that George's water dish was empty.

Dad took a sip of his and set it on the floor.

George was on the mantel paying close attention to everything going on.

When the glass hit the floor, he lit from the fire place.

He glided down behind the back of dad's chair and to the floor.

No one noticed where he went until we heard dad yell out "George!" Here he sat with his beak fully submerged, up to his feathers, into dad's glass of brown brew.

We all roared again!

He lifted his head straight up, foam around his beak, and swallowed. We laughed again.

A few seconds later, he dove for a potato chip. Mom said nothing at all. It was the first time we know of that he bothered with table food or beverage.

CHRISTMAS REMINISCE

Christmas Eve arrived once again. It was a fun time.

We helped mom and dad hang painted glass ornaments on the tree and loaded it with tinsel.

She had something new—some glow in the dark ornaments.

This year it was in the corner near our front picture window.

We all sat around the fire place, with the tree lights on. Someone began reminiscing in front of the tree. We traveled back over the years with our memories. We chatted about some of our favorites from years long before.

There were two that have always been among mine.

The first happened when I was in about second grade.

Christmas was always a big event in families with a Polish heritage.

When I was younger, no matter how big the family got, everyone always tried to get together on either Christmas Eve or Christmas Day.

I sure embarrassed both my parents at one of those gatherings.

Before I can get at the heart of this story I need to tell you that Grandpa Ben, my Dad's father, was always very kind to his grandchildren. He always called me Sonny, as did everyone on my father's side of the family, although my name is Ed—after my dad. Actually they could have gotten by without it because they also called me Ed and my dad Eddie. But, Sonny it was for years!

Just to confuse things a little, my other grandfather, Frank, used to call me Kenny. Grandpa Frank used to care for the horses that ran the various wagons for the city of Milwaukee.

Grandpa Ben often visited us on Friday evenings when we still lived in South Milwaukee. Jim and I would wait for him on the front porch. He'd pat us both on the heads and give us a quarter—a lot of money to us at that time.

On rare occasions, he would use a few choice cuss words in Polish when he would talk with dad.

Well, I always did learn fast.

Anyway, back to Christmas and how it unfolded at the home of my mom's sister—Aunt Emily Mankowski. This was a special annual occasion each year in Milwaukee a short distance from St. Lawrence Church on 27th St. In later years she would live at 1568 South 26th Street; however, at the time of this occasion she lived in the house directly behind it. There were two houses on the same lot and we always approached her home through the alley way in those days!

All of the family gathered.

Every child was as excited as can be.

It is hard to imagine how big this family was!

Remember, each of my parents had at least eight siblings. Plus, the great Aunts and Uncles came too—including my Godmother, Aunt Lucy. Even our second cousins came. You got to know them all. One of them became one of my best pals in college.

The big family made this a truly colossal event. This would have been true even if it wasn't Christmas.

The windows and doorways were decorated to the brim.

Mega platters of pot luck and specialty foods crowded the table.

It pushed the capacity to its very limits including a Polish ham, Polish Sausage, Kieshka, potato salad, green onions and raw beef and sliced raw onions to put on rye bread sandwiches. There was even a Nesco Roaster there to keep the beef and the ham warm.

The images conjured by this memory are truly of a special and festive time.

Everyone was decked out in their finery!

However, the real catalyst was my Godfather. He was also mom's Uncle Joe. Joe Nowicki! A wonderful person!

He had the most beautiful silver gray hair and a very resonant voice. It just so happens that he helped Santa out each year by dressing in a red suit for the Allen Bradley Company in Milwaukee. He did this for forty years. Countless numbers of kids got to enjoy his show every December. Therefore, he was well qualified to do the same for this family. He was very proud of that!

Uncle Joe and Aunt Helen did not have any children of their own and I think that they adopted all of us in their own way and we adopted them as some very special people in our lives too. They lived on the southeast corner of Howell Ave.—near Mitchell field in Milwaukee.

Uncle Joe built a musical platform that held their Christmas tree each year. It rotated slowly so that you could see all the lights and all the ornaments.

Anyway, this fits in well with the importance they both placed on Christmas. This year was no exception.

On this Particular December night, by the time everyone was stuffed with food, it was dark outside.

Red, blue yellow and green tree lights added a special effect that always turned the excitement up a few million times on the scale—and still does for me to this very day. The tinsel seemed to reflect them all many times over.

Suddenly there was this big ruckus outside.

Someone was pounding on the doors and banging on the windows.

It seemed as if all of my uncles and great-uncles were like hornets scurrying everywhere. They acted so excited about something that it churned up the level if many stimuli in each one of us youngsters.

We were also somewhat frightened at the same time!

"Santa's really concerned about something!" Some of the uncles chided.

"Somebody here has not been helping mom with the dishes!"

"Some children have not been exactly as good as they should be!"

"He wants one of to come out and promise him that you will all try harder before he comes in to visit," mom's brother, Uncle Ray Cerwin called out in his gentle voice.

"Each one of you has got to really try! You all have to promise you'll be good! Santa is asking if you will—or no presents!"

Well, I'll tell you—it doesn't take a Rhodes Scholar to guess the next sequence of events.

All of us kids stood there and ensured our parents we would be ever so good from then on—and with the purest of intentions. And so, they let Santa come in.

He wore his best red suit with the shinning black patent leather belt and the soft fluffy white fur.

He had a long black leather belt that looked as if it was a harness for the reindeer with a number of glistening silver bells attached. He shook it as he walked—for a very special effect on us all.

His "Ho, Ho, Ho," was even more convincing! He must have stood about 5 foot 8—well—just about exactly the same size as my uncle Joe and with the most beautiful white whiskers.

Meanwhile, no one noticed that Uncle Joe was missing. None of us under the age of ten knew he was helping Santa out tonight.

Santa was a jovial sort. He strolled slowly over to a big easy chair near the Christmas tree.

All of us cousins formed a line and, one at a time, got to sit on his knee.

He would ask us lots of questions. And, he sure seemed to know a lot about each and every one of us.

At the conclusion of each cousin's perch Santa would ask "...and can you say something in Polish?"

Now, the two cousins directly in front of me, Bob Slawny and Bob Mankowski, did that with so much ease.

Santa's praising response of "Good Boy," did not miss my attention!

Again being quick to learn, I hoped for some of the same praise from someone as great as him.—Well let's face it; he's almost the greatest living person in the world to a kid—outside one's parents.

Well, when he asked me if I could speak some Polish, I wanted to keep up with my cousins. I wished I had known some phrases like dzien dobry that means good morning, dzienkuje which means thank you,

146

dobranocs which is good night or choina which means Christmas tree. But, I didn't!

So I proudly let loose with two or three of the choice cuss words that I had heard occasionally on Friday nights.

Unfortunately I did so without knowing what they meant yet. Not smart! No! Not smart at all! Never use words when you don't know their meaning. Look them up first. Check them out. Moreover, don't use them unless you really know them.

I found out quickly that their meaning wasn't good. It was truly much to the chagrin and the surprise of both my mom and my pop.

Even more significant to me were two or three firm hand placements on my behind from Santa after he took over his knee.

I was totally embarrassed. I think Santa was somewhat surprise too by the spontaneity of the sequence of events.

Somehow this old Santa knew what to do next. He made a great recovery for both of us.

"Edwin," that's what he called me, "Kiddo, it's important not to use words you don't know—even if it seems important to you to say something." Then he picked me up and held me in his arms.

The word Kiddo should have been a dead give a way because it was an innate part of my uncle's vocabulary. That night, for some reason, it didn't!

That warm comforting hug from Santa felt strangely as comforting as the one my uncle Joe used to give me every time I saw him. Somehow, it was even stronger and warmer this time.

He also made a big point to everyone that his message was one for everyone—not just for me. He went on to stress that I had been a good boy during the whole year and that he knew this slip was an accident.

At that moment he gave me a great big red fire engine with long yellow ladders.

Thereupon, Santa gave me an even bigger second hug that made me feel tons better.

In fact that was the same Christmas that Uncle Joe came to our home and gave me my second all time favorite gift as a child. It was a carpenter box he made with a hinged lid on top that lifted to open.

The box itself was approximately 3 1/2 feet by 2 1/2 feet and about 7 inches deep. He said that Santa loaded it with small—yet—very good carpenter tools including a hand drill, a saw, hammer, miter, a plane and a small box with compartments full of nails.

Uncle Joe Nowicki headed the carpenter shop for the Allen Bradley Company. I know he was sharing something very personal with me.

He was a personal friend of Mr. Bradley and was responsible for me working there for three summers during college and for my first job offer after college.

It seems rather interesting to me, as I'm writing this now and reflect back, how his name was Joe—and another carpenter named Joe played such an important part in a much earlier Christmas. Just maybe that's why Joseph was the name I chose for Confirmation.

BILLY THE BROWNIE

There is something I probably should have gotten a spanking for relative to Christmas time—a few years back!

When one tells a story—they should fess up and tell the good and the less than good decisions one makes in their life. Hopefully, we make progressively better ones as time goes on!

While the Christmas tree lights are shinning in my memory, it is only fair that I disclose this tale of well intended but definitely misconceived effort.

I will admit—it was creative—but not as funny or as short, in terms of lasting impact, as when it was first conceived. In fact it was thought of as a simple idea to make things better.

As I look back, better, probably meant better for myself in terms of making chores easier.

My sister Jan reminds me of it now and then to this day, even as I near the age of seventy! It is now a standing joke between us—but it wasn't always so funny to her and Jerry—although that was never intended.

With mom and dad both working, they relied on me to be the keeper of the house at a young age.

With this responsibility, went the tasks of keeping our home clean and taking good care of my younger brothers and sisters. I really didn't mind because I knew how hard both of my parents worked! Plus, I loved my brothers and sisters very much!

I tried to split up the chores best I could to be fair to everyone!

I also tried to help provide some of the entertainment and ways to help make the days interesting, fun and more pleasurable! This would often including drawing with Jim, Judy, Jerry or Jan—or just making up things to do—many of which would stimulate or challenge the imagination.

In the summer time this was simpler to do with so much open space and so many more options.

We would take what ever we could find and adapt it to games we already knew or make up our own.

An example includes taking the long handle from a farm implement that had a curve at the end of it sort of like a golf club. And so guess what! We would adapt it and use it for a golf club—create some holes around the yard, which was certainly big enough, and play golf even though no one in the family had played golf prior to this time.

Dad even joined in our game. He would later become a low handicap golfer, but that was years after I grew up and started my own family.

Or I would just plain make up games we could play indoors.

For example, I would create imitation pin ball games using a piece of board, drilling holes in selected places, using small nails as pegs and using rubber bands to bounce the balls off of them.

Then I would take some of the steel balls from scrap bearings to play the game.

Or, I would take modeling clay and make pieces for board games I would make up.

Or we would make playing pieces out of paper with a scissors to fit the games I would invent. Etc., etc., etc.

Once, long before we could afford actual chess pieces, I made playing pieces out of light cardboard and the bases for the pieces out of modeling lay so that we could play chess!

Some of the ideas were much more imaginative than others. At that time, there were no TV shows to show you how to do these things. Maybe that is why it is difficult for me to be bored today. We learned how to amuse ourselves at an early age.

Well, how then does that get around to the spanking—I probably deserved?

It was several weeks before Christmas, and I was having a difficult time getting my younger siblings to pick up after themselves.

However, they did enjoy sitting in front of the radio and listened to a daily pre Christmas show called Billy the Brownie sponsored by Schuster's Department Stores in Milwaukee on radio station WTMJ.

The format for the show called for the brownie named Billy, one of Santa's chief helpers, to open the show and ask all of the boys and girls to face the radio.

Billie would then ask the children to call out "Yes" if they had been good.

Then Billy would say, "If enough boys and girls are good today, the magic story book will hear you—and—it will open and tell you a story. If not, the book will remain closed.'

When the response from the children was not judged to be positive enough, Santa would come on the short wave radio from the North Pole and explain to the children why it is that they need to be good!

Santa was pretty convincing and encouraged his listening audience to be better during the pre Christmas period—and year around!

It was pretty effective on those days that the magic book didn't open. Because of the power radio had on young imaginations in the pre TV days—the young imaginations would rise to pretty high levels—with a fair amount of putting their hearts into the validity of what Santa had to say.

One such day, when the magic story book did not open and Santa admonished the children to be good—a new idea was born.

My brother Jim,—also very imaginative—and I came up with a scheme to get a little more help with the household chores by building on the framework Santa had set the stage for on the radio.

Jim and I went out into the corn fields and plucked some of the corn silk off from the top of the ears of corn that had not been picked that year. The corn silk was used to form a beard and mustache for Jim to wear.

Taking an old clown's costume from a trunk up in the attic including a long pointed hat, we dressed Jim up as we imagined Billy the Brownie to look.

Then Jim sat in the back of a deep upstairs closet—in a far corner. We used a small flashlight with a green lens for the dim light in the closet to illuminate Jim, but not so much that you could possibly catch a really good look at him.

Then I was the culprit that did the dirty work! It was up to me to convince both Jan and Jerry that someone wanted to see them upstairs!

When I was put in charge by mom and dad, I never had a problem with my brothers and sisters doing what they were asked to do with most things. And so they faithfully followed me up the stairs and into the closet.

And there—Billy the Brownie (my brother Jim) delivered a short speech with his best effort at disguising his voice. "Keep the house clean or Santa won't come to your house this year!"

Well, it worked! So well, did it work, that Jan didn't forget the episode for years—and we never knew the impact it had on her until a good many years later.

She decided to break years of silence and brought it up during a visit to Jim's home in Arizona as we sat around a Christmas tree.

First she let Jim and I know how much she loved us—and then she asked what in the world made us execute the Billy the Brownie plot! She said that was so out of character for either of us—she couldn't believe we did that!

We explained, we didn't think it was that big a deal—and just a simple motivational gimmick that seemed pretty harmless at the time.

It was priceless to see mom's face when she heard about what happened on my watch!

Once in a while to this day, on the phone, she will say Billy is calling or ask if I have seen him. And we laugh. The more the years go by, the harder we laugh!

But a spanking, or something along that line, could well have been the appropriate order of the day for her older brother, even if no harm was intended!

JAN, JUDY, JERRY WITH SANDY AND HER PUPS

jIM STRUMMING HIS GUITAR

MY OTHER FAVORITE
EARLY HOLIDAY FAVORITE

Another famous December day for us was always St. Nicholas day, December 6th. It was a very important day each year in Polish families. It was a reminder that Christmas was coming and that you needed to prepare yourself for the great event.

For us, it meant giving up something for four weeks or doing something special for someone and trying to deepen your faith life.

It also meant hanging the biggest stocking we had over a chair before we went to bed on December 5.

Mom made sure we each had a pair of long light brown stockings that went up over our knees.

When morning came, they were always full of peanuts, candy, fruit and popcorn balls. Sometimes we would even find a freshly baked cookie in there.

It was such a big day that the nuns talked about it in school the next day and the kids compared notes about what they found in their stockings.

Christmas was close behind.

Christmas to us was always about the receiving of the gifts of Christ and about giving what He expects of us. Yet there were always a lot of the traditional fun things that underscored December the 25th!

It was only a year after the Uncle Joe incident. Mom reminisced about how it started out in a way that only dad could start it. I alluded to the fact that he was quite a character at times.

It is the only December 24th like this that any of us could remember.

What made it stand out in our minds was that some quite convincing amateur acting persuaded us that, maybe, this year we wouldn't get anything from that great fellow in the red suit.

Here's how it unfolded.

That particular Christmas eve it was already dark outside when dad set Jim, my sister Judy and me on the couch near the glistening, glimmering tree.

In those days there were no artificial trees—only the real McCoys.

The smell of fresh pine filled every niche of our living room. I still love the fragrance.

Bright tin icicles hung from the branches. Silver paint coated one side of the twisted piece of tin and a bright shade of red, blue, gold, green or yellow the other. They spun when someone walked past them spraying reflected light everywhere. They also shimmered as they mirrored the many multicolored electric light bulbs strung around the branches.

Shinny foil cones of varied colors hung from the tree loaded with peanuts and hard candies of all kinds.

Red cellophane covered bells decorated the windows right behind the couch—flashing on an off adding a special touch of Christmas warmth.

It was in this very exciting setting that dad did his thing!

He ran upstairs to the second floor to help Santa by carrying down the presents that Santa was bringing. We were really excited when he announced his intentions.

However, When he came back downstairs, he was empty handed and had soot all over his hands.

"Santa," he started, "was upstairs stuck in the chimney with our presents."

The soot on dad's hands was unquestionable proof.

Visions almost went out of control of maybe never seeing the presents Santa had for us this year. Also, what about poor Santa stuck up there in that Chimney!

Then dad whispered. "Maybe," he started, "if we were to sing jingle bells as loud as we could, it might encourage Santa. Maybe, it would even relax him enough so he could take a deep breath and maybe wiggle his way loose."

Dad continued to whisper, "If you sing really loud, I'll run upstairs and see if I can help him work his way out of his predicament."

And so, we started to sing.

Time after time he would run upstairs. Then he would come running back down to tell us we had to sing louder!

Well wouldn't you just know, that after about five or six of these trips up and down the stairs—I did say he went a little overboard sometimes, -- he had us screaming Jingle Bells at the top of our lungs!

All I knew then was that our efforts must have helped. Dad came running down the stairs yelling, "He's out! He's out! Poor Santa's free of the chimney!"

Oh, and were we ever thrilled!

He told mom to get a broom and come upstairs to help clean up the soot.

She came back down with dad carrying my desk! It was one that I was to use for many years. However, the desk was not half so precious as all the memories and the efforts both of our parents put into making it so special.

Judy got a set of building blocks.

There were two sets of modeling clay under the Christmas Tree, including one strip in each box that was luminous. One was for Jim and one for me.

You could mold the most wonderful and exciting things with regular modeling clay.

Using your wildest imagination, you could be strategic in your placement of the luminous clay to outline shapes, make headlights, create faces, a skeleton, a snowman, a rabbit or create most anything.

Then, for the fun part!

Expose the masterpiece you just created to a bright light. Turn the lights out. Then, wow! Watch your creation glow in the dark!

Any of my kids today can tell you that this enchantment with glow in the dark never left me. I would later incorporate this fascination into some ideas I would develop including a game I invented and sold called Fling as well as some other creations. Over the years, I would also do many, many glow in the dark ink drawings for others.

We each got our first kaleidoscope.

I got my first jigsaw puzzle with the picture of a U. S. Navy airplane—the Hellcat. Mom used to love to put these together and helped me start that first one.

A little bit of irony is that later that evening dad had a little trouble getting us to sing Silent Night—softly. Somehow our thoughts were still somewhere up that chimney. To this day, the memories still echo loudly! The warmth of it all lingers on.

These two Christmas's kept us laughing most of the night as we reminisced about a lot of things including some of the legends already created by George, Tiger, Goose and Sandy.

MIRROR ABOVE THE MANTLE

George was coming home more and more often in recent months. Sometimes, he would peck at the glass, totally unannounced, and pop in for a visit. Then, when he was ready to go, he would scoot up on my desk, peck gently on the glass covering, protecting the desk top, and let us know his visit was over.

Also, his visits were much more extensive.

He would make his way across the hardwood floor and over to the bedroom door. Then, he'd just stand there and wait for us to open it.

Once open, he'd walk down the short hallway and over to the top of the stairs.

Next, he would give a small hop up into the air.

Then he would glide all the way down with his wings outstretched and turn to the right at the foot of the stairs.

The flow of his descent carried him through the front hallway and on into the living room.

Usually he'd swing over to the mantel and gracefully land there.

Then he would parade in front of the mirror—back and forth, back and forth canting his head one way and then another.

He was a good flier because the hallway wasn't that wide.

If someone was in the living room, he'd walk across the mantel to the end closest to them and start his chatter. If Sandy was there, he'd hop to the floor and walk over for a visit.

It was 1955 and heading toward spring.

Jerry was ten years old at the time and he liked to sketch. In fact, most of the kids in our family liked to draw and it showed up in different ways over the years.

Jim stayed with art in one way or another since his childhood. He did many very fine portraits of people with colored pencils. Later he would work with acrylics and oils doing some great scenery including farms and scenes of the Southwest. He always liked people though and they kept showing up in his work including a period of very strong pastels and conte' pencils. He also did some very unique wood burning of all kinds of things including people and animals.

Jan would later take an oil painting class with me at Wustum Museum in Racine. She later took a class or two in art within Phoenix, Arizona. She still harbors a real love for art and will probably spend more time with her avocation as the years allow. She would later pass her love for art on to her son and our Godchild—Scott—who would really loved sketching super heroes.

Dad continued to sketch every now and then, but would later in life do a number of single panel cartoons. The only painting I ever remember seeing by him was an oil of a man sitting on a park bench.

Jerry liked to sketch all kinds of things and later would later take lessons in oil painting—with a strong interest in scenery. He loved the mountains and could not get enough of them. He took an interest in watercolors when he lived in Prescot, Arizona.

At any rate, back to 1955. During one of George's visits that spring, Jerry did a pencil sketch of him. It is an excellent likeness and the clearest representation we have of George today. Years later he gave it to me as a gift—a very special gift.

Judy had a very big interest in the music of the times and would bring home 45 rpm records of the day. We all loved music and she would share them with us, playing them on an old victrola that we wound with a crank. Jim would then pick up on some of them with his guitar.

Creativity, our love for the country and nature and our animal friends fit in very well together. This creativity would pass on down to our children and our grandchildren in many forms and for some of them become their professional careers in adult life.

It didn't make any difference if we were drawing, singing, playing baseball, basketball or football outside, George was usually around taking it all in. He seemed to be trying even harder to talk. Sometimes, it was almost as if he was trying to sing along with us.

I wished I knew how to teach him because he tried so hard.

Sandy always wanted to be around too.

The two were inseparable whenever George was around.

He always made time for Sandy!

George by Jerry

MY ALL-TIME FAVORITE TEASE

George wasn't thinking about law school or politics or the cost of tuition and books that summer. His focus was teasing the chickens. He played that game more and more often.

They would go cluck, cluck and he would go caw, caw.

He was in his prime and getting faster.

They were past their prime and getting slower.

They never did catch on that if they would only stop chasing, he would leave that last scrap of bread for them to fight over between themselves.

Some deep thinker might accuse me of being narrow in my interpretation of facts here. They could deduce that perhaps the chickens had it figured out all the time, but just enjoyed the game. Whatever,—they played it often.

Mom was the one who noticed it first.

George just wasn't feeling good one day and seemed very sluggish.

By the next morning, he was lethargic.

We tried feeding him and he wouldn't eat.

Dad tried to get him to take liquid through an eye dropper but he didn't accept it.

We took turns holding him because he didn't want to stay in the new box we had for him. We all seriously worried about our friend.

That night we all stayed up late until dad gave the ultimatum to go to bed. He made it clear that he would spend the night with George.

I don't know what time it was but, it was still dark out when dad touched my shoulder. Instead of the brighter ceiling light, he had turned on the desk lamp.

When my eyes came to focus, I noticed the tears slowly moving down dad's cheeks. No words were needed. We both went down stairs together.

"Too much playing with the chickens", he said. "George had picked up Chicken Lice. And for him it was fatal!"

It was so fast and unexpected.

The next morning was a solemn one in our home.

Everyone had similar feelings, but no one said a lot of words.

Dad placed George in a shoe box with a great deal of sensitively It was just as we had done not too long before for another friend. We went outside to put him in a special spot—next to his pal Tiger.

Sandy was with us when we did this and she took her place over the freshly turned soil where she kept watch for several days.

Something none of us could have anticipated began to happen around noon.

At first, a few crows settled on the branches of the small trees that formed the orchard and started a chorus like none we had ever heard before.

Within a matter of hours, the trees that formed both the North and South boundaries for our thirty-seven acres were filled with hundreds more of the black feathered birds. They added their feelings to an increasingly louder crescendo.

They seemed to stay until just before dark. Then, they returned early in the morning.

This continued for several days although they were less vocal during the last two.

Sandy also kept her vigil.

Then, as it started, so it came to a stop.

The crows disappeared slowly from the tree tops.

Sandy came home but was very quiet for some time to come.

Flashbacks of my favorite tease continue to bring smiles to my face and other feelings that I will never forget.

Every time I see a crow, I wonder if it might be a descendent of George. I have no way of knowing—but I wonder!

ON THE BRIDGE

Maybe dad was trying to get through the loss of George too. But, I think—even more so—he was trying to help me.

One Friday night after work, he asked me to come down to the basement and help him with something. Like a lot of men from his generation, he had a difficult time verbally telling you how he felt. Instead, he tried to tell you by the things he did.

He had some materials spread out in one corner. There was a heavy piece of wire, a large old porous curtain and a large spool of heavy string. "Remember what you used to help me make with this when you were a boy?" he asked.

I did!

We spent many an evening on the front porch in South Milwaukee at 1418 Manitoba Avenue.

He knew one of my favorite things back then was to catch live bait to go fishing.

Dad would use a net made with a rectangular shaped wire frame over which he would stretch old window curtains. Each side was about three feet long. He attached fish heads or raw liver as bait.

Then he would lower it, by a rope fastened to the four corners, over the bridge railing and into the creek below to catch crayfish. We just called them crabs.

This stream was usually slow moving and gentle but could get very rough when it rained.

It was directly across the street from the porch where we would sit and talk about most anything, and we did so. We also did things like listen to old time radio, drink Kool Aid and munch on popcorn.

Every fifteen minutes or so, we'd cross the street and pull on the rope to lift the net out of the water.

Shining a flashlight down into the net we would check to see how many crabs we caught.

If there were enough, we would lift the net by the rope until it came up to the bridge's railing.

We'd pick them out of the net, one by one, and put them in a bucket with fresh grass in the bottom to protect them.

One had to be careful how you handled crayfish. If I grabbed them wrong—those little creatures could really pinch hard.

Then, early on Saturday mornings and just before dawn, dad would take my brother Jim and I for a long walk through Grant Park, past the power plant and onto the South Milwaukee pier to fish for perch.

It was a beautiful walk—usually just as the sun was rising.

Much of it was along a winding path through the parkway sheltered by shaded areas. It formed the perfect setting for the many different kinds of chirping birds singing their rhythmic early morning symphonies.

We loved this walk and I know dad did too. We felt pretty important carrying the bucket and the stringer, for the fish he hoped to catch, while dad carried the cane poles.

The best part was sitting with him on the rocks that formed the South Milwaukee pier. We all loved to be out on the pier!

He was a good coach and he made sure you knew just how much tugging the perch were allowed to do on the crab tail bait before you set the hook.

I still remember that first fish. He somehow seemed to be able to catch them when no one else could. This was true even when he got to be an old timer and fish didn't seem to be biting much for anyone else— he could still get a mess of perch.

It's funny how, when you have something on your mind, your memory seems to skip around from one thing to another. That's the way it was early that evening.

I also remembered one particular time he went fishing without us.

Mom was really worried because he came home very late and was soak'n wet and very, very cold. A friend was with him.

His buddy told how the water was rougher than usual. Swells started to wash over the pier and swept a lady off one of the rocks and into the lake.

Dad tried to reach her from the end of the pier, but couldn't.

He quickly slid over the edge of the pier into the rough water holding on to a jagged rock with one hand and searching beneath the water for the woman with his other.

His hand managed to catch the woman by her hair!

He pulled her to the pier and his buddy helped lift her out of the water. He saved a lady from drowning in Lake Michigan that day.

He was a good swimmer, but that lake really got rough sometimes and the undercurrents are extremely treacherous. So, it was really dangerous even for him.

Mom was just happy he was home—wet clothes and all.

"Yes. I remember," I answered.

I slipped back into deep thought again. Dad just let me do it. He seemed to know I needed it.

I didn't think so much about our special pets. Instead, for some reason or another, my mind lapsed back to thoughts of my childhood and certain games we played as children outside near that old house by the old creek in South Milwaukee.

Like most kids at that time we loved to play outdoor games.

There was an old style plank bridge that crossed the creek.

There was a pedestrian crossing on each side of the bridge to connect the concrete parts of the sidewalks that stopped on either side of the creek. The pedestrian crossing was also constructed of heavy wooden planks and had a distinct sound when someone ran across it.

The foot of the bridge was about a hundred feet from our front porch.

A giant old Oak shade tree was well anchored just to the right of the bridge.

We used to face that ancient tree, lean into the crusty old bark and cover our eyes while playing hide and seek. We also played other fun games like Kick the Can and Red Light/ Green Light (I hope to see a ghost tonight).

We almost always played these after dark because it wasn't as much fun in the daylight.

It seemed as if trillions of fire flies lit up the area—probably because of the proximity of the creek.

Statue was another cool game we played.

One person was the statue maker. Their key role was to grab each player by both hands and spin them around and around and then let go.

As each person was released, they stopped and froze in what ever position they ended up after the spin—even if it they swirled to the ground.

Often their hand and arms would be extended in some unusual direction and they would be bent over one way or another at the hips.

Then the statue maker then went up to each player, one at a time and would then push an imaginary button on our heads.

In turn, each player had to act out anything they wanted to be—much like charades.

The catch was it had to somehow relate to the position in which you froze prior to acting out your part. Again, they could be anything their imaginations could invent. They could be a duck, a bird, a frog, a particular cowboy star, a ballet dancer, Superman, a cricket, whatever their imaginations could generate.

If the statue maker guessed what you were, you got to be the next statue maker.

The hard part was staying frozen in position until the statue maker got to you. If you moved, you lost your chance to act out your part.

Having the flair that children do, many froze in the craziest positions imaginable.

We used to ride scooters and roller skate all the way down the hill, past where we lived and up to the bridge.

"Hey, son," dad called out. I snapped out of my trip into the past and noticed we had finished making a net. We drove the short distance to the Root River bridge.

For the one and only time since moving to Oak Creek, dad and I went to catch crabs for bait off the Root River's bridge.

He woke me very early that Saturday morning.

We drove down to the pier in Racine and caught perch all day long—just dad and me.

It was one of the few times I got to go fishing with him alone.

We sat at the end of the long concrete pier until well after dark.

It was very relaxing watching the lights from the lake's shoreline reflect off the water's surface and listening to the sound of the water's ripples and small, quiet waves lapping around us in the night.

Sometimes there were long interludes of silence.

Then, again, there were long periods of time when we talked about anything and everything including George and Tiger.

We also talked about going on and how the good memories can be such an important part of your foundation for the future.

As we walked back along the pier that night toward the car he left me with a thought that was more like something my mom would have said. "Life has a lot of bridges to cross, but you have to cross them. God crosses them with you."

I've always had a special fondness of that vision since then and of the many bridges I've seen and crossed over the years. I love the sound of footsteps on a bridge or the sight of footprints in the snow approaching and crossing their span.

It was a very good day. Dad helped a lot!

DID I REALLY DO THAT!

Mom loved a good joke and was always a good sport. She seemed to enjoy teasing unless you went too far. It might have been this combination in part that attracted her to dad. Although there were a number of times he went too far!

Unfortunately, her children inherited the same teasing trait.

I was no exception.

I probably made a subconscious attempt to pick up where George left off.

I don't know how it started, but suddenly I started horsing around with trying to speak with different accents. I even tried to do imitations of different performers like Jimmy Stewart or James Cagney. I probably picked up the interest in dialects from listening to some of the radio shows like "Life with Luigi" or watching Charlie Chan movies. Grandpa Danowski talked in slight Polish accent and I used to try to emulate that when playing around. We also visited the Polish butcher shops and the Italian butcher shops such as the famous one from my Aunt Gloria's family, the Groppi meat market on Milwaukee's east side.

At any rate, mom ended up the victim of some my attempts along this line.

Every now and then, I would call mom from school just to say hi and chat a while. By the time I got home she was usually at work and the only other talk time we had was weekends.

I truly valued some of this alone time with her, even if it was just by phone. It only cost something like a dime a call at that time.

It was great because, during those chats, I learned some things about her and our family that I probably would never have known otherwise.

I learned that she loved to ride horses bareback.

I didn't know that her father, Frank, had a stable of horses that were used by the City of Milwaukee to pull the wagons for the Department of Public Works long before there were trucks.

I learned that her mother, Pauli, liked to play cards and have parties at her house all the time. Her maiden name was Datka and I know that I have a number of relatives with that same last name around.

I learned that my dad's mother Anna settled in the U.S. A. only because she was born on an American ship bound for Canada and automatically became an American citizen so her family settled in the Manitowoc Two Rivers area of Wisconsin instead.

I learned that my grandfather Ben met Anna only because he came to the Manitowoc area from Poland to paint ships that were built there. I didn't know, until then, that Grandpa Ben used to sing in a boys choir.

The first time I tried the practical joke on her, I wasn't sure I had the accent down quite right. I also gave it a lot of forethought and came to the conclusion that she would handle it just fine.

So, I called and pretended to be a guy with an accent from a laundry. She said, "Who?" I insisted that she failed to pick up the twenty-two white shirts and forty-one handkerchiefs she dropped off a month ago.

She said, "No way!"

I persisted.

She kept her composure and insisted she had never been to a Laundry like mine in her entire life. I started to say that she had to pick it up because she owed me tons of money

I couldn't pull it off any more and started laughing. When she found out it was a joke she didn't know it was me at first.

Then she showed the true sport she was. She said something about she would kill me when I got home—and then laughed along with me.

When I got home later that day, she was already at work.

However, there was a bag on the kitchen table bearing a note for me.

It read something like, "Please use this in the future to take all of your laundry to that laundry guy with the accent that you know so well. Signed, Ha! Ha!"

I tried this one other time that I remember fairly well. I made an effort to sound like Stashu, a fictitious Polish butcher. My friend Stanley who worked at Ray Bussler's helped me refine the accent. He was in his sixties and still spoke Polish fluently.

At first I asked why she didn't pick up the Polish Sausage she ordered two days ago. At first she thought that maybe dad did and forgot about it.

When she caught on—the gig was up. She suggested that maybe I quit school and try comedy or—no—maybe I just had better stay in school!

Fortunately for the world and probably most fortunately for me, I left this effort at impersonations far behind me.

No matter how hard I tried, I could never replace the character that was George!

Sandy and George

SANDY

Sandy was lonely, but found her own way of filling the void.

She filled it to overflowing.

Somewhere about mid October she gave birth to her first litter of seven of the tiniest, cuddliest little puppies.

There were no Georges or Tigers

However, there were these seven little furry balls—fourteen sparkling eyes that couldn't yet see—twenty-eight slender legs that wiggled at a pace that almost kept up with their tiny slender tails—and what seemed like countless tongues that wanted to lick everything in reach.

She just looked up at us as if to say, "How is that?"

She really helped us. Perhaps more than she ever knew.

I don't remember any of their names the others gave them except for Rex. Yet, they could have been names like Spooky or Cleo or Chester or Jasper or Linus or Bear or Tippy or any of a number of names that people and children everywhere give to the special animals. Pets we hoped others would take to their hearts and into their families as full fledged members with all the love and memories that they bring.

Yes, Sandy was special in her own way and so were the others.

There is one little secret promise I made to myself and never told anyone about while Sandy was expecting.

When I was alone with her, the morning after she had her puppies, I picked up the one I thought was the cutest. I held this little black and white puppy in my hands like I had held Sandy a while before.

I whispered my secret to the puppy's mother.

"Let's name this one George!"

Sandy, little George the puppy, and me

KALEIDOSCOPES
(Epilogue)

Family

Families are really very much like amazing Kaleidoscopes.

With each new turn—and each day—there are changes in the patterns of our lives.

Each family member grows in so many ways—and—does so many things. The interactions are ever changing.

Specific events of all kinds impact us!

Special non human living creatures sometimes enter in for us and provide us with lots of extras that God has created into them that are not even noticed unless you get the chance to experience them first hand for yourself!

The designs of life are never ending as one would expect in a real living kaleidoscope and all that makes it turn in real life. Images of the past and present are ever blending.

Every person—we get to know—has an impact on our lives in some way. This is no more so than within a family! For example, I remember just how important many of my uncles and aunts were in my life.

Aunt Bernice Dahnilik, my dad's sister, interested me in 3-D photography. She had the very first Stereo Realist Camera I had ever seen and it totally enthralled me. I didn't own my first one until I was in my early forties. It was almost an antique by then, but it was just like the one she had shared with me so long before. She would later, when she was in her seventies, share with me that she also loved painting with oil paints. I still treasure the one she sent to me from her home in Florida. She was also quite the entrepreneur who started out with a pony rink and a roadside hamburger stand and would parlay that over the years into owning a far bigger sized business. She always let me know I was important to her. When I grew up, she would remind me that she used to baby sit for me quite often,

Aunt Alice Mucha, another of my dad's sisters, introduced me to stereo view masters and pianos. She had the very first of either that I had seen. Later I would fall in love with the piano at my Grandma Anna's home at the top of Rawson Avenue in South Milwaukee on the corner of Nickelson Road.

Aunt Ruth Kozlowski, my mother's youngest sister, taught me to smile deep down inside, feel like I was growing up and to like her very special duck soup. I loved the visits with her when I would visit following my days of yard work for Judge Kletchka as a boy. She always treated me so special and was such a warm and friendly person.

Uncle Ray, my mom's younger brother, hooked me on accordions, guitars and electric trains.

And who of her nephews and nieces could forget Aunt Emily Mankowski? None of us could! She was famous to us all—because she was in charge of the molds for making the excellent chocolate Easter Bunnies for Easter and the chocolate Santa's for Christmas for the oh so famous Quality Candy Company in Milwaukee. They were the best! And, they were ever so large; you would break them up, piece by piece and eat away! It took days to finish one! I could never finish one off in a single day. Aunt Emily made sure we all had one each year when we were growing up.

She would also bring over chocolate bird nests. The coconut scattered throughout added the texture so that there was no doubt they were nests. And the several jelly beans in the middle added to the image. But the taste—ummmm—the taste was the best! She loved her job so much she was a fixture at her job until she was almost ninety years old.

I would get the chance to return the favor in later years when she lost her husband, Uncle Ben. Their son Bob, my cousin and one of my best friends as a young man, lives in Arizona. He tried to get Aunt Emily to move out to Arizona with them, but she loved her friends here too and the Quality Candy Company kept her job open all of those years.

Mardy, Greg and I would visit her in Milwaukee from time to time and try to help out with needs she may have had around the house like getting the carpet cleaned or fixing her furnace.

Those were always priceless visits because she was the last remaining of all of my mom's siblings.

Aunt Gertrude, she was mom's sister and was so very special in different ways, started my interest of classical music, brought the love for the rosary into my life and showed me how to deal with adversity. My first memories of her were seeing the crafts she made while living with my grandfather Frank Czerwinski on Lincoln Avenue in Milwaukee. She would bring out the angels she made with foil and lace. I fell in love with them. So did mom and so did her customers of which there were many!

Then there were three of my dad's brother's!

Uncle Pete interested me in business and the opportunities it presented and had me stay at his cottage on the Fox River in Waterford, Wisconsin for part of the summer. I enjoyed the water and the wooded area every year for a number of years. Uncle Len used to take me out there at the start of my vacations and bring me home when they were over.

Dad was the oldest of the boys in his family and Uncle Pete was next in line. Their twin brothers died from an illness when they were very young.

I listened to his stories of how Uncle Pete managed businesses. He was a real inspiration for me to eventually go on to college. I really grew in my love for the out-of-doors here and my love for the lakes and streams. And oh how I loved how his wife, my Aunt Sis, would cook the wild game that he hunted.

One of my favorite thing to do when I visited was to borrow my uncle's binoculars and search the water's surface and scour the weeds, the woods and the air looking for anything wild that moved or fish that would jump and splash back into the river.

Fishing in rivers would always be a special treat to me. My love for that probably dates back to my visits to Uncle Pete and Aunt Sis. Later when we lived in Oak Creek my brother Jim and I would spend hours at the Root River that was so much a part of the true story you have read here about George and the gang. We loved those times of sitting there and catching fish. But, I think we both also enjoyed the times when the fish weren't biting of quiet time to talk about so many things, watch the Herons fly by, listen to the waters ripple, tossing pebbles and watching them skip, eating the lunches we would pack, etc. I also enjoyed the quiet times too because they were also occasion for special reflections, thinking about what I wanted to do with my life and time for prayer. Prayer at the quiet of slow moving waters—it is hard to find a better setting.

I did find other places where the serenity and the beauty of it all formed such an excellent backdrop. One that truly captured my heart and gave me pause for prayer was when we visited with Mandy and Seb and stood at the top of some of Switzerland's majestic mountain tops!

Or, there were the times with our whole family at the edge of the Grand Canyon.

Or there was the time we visited with Jeff—when Jeff lived in Wyoming and was a sports reporter—and Mardy, her mom, Jeff, Greg, Dan, Cheri and our dear friend Father Howard Haase got to stand part way up one of the Grand Tetons and over looked the magnificence of God's creativity and what He chose to do with it including Jenny Lake and Hidden Falls!

Or there was the time when I got to sit and absorb the beauty of the sunset on a river bank in Kenya with my friend Al Hornish.

Or, there were times like Mardy and I standing on the Pacific Ocean's shore, listening to the quiet and the surf, with my cousin Bob and Betty on a many week trip we took up the west coast in their RV after I retired from Johnson Wax.

Or, there where the times we stood on Cannon Beach watching sunsets with our friend Father Gene Neuman or standing at the top of the royal and forceful Multnomah Falls.

Or, there was the tranquility of the Smoky Mountains in Tennessee with Do, his wife Betsy, and our grandchildren Shanna, Erin and Jessica.

Or, there were the outstanding sunrise moments of the eastern shore of Door County in Wisconsin with Cheri, her husband Tom, and our grandchildren Hanna, Paul and Mike.

Or, there was the splendor of the sites at the Wisconsin Dells with Dan, his wife Deb, and our grandchildren Kyle, Ben and Sam.

Or there was the inspiration of the Casa in Phoenix with my brother Jim and his wife Bonnie and their sons Mike and Chris and my sister Jan and her husband Al and their son Scott.

Or there were the many times on the Willow Flowage with its endless offerings of beauty in northern Wisconsin with Mardy's cousin Bill Bohn and his wife Chris and all of their wonderful children who have been brothers and sisters to our children these many years. (One of Bill's sons would turn out to be a hero many times over in Iraq.)

Or, for me, there were the times when fish were not biting and I would get to sit there with my dad and—any combination of—my brothers Jim and Jerry and my sisters Judy and Jan on the piers in Racine and in South Milwaukee to watch the sunrises on Lake Michigan! Dad was an early riser and so am I to this day.

Or—there are so many "Ors" it is impossible to count them all!

Solace, beauty and serenity—all can be such beautiful gifts and opportunities for contemplation and communication with the One who created it all. He is such a master artist and a master sculptor and painter of strikingly marvelous things. Did He create these things to give us such pause and unique opportunities including for reinvigoration and for prayer—and—knowing Him and His love better? One has to wonder!

Uncle Leonard was only nine years older than me and took this to yet another level! He was and still is—well—more of a big brother. He took me everywhere and really interested me in fishing and the out of doors. I still call him big brother and he, in turn, still calls me little brother even though I am almost seventy two years old at this writing.

My Uncle Larry was much the same way. He would carry me on his shoulders to the movies and took me swimming at the old gravel pit in South Milwaukee.

They were all great people who took the time to care about me and teach me.

When this is going on, one almost takes it all for granted, that they are there and that they do what they do and will be there forever.

It took me years to realize that all of this comes down to one thing that is so obvious and yet so often not clearly identified for what it really is. Those who genuinely, unselfishly have taken time with us along the way and those who take time with us now are really giving us their own very unique and very special gift—their love! Even more importantly, they are God's gifts of love to us—each and every one!

I wonder if it would make a difference for us if we started to pause before going to bed at night and reflect back on the day completed. Then, if we were to think about those who spent time with us in whatever way they could—no matter how busy they were or just how convenient or inconvenient it might have been, what would we take away from it?. And, if—in our mind—we converted time and whatever other gifts of self they gave us into what it really is—love—would it make a difference? Would it translate into a unique appreciation for what gifts they are in our lives? Would we feel much richer than we did only moments before?

It could—if we do not look at these as expectations on our parts, but as gifts of self that they give to us!

SOUND FAMILIAR?

While a lot has happened since the beginning of this true story about George and friends—some things certainly have a familiar sound to them.

The creativity, the lessons and the love—that were all a part of what came before—did verily take a quantum leap with us into the future.

Today, most everyone in our family loves the mountains, hidden streams and glistening waterfalls, waves upon the sand, lighthouses and beautiful sunsets.

You will probably never get the country out of us.

We all have a bit of a tease in us and love to laugh and have a good time. It is just a part of the fabric of who we are!

Our roots still show through strongly—in all of us—and in our families.

God is paramount!

Family is so very, very important.

The last two homes for Mardy and I and our family have been in the city, but always close to the wide open spaces on the edge of town.

The beauties around us—the trees, the flowers—their smells, their colors and their splendor in the rains, the sun and the breezes are so very special.

AIMING THE SCOPE FORWARD

Those who have heard the story over the years have always asked about what happened to the boy who loved his crow when he grew older. So, turning the Kaleidoscope forward looking—here is a glimpse or two or three of the years after that transcended the days of the adventures of my four wonderful pets. While trying to take you for a look forward, at the age of almost seventy two, it will require me to look back a bit. I will try to share with you some of the things that folks ask about regarding a family love for creativity and other things in our lives. Some of the names will have a familiar ring to them since you read the first part of the book, but the effort will be to put them a little more into the context of my life.

GOD'S OTHER LIVING GIFTS TO US

Who can't help but feel good at the sight of a wild crane, hawk, eagle, duck, goose, pheasant, chickadee, nuthatch, robin, wren, blue jay, cardinal or many of God's colorful feathered friends in their natural state.

We all love the wide open skies where the crow flies.

We all love little kittens.

And, puppy dogs—will always melt our hearts away.

And so do feathered creatures like Mickey—our son Greg's bird with whom we all fell in love! Coated in beautiful green feathers, she is a small sized parrot—and was so special to Greg! Mickey was as close to Greg as George was to me. I saw it in the interactions between the two. Greg taught her to do so many tricks!

She would sing with Greg.

She would dance with Grig.

She would spin a round with Greg!

She would kiss Greg.

He taught Mickey so much more.

However, what I remember most about Mickey is when Greg did something very unselfish with her!

Even though he knew he would miss Mickey a lot—he gave Mickey up to an older woman, with a special need for Mickey in her life, who had also grown to love Mickey! Mickey was also very important to her. She too had known Mickey for a long time. Greg knew it so important for her to have Mickey as a part of her life! So, my son did something very special. Even though he really raised Mickey and trained Mickey and grew to love Mickey, he gave up Mickey—to her!

The real live adventures of Mickey are fascinating—but—that is for another book!

Variety is good!

Cuddly animals and friendly feathered friends plus the big wild ones too—are loved by us all including my wife and children and now grandchildren.

If you need proof, Mardell once collected lots and lots of Beannie Babies—cute little reminders of the real live animals and birds around us! She doesn't keep them. Instead, she has been sharing them when they were the in thing and still shares them with those near and dear to us and to those in need!

LICORICE

While speaking of animals in our lives, it wouldn't be proper to overlook Licorice.

No, I'm not referring to candy!

She was a real live genuine dog who came to live with us! And—she did for almost thirteen years.

Mardell named her!

We loved her!

A real part of the family—she had the greatest of times with Jeff, Don, Cheri, Dan and Greg, our five children who grew up in our home.

Licorice's pedigree—part collie, part beagle and part terrier—blended so beautifully.

Her graceful nose fit perfectly on her pretty face!

A big white star adorned her chest—and was about the same size as the star on the chest of the special Sandy from my past. Her colors were what one would expect from a dog that was part collie and part beagle. However—mostly—her colors resembled those of a beagle.

She had the pointy nose of a collie.

As for size, that was closer to that of an over sized beagle.

She fully entered the hearts of our entire family during the simple short drive from the pet shop in Milwaukee!

It didn't take long!

Heart stealing—this little puppy sat in a cardboard box on our children laps! The cardboard motel in the basement of my boyhood past was just so much like the cardboard box on the laps of the youngsters in the back seat of our station wagon! While driving the car taking Licorice home, I could not help but think back to Sandy and all of her close friends in our basement in Oak Creek!

Licorice took in all of these little human faces in the rear seat—all of them grinning at her from ear to ear. She certainly thought she was a part of this family! There was no doubt about it!

Yet—Licorice didn't think she was a dog as the Tiger of my past once did. Instead, Licorice thought she was a human and—at times—acted like it.

Agile, fast, and fun—she loved to play football with our five young children!

A smart little one—she knew what to do on defense! She tackled with her two front legs! It seemed like such great satisfaction to her as she would catch one of our youngsters and stand over them when they would playfully fall to the ground!

On offense—she made like a half back! Licorice carried the small sized ball in her mouth! Could she ever run!

She played with them in their snow forts and their bedrooms! She loved them each in a hundred ways! And they certainly returned it!

Once, when I came home from a business trip, I brought something back for each of our family—but not for our dog! Licorice came over to my knees where I was sitting and just stood there looking at me as if to say "Where is mine?"

She even looked for her own stack of wrapped Christmas gifts under the tree—and Mardell always obliged! Did Licorice love them? You bet! Would she miss them? Yes! How could one not tell?

Well, as each left home—she let them know just how much she missed them.

When they came back home for their first visit—after being gone for a while—she literally stretched out on the floor—legs outstretched. Then, adding insult to injury she would turn her head away from them and totally ignore them.

If they moved around her to where she could see them, she would turn her head the other way—continuing the cold shoulder she was giving them. And, she didn't relent—at least not until they went out of their respective ways to let her know she was still important to them. And then—she would slowly let her love for them show again!

We all have one particular memory that illustrates this well!

Our second oldest son Don—returned home to visit for the first time after the honeymoon with his bride Betsy!

Don was the first of our children to leave home!

I can still remember Don and Betsy entering the front door!

There were lots of hugs and kisses! Homecomings are always a monumental event!

After greeting all of the siblings, Don started his search for Licorice. He called and called!

No Licorice!

She didn't come to greet him!

This was really strange! She always came running when one of our children called—always!

So—Don started a room to room search!

I looked outside to see if somehow Licorice had slipped past them! But, no—nowhere in sight!

Finally, I heard Don call out, "There you are!"

Yup! And there she was!

Licorice was defiantly sprawled out in front of our patio doors—looking straight ahead out the glass window.

In essence, she presented her back side to Don—making a very definite statement!

Don called to her several times!

She paid absolutely no attention to him!

Finally, our son patiently reached over to her to pat her on the head. His hand approached!

Licorice again turned her head rebelliously—sharply—away from him!

Don approached her from both sides—again and again!

Licorice, again and again quickly turned her head the other way!

Licorice then continued swiveling her head so that she wouldn't have to look at him!

Better than old Abbott and Costello routines—it was one of the funniest comedy routines I ever saw!

At the time, Don didn't think so! However we did!

How did it get resolved?

Well, Don just lifted Licorice up into his arms and hugged her! Then he carried her out the door and placed her in their car!

She continued to show her defiance by looking the other way all during the drive!

When they arrived—Don and Betsy gave her a tour of their new apartment. She didn't seem so defiant—yet—still kept her distance.

Sometime during that stay over—it happened! They made up with each other—and everything was fine once more!

Over the past forty some years we have deliberately lived near where there is an abundance of wildlife from the Finch and Cardinals on the bird feeders to the Blue Jays occasionally steeling their share to the squirrels, rabbits and raccoons in the backyard and to the occasional fox and deer who visit in broad daylight.

Watching my grandchildren, I know that they all have their own special stories about the furry and feathered creatures that have made their way into their hearts over the years! None of them are as dramatic as the dog, the cat, the crow, and—yes the goose—that provided more than a little love and oh so much enjoyment!

A LEVEL OF THOUGHT PROCESS
AND FEELINGS THAT WE MAY NOT
YET FULLY APPRECIATE

No one can ever convince me that the creatures God sends us—and who become our pets—do not have feelings on some level.

Nor can they convince me that they do not have their own way of somehow sorting things out in the minds God gave them! They have their likes and their dislikes and they definitely have their own unique personalities, qualities, characteristics and even their own quirks between creatures of the same breed!

Nor can they convince me that they do not love.

They do!

The world would be a far emptier and lonelier place without them and a lot less fun.

I believe that those who don't agree—have never fully taken enough time and made enough of an effort to really experience what the living creatures do—and how they behave when exposed to a human's presence over an extended period of time!

Or maybe they have not been given an open enough opportunity to form a relationship and interact as some people do! If one doesn't take the time required—they operate by thinking in the vacuum of their own inexperience—whether by choice or otherwise.

Sometimes it is more of a false sense of sophistication about assuming an amazing level of inferiority of other creatures. Why do some sort out the need to save lives—and then do it?

True, they are not made in God's image and do not have the same stature that humans do, but just maybe they have more sophistication and capabilities than are attributed to them. It may just be that we haven't learned to appreciate them yet or the unique qualities God created just for them—including many we just don't have—i.e. built in sonar, an ultra good hearing and a superb sense of smell!.

Just like all other stereotypes—what one doesn't know—is easy to ignore and sometimes safer to put in little boxes with closed lids! Then, many just say "That's just the way it is!"

Who can doubt that these living joys—we call pets—have memories?

Pets can learn—despite the fact that some would make their learning trivial! Some merely call their mastery of what we ask them to do—tricks! Yet, somehow they master what it is that we want them to do!

But—they definitely do learn!

George was the first one to teach me that!

If animals, birds and other creatures of God can play such an important role in the lives of children and adults alike—and they are not made in His image—I have to wonder and imagine just what expectations He has of people in the lives of others.

It is an interesting ponderance as to just what roles people may be expected to play through their roles and opportunities during their life's journey—in terms of the lives of those around them—and, those whose lives they may be able to touch in some significant and/or meaningful positive way!

My feeling is that this question may certainly have relevance to those who have real obligations whether they sought them out or not. It is also possible that it just may be relevant for those who are entrusted with special gifts and opportunities. When we are faced with challenging times, we may not think of it in these terms for a whole variety of reasons, but the question may still apply because how we attempt to address our challenges can definitely affect those around us in a multiplicity of ways.

LESSONS

Consciously or unconsciously, I used so many lessons—lessons that I learned back in my youth!

So have my brothers and sisters!

We learned to really try to listen to each other during those times that were of the greatest challenge! I am sure that all of us are better listeners today—because of our experiences of yesterday.

We learned what family really means!

When you just have each other for a while—and material things are scare and everyday needs are sparse—a strong dynamic takes place!

I learned to work hard!

We learned just how much effort, togetherness, courage, leadership, faith and prayer really mean and just how critical they are to us all!

We learned how much a needed hug can mean!

Mom taught us not to be afraid to fail. Fear of failure is one of the biggest deterrents to learning how to succeed! Mistakes that we make can become the cornerstones for success if we digest what they have to offer!

A big key, I think, is not to be afraid to start over and over again!

Access the possibilities!

And—if the window of success can be opened in a particular direction and one is willing to pay the price—never give up—no matter how long it takes or what the odds are!

God is always there for us—particularly when you need Him most—and you feel His presence least.

Just keep reaching out to Him.

Opportunities to learn are lost—and—we grow so much slower if we are hesitant to try through lack of confidence, fear or anxiety.

A big key is willingness to try and try again and again! It can be slow—but it can also be potent—dusting one's self off each time and getting up anew!

It can mean not being unafraid to take chances in order to possibly succeed!

It can be important to search for and try to find better ways to achieve one's goals!

It just might be that a given goal is not the right goal at the right time or the right fit under the circumstances.

However, then it may also be important to search out and find new goals that are attainable!

We need to make a more thorough assessment first of where we are at, where we want to go and what we can and what we need to do to get there. And—then we need to better prepare ourselves, develop a workable plan and gather the appropriate resources before embarking on the journey!

Along the way, it can be beneficial to access our process, make any modifications that may be needed and keep your eye on the target!

After each journey, many do not take the time for an important step—to look back and evaluate what one did well and where one could improve. This can be an invaluable learning process.

One truly achievable goal for each and every one of us—is to make God the center of one's life! He will help us with that goal if we extend the invitation to Him! It truly is THE most rewarding goal—an eternal one!

Paraphrasing my dad—he used to say—focus on ways to meet and beat each challenge! Look for the "How To" in each situation. Spend your energies finding the ways it can be done—how to resolve or overcome each formidable task.

When we had it toughest at home—and when I would go with dad on his jobs as a painting contractor—we had lots of talk time.

He had lots of mountains to overcome in his life and he would say over and over—don't get caught building lists of reasons WHY NOT! Search for and discover the "HOW TO's"!

Starting down the road of "why something can't be done" almost assures that it will become a self fulfilling prophesy!

And, guess what? Then it probably won't get done—or even have a reasonable chance to succeed!

A far better tact is to spend our efforts and energy figuring out HOW TO forge through, get around, and change directions or tactics as well as ways to overcome what may be or seems to be or in fact truly be an obstacle.

Sometimes it may even help to shift gears and to choose another direction instead of stalling or going into a needless nose dive.

This approach has potential to help one to avoid spinning their wheels in the mud of despair!

There may be a time and a place for taking advantage of planning different positive objectives and setting realistic strategies for achieving them! Honesty—true honesty is the key!

Dwelling on—why we can't do something—is a needless waste of time, energy and resources!

Dwelling on truly honest why nots—is unproductive.

Acknowledge them for what they are!

Then start down the road of redirecting one's attention until we find attainable goals that do fit us and our circumstances no matter how big or how small!

I tell my children—make sure your most important goal is God! It is one my mother planted in me as a boy and my Aunt Gertrude nourished! My mother-in-law, Vivian believed in it—and life has proven this to be true over these many years for me!

Scriptures lead us to this same conclusion over and over!

It's not what you can do alone!

It's what you and God can do together that makes the best music!

This is harmonious!

This is symphonic!

This reverberates beyond the mountain tops of what one can do alone!

PERSONAL

Some of the vignettes that follow—are far more personal than I have normally shared publicly all of my life. A person who developed an hour TV program about creativity in our family encouraged me during the taping of the program to share more of this because it may in some way encourage others along the way.

Others have encouraged me to do the same because, as a person with a serious disability, there have been so many blessings in my life and maybe it would bring some degree of support to others by sharing more openly.

Some of my children have encouraged me to do the same.

So—through the behest of their encouragement and hopes that maybe someone may find something of value in my doing so and in this spirit—I open my heart and memory bank here a bit for you.

The intent of bits here and there is not to be preachy, but to share a little about some of my experiences, inner thoughts and some of the challenges in my life.

And, in truth and the spirit of actually sharing—there have been some truly major tests along he way to address, but there have also been some amazing opportunities!

HERITAGE

It is a little hard for me to trace the heritage in my family tree. Some work has been done by others, but I have not personally had the opportunity to confirm a lot of it.

My brother Jim has done the major work so far and I have heard some pieces here and there from others.

There is definitely a strong Polish influence, but with the way borders have shifted in Europe and Russia over the years—it is even harder to be certain. There are some traces of a bit of German. There may even be a touch of Jewish.

However, a particular lady's last name—of years gone by—has been fascinating but impossible for me to fully track.

My mother's mother was Aplonia Datka. Some think they may have traced us back to a queen with the name of Datka. The queen's full name was Kurmanjan Datka and was known as the Tsaritsa of Alai or the Queen of the South from Kyrgyzstan. She was born in 1811 and has an interesting history with Russia and even spent some time in China. She had a reputation as a great military leader defending her nation along an important east/west trade route. Our source said she eventually went to Poland, but others trace her to Russia where she was honored. Yet, I have not been able to substantiate it.

There are a few pieces of family history that I have more comfort with in terms of knowing that they are correct.

I do know that there are musicians on mom's side and business people. I do know there are some business people on my dad's side.

I do know that my dad's father worked in Gdansk Poland, but was born in Kadonia, Russia. He worked his way across the Atlantic as a finisher of wood on ships and settled in Manitowoc, Wisconsin where there is a history of ship building.

He met my grandmother Anna Welnick. Anna was born on an American ship enroute to Canada. So, her parents changed their plans and moved to the U.S. in a city called Two Rivers near Manitowoc and enjoyed immediate American citizenship.

DEEPER THOUGHTS

We learned to appreciate the people in our lives!

We also learned to value the non-material things that can be true gifts to treasure!

Some of the most solid rocks on which we can build our foundation—are the humble periods in our lives—if we do not let them humble us.

We learned that humility is not weakness! It requires great strength, resolve and commitment!

Personal recognition and gratification fit best—on the far back burner.

We also learned a lot more about finding our Lord in our daily lives. Two particularly hard to achieve goals are the crux of trying to follow His way.

One is to try to find Him looking back at us each time we look into another's eyes. It can make such a difference in what one decides to say or do, to, for, with or about that person.

The second major challenge is to try and let Him work through us by trying to:

let our ears hear as He would

our feet walk where He would go

our hands serve as He would serve

and—our mouth speak the things that He would speak to others.

This surely is not easy all the time—every day—in every situation!

I'm not sure I've captured this completely enough, but I think this might be some of what He meant when he asked us to "Follow Me"!

The old saying—"What would Jesus say or do (WWJD)?"—can make a difference if we believe it and put it into practice every moment of every day of our lives. It should never grow old and should always be current and so meaningful for us daily!

Imagine thinking about the answers we would come up with—if we were to apply the WWJD question to all of the things we did or said during the past few days of our lives.

Imagine how different some situations could have turned out or been handled by asking the WWJD question first and then actually applying the answer!

One should truly ask one's self—if asking this question first can make a difference in how one lives! What would happen if one were to honestly apply the question before things are said and done? It can be a great self inventory to do this from time to time!

In a time when people are searching for ways to teach values to the young and growing and to guide the teens and young adults—the answer is not hard! It really isn't! The answer is to WWJD and the guides to this are found in His teachings which are not allowed in schools while all sorts of absurd influences are allowed in the name of free speech.

Somewhere we in this country have really messed up badly when we deliberately keep the true guides to life out of our educational systems and yet allow all kinds of terrible impactful influences in—and—they are allowed to repeat their mantras minute by minute in misguidance and misdirection over headphones and the gatherings of the young and in the guises of the various media outlets. Instead of following the guides to life God gave us—people are constantly trying to invent our own—i.e.—how can we find a way to give our school children values that are good? When you can't mention God in schools—naturally there is going to be a void!

Something has gone askew with a culture that directs so many young away from the teachings and directions of their parents. Yet, we adults stand by and have been letting it happen. It seems like a false syllogism to me to allow what is wrong to exist and what is right to decease and disappear. At this point in time, we have become a society of pulverizing that which is right and protecting that which is wrong!

As I reach my current age of seventy-one plus, I realize just how many older folks are viewed as old folks.

Older doesn't mean less intelligent!

Nor, does older mean that one is elevated above either the genius— or the creativity—that is thriving in the young of our time.

I feel it is so good for everyone if all concerned respect what the other has to offer which—is much—because of the generosity of God! He gives the young the opportunity to learn from the experiences and wisdom of those older.

He also gives the older ones the opportunity to rekindle the sparks of hope and vision and the many other gifts of youth.

Plus, the young of each generation are given so many potentially wonderful tools to use that the older generations could only dream of if in fact they could even be imagined.

It is possible that maybe older, for some, could mean seasoned—in a personalized way—by many of their own life's experiences and of their experiencing of history to interpret what is being represented or presented.

ENTITLEMENT

There is a dangerous trap that folks can fall into. Sometimes I think folks make the mistake of thinking that God's many and varied gifts to us are entitlements!

It is when we recognize them as what they really are—gifts entrusted to us that we begin to realize just how special He is and just how special He thinks we are.

Then—if we know He thinks of each of us as really special—we can come closer to being the gem we really are capable of being!

Perhaps the greatest of these gifts is faith! It is one of the greatest treasures here on earth!

What we do with the gifts He entrusts to us—will go a long way in determining our journeys and our destinations.

If we treat them as entitlements, we can miss the mark by galaxies.

If we treat His gifts as entrustments, then—just maybe—there is something we are supposed to do to nurture, develop, utilize, share and put them to the purposes for which God may have intended!

Entrustment requires us to accept what has been entrusted to us and then to provide our response to it. The entrustment is God's. What we accept and how we respond are essentially ours to choose—an important choice!

INFLUENCE

Certainly there were many fine exemplary people who have influenced me along the way—and—have helped to form the ways that I travel in this life.

George, Sandy, Tiger and Goose were among my early teachers! They, in their own ways, added their contributions too! And, surely—in that sense—who can deny that they are gifts God sent to be here for us?

CREATIVITY

God gives each and every one of us unique gifts. That is one of the things that makes us each so distinctive!

Creativity is one gift that has always been very much alive in our family and continues to flourish today.

For example, over the years our family has been filled with performing musicians including great uncles with accordions, uncles with multiple instruments, mom with the piano and dad with multiple instruments. All of my brothers and sisters loved to sing along with mom and dad. This was an especially real gift to our family during those times were tough for us for several years. We always enjoyed music, but we could also find a great deal of enjoyment with ways in which we could jointly participate and share.

There are nephews who pursued songwriting and playwriting.

My cousin Romelle Bintz, Mel, is a writer for newspapers in Northern Wisconsin. Her sister Donna loved to draw. They are both daughters of my dad's younger sister Leona. Another of my dad's sisters loved to paint—his sister—my aunty Bernice—my one time baby sitter.

My brother Jim loved the guitar and loved to sing!

There are cousins who played in bands including my uncle Len's sons Bob and Jim. Jim played with a band that was featured and many major events throughout Milwaukee and went on tour with his band, the Bosz Brothers Review. So did Bob.

And now, our children and grandchildren are into music in a big way.

So, the roots have been there for a long time for things from the heart and a means of expressing them.

There are also so many other avenues for creative expression that continued to grow from the times of our youth.

A TV special was made about some of us providing an overview of some of the ways creativity flourishes in our hearts! And, in full truth, we know they are gifts from God.

So, what are some of these?

The next few pages will open the curtain a little more.

It is so hard to fully explain the workings of the seeds of creativity other than to try to show some of what comes to the surface and is visible to others.

Enhancing these gifts—are the wonderful friends that God has put into our lives. It is a lot like mixing colors. For example, yellow is a very distinct color with its own unique qualities. So is blue. So is red. Yet, when they touch each other, something else emerges creatively. These provide the wonderful blends of life—the greens, the purples, the oranges, etc., etc., etc.

WHAT HAPPENED TO THE BOY WHO LOVED GEORGE?

I try to tell our Grandchildren, in different ways, about the living friends God sent into our lives. I also try to share with them how the various unique touches have impacted each other—and the beauty of it all!

At this writing, there are eleven grandchildren with whom we can share our stories and shower with our love. Shanna, Kyle, Erin, Ben, Paul, Ricardo, Sam, Hannah, Jessica and Mike! A new name, Kira, is the newest treasure added to our family! They return what we have to offer—reciprocating many, many times more what we try to give them.

Staying with creativity as an example, hopefully, through writing what I remember—and in sharing these tales and our love with them and those yet to come and with their children and so on and—with your family too—we are doing some of what we can to show just one example of these kinds of special workings of God in our lives!

Today, if you asked my grandchildren what I was—they might tell you, "He is Grandpa!"

They might just say that I don't have a nose—-just a long black telephoto lens to perpetually take their pictures.

Or, our grandchildren might say an artist with works in many galleries or shows.

They have all had occasions to participate with me in my avocations as have their parents—successful artists and writers in their own right.

My children have met some of my very close artist friends like Berta Sherwood, Elton Dorval, Bob Johansen and Zoltan Szabo and have been mentored by some of them at different times.

Some could remember me for being an artist in residence at their grade school, making guest appearances at others, or being a member of the Wisconsin Watercolor Society.

Then they might learn about other directions in which my life has taken me.

Some would learn that I taught business courses, lectured at universities and that I headed a number of professional and church organizations over time including President of the Racine Manufacturer's Accounting Association. They might learn that I was an instrumental member of a number of Human Resource and professional Associations and that I delivered addresses to their national meetings. Those that know me as a fun loving grandpa have difficulty seeing me in these roles. Some of my classmates from my youth would probably be surprised because I was a bit shy once upon a time, but again, I think the teaching experience I had at Oakwood Road School helped to break me out of that.

They will; however, probably never see the countless self published business books I wrote for clients over the years—at the request of CEOs and Presidents of corporations and of organizations—to guide them and the top management of many companies or that, in key situations, I became their confidant. Nor would they know that I worked with, consulted with and made presentations to and worked directly with their Boards of Directors. I will mention more about this later.

Some might know I love to write poetry or that I wrote for one of the world's top art magazines.

Most will remember that initially I initially wrote the first part of this true story just for them about my youth—because it was about a very special time in the lives of me and my brothers and sisters! Some may remember that I was later to expand the Kaleidoscopes portion of this book to share other personal experiences for generations to come— because I was asked by some in my family to do so—so many times.

Or, they may remember the many individual stories I wrote just for them over the years including "The Green Turkey", "E Bunny", "The White Wolf of Christmas" and many, many others that I gave them at Christmas or Easter celebrations over the years! Or, they may remember my first non business published book "The Green Turkey and other Holiday Classics". Our sons Don and Greg helped me to illustrate the cover for this book. "The Green Turkey" would probably never have happened if my son Jeff hadn't pushed me to do it.

Encouragement from Mardy and our children have been a constant in stirring me to move forward in some arenas. They have all been responsible in one way or another for my moving forward with things I love to do.

Another key contribution that my children give me is that we can talk about most anything and in depth. All channels remain open and that too is a gift.

They would probably laugh if you remind them that the first book I put together and was formally published was called "How to Talk to an Actuary". Stuffy—as the title sounds—it was a major accomplishment because it saved the company I worked for a lot of money! Folks actually did laugh when I first came up with the idea because they said it was too technical of a subject to condense and make easy to understand. I have to admit, that when that happened my motivation shifted a little to prove that I could do it. I seldom have been motivated that way, but this book was. And it did work. Johnson Wax sold it to other companies to help them in their international operations—the real target for the book.

There are three more books in the pipeline that are in various stages of completion. Two of them are being co created with persons very near and dear to me and are true stories. The other is a book on effective planning which has been encouraged by some of the CEOs for whom I once consulted. I learned a lot about the subject in the real life laboratory of my years of studying and working with management at all levels.

Certainly they will not forget our son Jeff's first published book— "The Teddy Bear Necklace" or his two volume releases last year—"In

Flying Colors"! They may also know how I illustrated the cover for volume one, how Greg illustrated the cover for volume two and how painting from Greg, Don, our daughter Cheri and me are found inside of Jeff's new books. Jeff also has several new books in the works.

Over the years we have had a lot of fun with our grandchildren and their interests in creative things. Years ago when Kyle, Ben and Paul lived in Milwaukee and Shanna and Erin lived in Racine, I would make a run up to Milwaukee and pick up those that lived there during the summers and bring them to Racine so that they could have a day together each week. Often we would do creative things—including drawing. Each had their own plastic box containing their own drawing pads, watercolors, crayons, colored pens, modeling clay, etc.

As the years went on that became harder to do so it became more individually oriented—more one on one time with Mardell and crafts or art sessions with me—including the newer additions like Jessica and Hannah and Sam. Some of them even helped write some poetry for my book "The Green Turkey."

In what has now become a family tradition, our grandson Kyle Danowski who is mid way through his senior year in high school contributes this special poem for this book. I so appreciate my children and grandchildren reaching back—each and everyone in their own ways—and keeping those special lines open with their grandparents.

Kyle shows a great interest in creative outlets including music, writing and perhaps film directing.

One can not miss the feeling that is in his heart in this piece. Actually, Kyle gave me a choice of three pieces making the decision a difficult one at best. They are all very special.

But a decision had to be made.

All of them have such depth of thought, imagery and beauty in handling. This particular one touched me because it also uses a subject—that I love to include in some of my watercolors—as the thread that weaves his thoughts together so marvelously. Snow!

"SNOWFLAKES"
By Kyle Danowski

Under the stars I stand and wait,
restless mind in locked debate.
Looking for symbols, signs and keys,
to assure and put me at ease.

The air is cold, but I am warm,
the sky is calm; my mind's a storm.
Snowflakes around me falling in peace,
nothing disturbs them as they twinkle and freeze.

A sweeping wind blows bits of snow,
and under lampposts; grains do glow.
Tossed about in the open air,
jubilant with no despair.

And when they settle upon the ground,
they do so gently without a sound.
Building up to fluffy banks,
adding snowflakes to their ranks.

In silence they proliferate,
as my thoughts reciprocate.
And slowly I do realize,
what's happening before my eyes.

Goosebumps forming on my arm,
not in fright or dread alarm.
I now begin to understand,
as if this moment had been planned.

~continued~

A metaphor in passing then,
a void where all my doubt had been.
The snowflakes falling silently,
helped in reassuring me.

The world itself is not that bad,
if you look past the growing sad.
All the cries of those in rage,
and all the wars we have to wage.

If you can stop as I did then,
and press your paper to a pen,
words will come from deep inside,
and you shall understand my mind.

Why I stand and ponder these,
and why my body does not freeze.
What keeps me warm and keeps me whole,
and why these snowflakes touch my soul.

A madman some will say I am,
and in my mind I laugh at them.
For I have found what they all need,
to help them conquer worn out greed.

Happiness in silent hum,
powers; great: to overcome.
All are found with what I ee,
in tiny snowflakes white and free.

~continued~

For snowflakes have no evil core,
they do not starve or go to war.
They simply fall form starlit skies,
as if teardrops form some dying eyes.

They blow and fall in any case,
regardless of their time or place.
And do so without heed or care,
without permission through the air.

Whit and pure in unique shape,
they bring about a gentle drape.
They hide the Earth in monochrome,
and all the things that we condone.

So stand as I, in lonely nights,
and bring a peace to inner fights.
Close your eyes and stop to feel,
and you shall remember what is real.

Take belief in tiny flakes,
to teach you now of your mistakes.
Discover the eye in worldly storm,
and in the snow, become reborn.

They will not forget the art of their uncles Don and Greg and their aunt Cheri or of our newer family members Jiade or Ting or the more recent drawings by their newest Aunt—Mandy. They will also be familiar with the wonderful art of my newest brother Jiade.

Some might say I'm a magician because of the tricks I show them including one I learned from my Grandpa Ben or my favorite called Mr. Wizard".

Lesser known might be my award in photography. Yet, they certainly know how much I love taking photos. And as the have been getting older, I see cameras in all of their hands.

Creativity has been such a great outlet for us in so many ways!

Yet, there were other areas that God let me explore!

WHAT HAPPENED TO THE SEED OF MUSIC THAT DAD, MOM AND JIM NURTURED IN ME AS A BOY?

Those nights of singing with my brother Jim up in our room or singing as a family in the car or around a camp fire in the backyard didn't die with the embers of the past!

Some of the grandchildren might know about the music I co-wrote for church with my dear friend Jim Holt and was sung by our church choir in church frequently.

However, the may never know just how special it was to share our thoughts and ideas and discuss our philosophies and come up with the many songs that we did and would be sung by our church choir. My favorite of those is one where Jim Holt and I co-wrote the lyrics for an Easter celebration and I helped with some thoughts about the musical direction. There were hours around the piano in our home or the key board in Jim's apartment. The friendship that grew was so very special!

Some day they will know that I wrote the wedding song, with Jim, for the weddings of their moms and dads and for them and their children etc., etc., etc. The opening words for the bride and groom are "Love—my gift to you! Love—your gift to me!" They would probably not know that I wrote the lyrics on an airplane bound for Boston on a business trip to meet with my friend Tim Haigh and polished in the hotel that night. Before writing them I thought of each of our children by name, said a prayer and also dedicated it to all of children and grandchildren and heirs for all generations to come. So far—it has been performed by Jim at four family weddings and sung by his marvelous vocal accompanist Jan at each of them. The latest was our oldest son Jeff's wedding where part of the lyrics were translated into Spanish and sung in both languages. This song—like the others Jim and I did, came from the heart!

For the first time publicly, here are the lyrics:

LOVE'S VOW

Lo—ve!
Your gift to me
Lo—ve!
My gift to you.
It glistens like the snow.
It sparkles like your eyes.
Bounding from our hearts
Like rainbows in the skies!
Oh, Lo—ve!
Lo—ve!
A gift that gives us life!

Standing here before you—
My heart opens wide!
A promise of life—
A love that won't hide!
Unselfishly—
You give to me!
Season of life
This is our spring!
Receive—
My ring!

(Refrain)

Lord…
Hold us…
Lord…
Blend us…
Into one loving vine.
May the fruit that we bear—
Drink from your wine!
Lord…
Love us…
Lord…
Bless us…
And, every day ahead,
Sit down at our table—
Share from your bread!

Standing here before me
Reach for my hand
A promise of life
And a love that won't end
With all of my heart
I give to you
Season of life
This is our spring
I'll wear your ring!

Lord…
Hold us…
Lord…
Blend us…
Into one loving vine.
May the fruit that we bear—
Drink from your wine.
Lord…
Love us…
Lord…

Bless us...
And, every day ahead,
Sit down at our table—
Share from your bread!

Standing here together—
Growing through the years.
Becoming one...
Some sorrow
Some tears.
Let the journey take heart—
To promising dreams,
Season of life—
This is our spring—
True love we bring!

Lord...
Hold us...
Lord...
Blend us...
Into one loving vine.
May the fruit that we bear—
Drink from your wine!
Lord...
Love us...
Lord...
Bless us...
And, every day ahead,
Sit down at our table—
Share from your bread!

(Written by Ed Danowski on behalf of Ed and Mardell for all of their children and grandchildren and heirs for future generations to come in celebration of their weddings—1987)

My dear friend Jim Holt added the beautiful music to my lyrics and has performed and sung it at all of the weddings of our children—traveling all the way from Kansas City to do so. Another very special friend, Father Howard Haase has performed all of the services for the weddings. What a dynamic duo they have been at these all important junctures of their lives.

Jim sang the duet along with a lovely lady and another special friend Jan.

I love him and my children do too. He has added so many wonderful moments to our family's memories. I can never forget the talks we had into the wee hours of the night discussing the meaning of life and the fun of marrying lyrics and music. I treasure the basketball games he had with our children in our driveway. Mardy and I love been Godfather to Elliot, the son of Jim and his special bride Lorie! I can never forget what a special gift he has been to my life and the life of my family. There would be a major piece missing without him.

Our coming together had an unusual start! Over the years, I would create a serigraph for each of our children as they graduated from eighth grade. When Greg came along as our youngest, he asked me if I would also stretch myself and write a song for his graduating class.

I didn't know quite where to turn with this request and so I asked our music director for our church, Jim Holt if he would help me. And he was gracious enough to help by adding music to the lyrics I wrote for a song about God painting rainbows and what those rainbows mean in our lives. He not only added the music, but made a recording of it and performed and sang it at the graduation mass for Greg and his class. It was the first song that I worked on with Jim and will always be a very special memory:

Lyrics for Greg's graduation class and the title they selected

TIME AFTER TIME

Refrain:
May we always find rainbows.
Master Painter, fill our skies.
May God's colors bring comfort
And dry life's tears from our eyes!

Bands of reds, blues and yellows,
Tints racing up and down slopes,
All brilliant slices of life,
His gift brings us new hopes!

Velvet wings touching the breeze!
Dazzling hues dancing in flight!
Graceful messengers of change,
Out of each dawn's warming light!

Butterflies, new beginnings,
May our lives be truly full!
May each start be ever better
And more beautiful our soul!

Our time and God's time
Run together hand in hand!
May our love and His love
Blend forever like the sand!

That was the beginning of an ever deepening and wonderful relationship and friendship with Jim and all of us in our family.

We had a fun experience with the wedding song when our daughter Cheri was at the rehearsal for her wedding. Everyone thought Cheri went with someone else from the rehearsal to the rehearsal dinner. When we all got to the hall, there was no Cheri. No one brought her.

Both her husband Tom and I got up at the same time to rescue poor Cheri from in front of the church—a good fifteen minutes away. It was dark outside by now. We only hoped that someone would know that Cheri was left behind and would stay with her at the church.

Tom panicked! I wasn't far behind!

The large dinning room was full of people wondering what was going on!

As Tom and I were preparing to go back to the church to get her—there was Jim! Jim Holt stepped into the dinning room at the restaurant.

The first thing he said was, "Where is Cheri?"

Then, to the relief of us all, there she was!

Cheri stepped out from behind Jim.

Not only did Jim come to the rehearsal dinner after rehearsing the music for Cheri's wedding including "Love's Vow", but he also rescued Cheri from being left at the church alone!

As it turned out, Tom thought that Cheri left with us.

We never gave it a second thought. We were sure Cheri left with the man she was to marry.

The greatest thrill about writing the music together is the synergy of sharing what is in one's heart and trying to reach others with what it is you are trying to say!

There is a special thrill that comes from hearing something from your heart performed by the many options available including choirs, soloists and duets.

One of my other favorite memories is the song Jim and I wrote and he performed as a duet on Easter Sunday. I have to admit to having tears in my eyes as I heard it performed. Often times, those feelings are something I can keep inside, but that was truly an exception. I think we have written nine songs together now.

I really appreciate how he packs up and makes the trip from Kansas City for each wedding since he moved there. I miss those times we had together including the moments we spent writing music together. I miss not being closer to Lori, his bride, and their children. However, I treasure with all my heart the gift he has been from God to me and my family.

I also treasure how my lyrics were translated into Spanish for the wedding of our son Jeff and his wedding to Sonia!

I think the lesson here, is to treasure those gifts of special people that God put into our lives while they are here or close at hand. It is good to fully appreciate this while they are near. Each day, each minute with a special friend or relative is a true jewel in the crown of life!

WHAT HAPPENED TO THE INVENTING OF GAMES TO SHARE WITH MY BROTHERS AND SISTERS WHEN WE WERE GROWING UP— AND—I WAS THE CHIEF BABYSITTER?

There are many card games Mardy and I have enjoyed over the years that we have played with our children and with friends. We enjoy a variety of card games such as bridge, sheepshead, hearts, spades, etc. Some of us have really enjoyed some of the first computer games such as electric football and baseball. Perhaps the favorite game for us to engage in as family has been Mastermind. Some of us have enjoyed Pictionary, chess and checkers too.

I never lost the desire to invent. Games were a lot of fun. My brothers and sisters were so patient with my efforts and never discouraged me.

Even dad got in on trying tome of my early efforts! Using whatever was available, it was always fun to come up with ideas that others could enjoy spending their time playing.

Some of our grandchildren might know about the games I invented and those I sold to Western Publishing and to other companies—or the Golf Game "Tee Time" that I had published in a magazine many years ago or a game called "Fling" or another game called "Stumble-O" or the very first one I created and sold called "Brontosaurus Hunt".

They will also know of the learning curve I went through with several of my best early ideas being stolen because even though I had them protected, they weren't protected adequately enough. One of them was Tee Time which was protected by my employer with a copyright for me and with their help we were moving toward a three dimensional game to be sold by the company that published the company magazine that the game appeared in. It was to be published by the game company in conjunction with a major professional golf tournament at the time. Their copyright was not foolproof enough. I found that I had to go for patents later on with other inventions.

It was a lot of fun testing the games with my family. Mardell and her sister Bobbi were my early test panel when we were young newly weds. Later, I would get to share the ideas with our children and Grandchildren. Our children had lots of fun testing for me and I had a lot of fun watching them.

I do have one very special memory however! It could have been very intimidating!

When I was a rookie at Johnson Wax, I sold my very first game to Western Publishing. It was the first game I developed since my youth in Oak Creek. It seemed so simple.

It was called "Brontosaurus Hunt"!

I developed it based on my love for the Flintstones on T.V.

I couldn't believe how easy it all seemed.

I developed the concept I had, made a prototype and took it into Western Publishing for their consideration.

They tested it for several weeks and called me to give me the good news.

Then the newspapers got wind of it and published an article about it.

Well my desk, at the time, was located in the very front of the Great Workroom that for Johnson Wax that was designed by Frank Lloyd Wright.

At the time I was the inventory accountant for the company.

One morning, I was bent over my desk hard at work.

Suddenly, I heard this loud booming voice, "Are you Ed Danowski?"

I was startled and looked up!

There, in front of me, stood a distinguished looking gentleman. He said, "I don't think we ever met! My name is Howard Packard—your President.

Later, I would learn why his voice was so booming. Howard was hard of hearing. Not only was his voice booming, but it was very resonant!

Howard then said, "Ed, come with me!"

Without delay, I did just that!

He led me to one of what they called the Bird Cage elevators. It was a barred cage like structure that allowed one to see out into the great workroom as it ascended.

Howard led me to his office on the mezzanine and bid me to sit down across from him on his desk.

Then he looked up at me and asked me, "Ed, how do you go about inventing a game." He was serious and wanted to know.

So, I described what I went through to develop "Brontosaurus Hunt".

He leaned forward from the other side of his desk looking very interested and took some notes.

"Ed," he asked next "What do you need in the way of materials to do make a cartoon?"

So, I listed the paper, pen, ink, colored pencils, etc. that I needed to make a draft of a cartoon.

Then he caught me totally off guard!

Howard picked up the phone and called the Art Department and asked them to bring over all of the materials I had just enumerated.

Then, he turned to me and said, "Ed, I would like you to draw one for me."

I replied, "That is OK Howard, I have the materials need at home."

"No, no," he continued. "I would like you to draw a cartoon here for me about Johnson Wax."

He meant at his desk—with him watching.

That is when my knees started to shake a bit.

I had never met him before, and here I was in the company's top officer's office and supposed to come up immediately with the idea for a cartoon and then draw it!

Ooops! I wondered to myself, "How did I get here?"

And, so the materials arrived.

I had to quickly come up with the concept for the cartoon which I desperately thought of—while trying not to look desperate!

So, Howard watched and watched and watched.

And, so I drew, and drew and drew!

With only, one small blotch, I finished it!

The good news was that he liked it!

Weeks later, he would call me and invite me up to his office.

Then he led me out to the causeway outside of his office that connected two of the Frank Lloyd Wright buildings.

There on the wall hung the cartoon I drew for him! It hung there with the many cartoons by some of the world's finest cartoonists over the years. There were their cartoons that appeared in many of the top magazines of the time. And here was my cartoon.

What has surprised me even more is that fifty nine years later, it still hangs there and all of the thousands of folks who tour the famous Frank Lloyd buildings get to see it.

When ever I go on a tour of the building, now that I have been retired from there for a while, I think back to Howard Packard and the nerve wracking session I had in his office.

Howard did not, however, let me off of the hook yet!

After taking the cartoon from me, he looked directly at me. "Ed, how long does it take you to invent a game?"

I thought for sure that he was going to have me invent one on the spot.

Then he went on.

"I would like you, to invent one that the company could put into our quarterly magazine. It will be a special addition that will feature the new art collection that Johnson Wax is assembling from the greatest living artists today including Andrew Wyeth!"

"When would you need it?" I asked.

"In two weeks," he said.

"Oh, Mr. Packard," I tried to weasel out of it. "I go to two weeks of Army Reserves at Camp McCoy Saturday."

I thought for certain that this would get me off of the hook.

Wrong!

"That is OK," he continued. "I know how that works. You will have Saturday afternoon and Sunday as free time. You can do it then.

Well, I had no choice! There was no room for choice.

So, the weekend between week one and week two at camp McCoy found me in my Officer's quarters, up late, developing the concept for a game that would appear in the magazine.

And, when I arrived home the following Saturday afternoon, I started on the prototype. I finished it Sunday and delivered it to Howard's office on Monday morning.

He liked it and it appeared in the magazine, which won a national award. It also included an article about the first game I invented and sold "Brontosaurus Hunt."

The game was "Tee Time".

Oh, and yes, he asked me to create several cartoons for the magazine. One of them, shown here in the next several pages, was about a boy and his father and some fish.

While my creativity sort of put me on the spot, it did something else for me. It developed a good relationship between Howard and me.

With his blessing, I accomplished a few things several years later that had never been done before in the corporate world.

Howard endorsed and supported two particular programs that I developed that were firsts. We were able to recognize alcoholism as a covered disease under our company's medical program instead of letting those folks go from the company as terminations. Then we introduced a first of its kind pre-retirement- counseling program that included both the employee and the spouse so that the spouse would be a part of the decision making process that would affect the rest of their lives. Because those decisions could be complex and the options not readily understood, we found that many employees made those critical decisions by talking to their locker room partners rather some feeling embarrassed about asking for more information. The results were sometimes tragic such as a retiring employee choosing a life annuity instead of a longer term annuity that would provide income for his or her spouse in the event of the retiree's demise. The program would later be expanded and received a national award.

These are a few examples of how God allowed me to apply the creativity He had given me to the workplace.

Another example occurred some years before, which would bring a smile to my face about twenty five years after the innovation. It started out because I was spending many a weekend, evenings and even holidays away from my family during my days as an accountant scrambling to develop and update the cost of the products the company produced. This periodic process was always fraught with tight deadlines and a complexity of information had to be gathered and analyzed.

One weekend I was home and Mardy and I were talking about how one of those late at the office periods was approaching again. Like a lot of problems, they can sometimes become opportunities. Later that day, I wondered why this process was never computerized.

It was dealing with a bunch of variables that would change from time to time and there were accepted accounting principles for dealing with those variables.

So, I instigated a search and no one could find such a system anywhere. My supervisor told me it couldn't be done because the consultants said the variables and the choices that had to be made were too complex. He said he had checked with our best resources.

Well, it was obvious that the problem wasn't going to go away unless someone found a new answer for it.

As things stood, the overtime and missed time with my family still loomed ahead!

So, I sat down and tried to develop the logic trails that were followed to make the various decisions and come up with the sought after conclusions. The old saying definitely is true about necessity being the father of inventions. The more I studied it, the more definitive patterns evolved. By the time I went to bed, we had flow charts for how a computer might do it.

I told my supervisor about my findings and he again said he didn't think it could be done.

So, I went to the computer folks and showed them the flow charts and explained the idea.

They kept it all for a few days and came back saying they thought it would work.

And so it did.

And, so was all of that overtime!

A year later, the company had a professional business group come in to tour their computer area and they featured our new product costing system as the first of its kind that they knew of in the country. I don't know how true that was, but I did know that the added time with my family was an enjoyable reality!

The reason for sharing this story here is because it does have a bit of a tie in to my love for art. How you might ask? Well, it does, but in a very unusual kind of way.

Oddly enough, my work on this particular project caught the attention of management because they were looking for some innovation in the Human Resource area.

I liked what the opportunities looked like and the chance to grow in a new direction. And, so I changed career paths.

A friend of mine, John, stayed in accounting while I headed off to work in Human Resources.

One day many years later, John came to see me.

"Ed," he said, "they are trying to link the budgeting process and the production planning to our cost accounting system. If you will remember—that product costing system you developed had a form that was divided in various parts using the colors of green for some and red for others."

Then he laughed as he told me a bye the way. "Did you know that they have dubbed your form the Christmas Tree form?

But, now they want to know, why the two different colors. What's their significance?"

I smiled for two reasons. First, I was surprised that something I had created that many years before was still in existence. Secondly, I was almost going to be embarrassed to tell John why I used the colors red and green for the parts of the form.

"John," I said, "Get your pencil ready"

John did not miss the big smile on my face.

After watching me muse, he asked the question! "OK, why the grin?"

"Well, John, it was a Sunday night when I was laying out the form at home. The stores were all closed and all I had at home were two colored pencils. One was red and one was…?"

"…Green!" came his response!

And then John laughed!

We both laughed and I am quite sure the computer professionals had a smile or two. John and I both laughed wondering how many hours the spent in cogitation regarding why the color red and why the color green.

There was another carry over from that day in Howard's office. Years later, after retiring, I began my own management consulting business consulting with CEO's about management and serving as a confidant to the CEOs that retained my services. Howard was on the Board of Directors for the first company where I would serve the CEO and make presentations to their Board of Directors for ten years before deciding to concentrate on painting watercolors and creative writing. I will say a bit more about this later.

I also think this meeting and subsequent meetings with Howard, would set my comfort level for meeting with top management over the years. I do want to commend him here as a truly good person in addition to a sharp company President.

While talking about how creativity carries over to more than just those things that people conceive of as outlets, I found it such a helpful tool in the work place. It allowed me to develop unique solutions to other problems and certainly was a key tool in my career over the years.

So, my thought is to foster creativity in the young. I don't think we have this built into our educational system, but would be a good idea to do so. I strongly believe it would be very good for the country and good for the world.

WHAT HAPPENED TO THE CARTOONIST AND THE ANIMATION AMBITION THAT ONCE PULLED STRONGLY AT ME AS A TEENAGER?

Even though I did not go to work for Walt Disney, the dream never really died.

I think all of my Grandchildren have now seen some of the panels for the multi-panel Cartoon strip Happast VII that I co-authored with my special friend Elton Dorval and we had published in the newspapers.

One of the lead characters was Caesar Reaganus. We made fun of him. Then as time passed by we had Caesar Carter and we made fun of him. We planned to do that with every President that came along as Caesars who "did not measure up"!

Of course that really was in fun. We planned to roast them all and have a little fun with what they did along the way. That would have been an interesting way to use my Political Science major had we continued for long.

We were all set to do this when we had to stop for good reason. I will touch on that more latter.

Working with my friend of so many years, Elton was such a special gift. We had more fun!

Working with Elton was like working with Jim Holt. Both were and are such special friends and fellow artists at heart!

We painted together, went on photography escapades together, did air brushing together and shared the same strong love for cartooning and animation. We also knew each others families well.

I did try my hand at it off and on, but on a limited basis earlier over the years. Early on there were single panel cartoons which appeared in various newspapers.

One was called "Li'l Halo" about a young little girl angel with a pony tail and her innocent series of adventures.

Another was about a stylized character and his pet called "Denny and Dog"!

My personal favorite was my very first adventure strip, at age twelve, called The Nomad—about a wandering detective who ventured across the world—a super hero type.

I loved cartooning because it gave me a creative outlet that combined line art and verbal communications. It also presented the challenge of telling a whole story, be it humorous or adventure, in a short visual space and creative framework.

Early cartoons

This a cartoon I drew for the Johnson Was Quarterly Magazine. Howard Packard requested me to draw several for their special issue and this is one of them:

One of my early cartoon characters:

Combined cartoons

ACCEPTING WITH HUMILITY

Some of the grandchildren may even have copies of the hour long TV special done about creativity in the family. It was condensed from hours of video work and multiple visits from the producer John Poladna and aired on TV during November and December of 2007 and January of 2008. Everyone from the immediate family was involved.

Some may even have a copy of the special appearance Jeff and I had on Channel 4 television in Milwaukee on a program called "The Morning Blend" to talk about a father and son having books published at the same time.

At first I tried saying things that played down what has happened in terms of recognition given to my own works. It took a number of people including Sister Kathleen of the Racine Dominicans and my son Greg to tell me that true humility requires strength and is an open acceptance of the recognition that ones' work is given as acknowledgment of the gifts of God!

I am still working at this, but I understand now more than ever that I know that whatever I do that is worthwhile is because God made it possible! So I now sign all of my paintings with AFJ+M+J+F+H. Which, to me, means "All for Jesus, Mary, Joseph, our Heavenly Father and our Holy Spirit." Before touching a paint brush or a computer key, I start with a prayer dedicating my work to the God who gives me the inspiration and the gifts to do them.

WHAT ABOUT THE GIFTS WE ARE GIVEN?

I have come to the conclusion that talents should not be a source of self praise—but a reason for thanksgiving.

Each of us is so unique and we each have different gifts. Some are more understanding, more nurturing, better financial people, better problem solvers, better mechanics, better fixer uppers, better people persons, better technical people, better companions, better conversationalists, better speakers, better listeners, better at crafts, better with computers, better growing things, better at understanding others, better at solving problems, better cooks, better scientific thinkers, better abstract thinkers, better conceptual thinkers, better detailists, better leaders, better parents, have more patience, have more understanding, have more will power, etc., etc. etc. Some of these gifts are more visible, but we each have our own wonderful gifts.

What I really would like them to understand is that all talents and skills come from God. They are gems He sends our way! We don't own them for ourselves no matter what level we achieve with them!

They truly are His special gifts to us.

It doesn't seem appropriate to take the credit for special gifts so lovingly given to us or to engage in patting ourselves on the back. Instead they are truly cause to be humble and to realize what true gifts they are! Understanding that—, it would be appropriate to be ever so thankful!

I firmly believe that whatever gifts and talents we might have—that they are not ours to keep! They are not meant to be kept in our own little closet or for our benefit alone!

Instead, I believe that they belong to God and are for us to share and in the true spirit of sharing!

Gifts are a challenge! They bring with them a significant obligation—to the holder—to develop and use wisely and to use well for the good and benefit of others!

If persons everywhere were to share their gifts with each other—the world can be such a beautiful place—end to end—top to bottom and everyone would be so much more the beneficiaries!

Some will know how their uncles played at sports and excelled at them.

Some will know how good their Grandmother was at bowling.

They may only hear that I loved sports too even though my disability has prevented physically demonstrating some of the fine points of the various sports for them. Yet, I did try to talk them through some of those fine points that I knew to share with them like how to shoot free throws or how to swing a baseball bat—two of my favorite things to do as a young man—some of which I learned from my dad.

Yet, years from now, there are probably things my grandchildren probably wouldn't know.

For example, that coming from a very poor family at one stage of my life—where seven of us lived in one room for a winter, had cardboard stuffed in our shoes to cover the holes in the soles and made the meals stretch—I did have a wonderful and rewarding professional career. It began as a corporate executive at the global level for Johnson Wax where I enjoyed almost thirty four years.

For certain, they would never dream of just how much I learned from the challenging years of being on the poor end of the spectrum at the time and about what love really means.

Then, I would be fortunate to head my own management consulting firm for another ten years later in life and that my clients where exclusively CEOs and Presidents of companies.

Nor would they know that I helped build from scratch, along with my good friend Tim Bowers, and became Vice President of Operations for a company called MEI owned by six major employers in the health care field with a focus on quality. It became a prototype for others.

Nor would they know that I traveled the world often or was a reserve officer in the Army Corps of Engineers and up for Captain when my disability set in.

I think they will always think of me as grandpa! It is one of the treasures I love more than anything. I love the opportunity to get to know each of them and to enjoy our grandpa/grandchild relationships as they develop and unfold.

ANOTHER'S WORDS
ABOUT COURAGE

Lest I give the false idea that all things come easy for me, I share a very special memory with you!

One Saturday evening, Mardy and I were playing bridge with three other couples—all of them among our dearest friends. There was Jack and Barb Evenson, Tom and Joyce Rustici and Bud and Bunnie Ruter.

It was a great time. In fact it was so great that it was about two in the morning before we realized how late it was.

As we were getting up from the card tables to go home, Barb said, "In a few more hours it will be sunrise! Why don't we do something different and play till then and we'll have breakfast together?"

And so we did—on a lark!

Six AM came and Barb, true to her word, started breakfast!

Bacon and eggs—mmmm good!

Then—another surprise!

Our son Jeff called us on the phone. "Dad you lector at the 7 AM mass! Why aren't you home?"

I had totally forgotten getting caught up in all of the fun we were having.

And so without, helping with the dishes, Mardy and I rushed off!

We stopped at home to pick up the kids!

I shaved quickly and changed shirts and added a necktie and sport coat and headed for the car!

We got to church ten minutes ahead of mass.

I should have been there a good twenty minutes before!

Father greeted me as I am trying to go over the readings for that morning.

My sleepy eyes were not much help either.

Then Father broke the silence. "Ed, the singing at this early mass is not very good! I would like you to lead the singing!"

Well, enough members of my family had told me over time that my singing voice was wanting! This was so much so that they would ask me to turn on the car radio when I tried singing in the car!

So, I related that to Father!

"Father," I said, "You can ask me to do anything, but that! I'm sorry, but I think I would only make matters worse!"

However Father was persistent!

"Ed" he continued, "It is easy! You go out there and hit the first few notes! Then, the organist joins in. I guarantee, the parish will join in with their voices and no one will even hear you!"

"Father," I protested one more time! "I really don't sing that well!"

He wouldn't take no for an answer and time had run out!

So there we were walking down the aisle to the altar!

I approached the microphone, opened the hymnal, and did it! I started out as loud as I thought I could sing the first few notes!

Then—I looked up!

The organist was not in the choir loft!

And so—committed as I was—I continued.

Well after the first hymn, I gained confidence. I even thought to myself, "Maybe you're singing isn't as bad as my family is telling me!"

And so, I led the second hymn and later the third!

At the end of mass, I led the closing hymn!

Mardy and our five children were sitting there in the first row, which they often did when I lectured at mass.

I looked up at them from the lectern. Then I noticed an elderly lady coming down the isle. She was moving slowly and looking right at me. She wore a scarf around her head and a black coat. I'll never forget it!

And she continued walking right toward me.

I didn't know what to expect. Obviously there was something she wanted to tell me. And she did!

Taking my right hand between hers two hands, she clasped it tightly.

"Young man!" she said—with her voice trembling slightly. "Young man, you have a lot of courage!"

My family didn't know where to duck as they heard her words. In fact they elaborated that I sang way too loudly! My youngest son Greg told me it sounded as if I was using my military training and trying to sing with my command voice.

Yikes!

And so, every once in a while—my family would remind me of this! The reminders could come particularly when I would try singing in the car as I drove them somewhere.

However, this is not the end of the story!

Years later, when Greg graduated from high school, Mardy and I decided to drive from Wisconsin to Arizona to visit my sister and brothers there.

There were only three of us in the car—Mardy, Greg and I. Greg and I shared the driving of our Ford station wagon.

Mardy never said anything about my singing when I tried although she loved to tell the story about the lady in church and what she had to say to me.

So, I thought it was safe to try to do some of the singing I so loved to do.

Somewhere about the middle of Missouri, Greg finally spoke out! "Dad, if you really want to sing that badly, I'll teach you!" That too caught me a little by surprise.

But, I have always said that if you were defensive, you will impede your own chances for growth. So, I needed to back up my teachings.

And so we began.

Greg gave me voice lessons on the way down to Arizona and all the way back home again!

I should mention that I truly do have a lot of musicians in the family and good singers including my dad and my brothers and sister and lots of cousins who sing well.

Well, I logged those lessons away and felt less self conscious about my singing in church as a member of the congregation. I never did try leading the singing again.

I have steadily gained confidence in singing with others.

I don't think I will ever solo for anyone.

Yet, there was a day of redemption!

This past year I was in church with Mardy and I absolutely loved the hymns that were being sung. And, I guess I did put my heart into it.

After mass, two ladies who sat directly in front of us turned around and looked at me. I thought, "Oh no, here it comes again!"

Mardy gave me that look that told me she thought so too!

Only, they surprised us both.

Almost like dejavu! One of the ladies reached for my hand and held it with hers!

"You can sing for us anytime!" she said!

She may never know how much I meant the thank you I said. However for me it was rewarding to see the smile on Mardy's face. I never did ask Mardy what the smile meant!

I went home and called Greg to thank him for his courage in offering to give me lessons. I will never be a Pavarotti, but I am no longer self conscious about singing the songs I love in church thanks to a son who had the comfort and the courage to take on his dad.

DON'T GIVE UP—WHERE THERE ARE WILLS THERE ARE WAYS!

The road to what one can achieve is not always a straight one.

For example, my dear friend Elton and I had a great time developing our cartoon strip. It couldn't possibly have been more fun!

I had submitted ideas to Walt Disney as a boy.

Elton had submitted ideas to Milton Caniff who has been called the Michael Angelo of cartooning for his comic strips, "Terry and the Pirates" and "Steve Canyon". For Elton, this led to a life long close friendship with Caniff. In fact, Elton would visit with Caniff at his home and, with his video camera, recorded hours of Caniff actually creating cartoon panels.

Elton later donated his videos of these sessions to Ohio State University where Caniff was inducted into their hall of fame.

Elton also had a marvelous collection of original panels for Caniff's strips.

So, we both had strong ties to well established people in these creative fields.

Elton has been such a special friend and one with whom I was able to talk about most anything. We shared so many interests in common including various art forms, photography, old time radio, music and much more. ! When you share that much—you can't help becoming very close!

Fro me, it was much the same working with and times spent with Jack McMahon, Tom Newman, Bill Bohn, Jim Holt, Howard Haase,

Gene Neuman, Russ Oelke, Kathleen Bohn, Al Hornish, Ron Kuhajec and others.

Sometimes friendships can evolve to a higher level—more like brothers and sisters. This is the beautiful thing about some friendships.

It is a theme that I mention now and then. I just feel that God's blessings are so abundant with the friends we are privileged to have.

Like some other special friendships in my life, including some named in this book, my friendship with Elton was one of these.

In our case, we painted together—every Monday for years. Elton won the prestigious Watercolor Wisconsin Art Show twice which is a major achievement. We both had paintings judged, accepted and featured in the very competitive Watercolor Wisconsin Art Show at the same time which was really special to us.

One of our more infamous escapades included a photographing expedition to the Racine Lighthouse.

What is so special about that, you might ask?

We both had done it so many times before, but one cold winter's day, we took our Nikon cameras and traipsed around the grounds again. This time the water was frozen over near the shore. So much so, in fact, that we dared venture out on to the ice—walking out a ways. There we got some great angles with our cameras that we weren't able to get before.

I used one of the resultant photos as a reference for one of my favorite paintings "Windpoint Sunset". Whenever I part with a print of this painting, I can't help but think of our adventure out on the ice—and the reprimands we both got from our spouses for being so brave; however, I think the word they really used was more equivalent to—foolish! But it was thick ice—very thick—and we checked it each step we took out onto it's surface! We may have had fun, but weren't foolish like a certain boy I knew who once went on an unplanned rafting trip on a wild river.

The early days of our friendship had a unique push from my bride!

Initially, for me, I was trying to be responsive to Mardell's concern. She viewed that since the car accident I sat home too much after working hours. I no longer played golf, went bowling, played baseball, etc. She felt I needed something to do away from home besides work.

Then by happenstance—if that is what it really was—one day I was out shopping for and purchased five of the identical books on the history of animation—one for each of our children at a book store called The West Wind Book Store on Washington Avenue in Racine.

Standing about three customers behind me was a person I had never met before and was curious about my interest in cartooning.

He didn't ask me though.

Instead he asked the clerk at the cash register if she could give him my name. She new me well from my frequent visits to add books to my library at home.

She also told him that she knew where I worked and told him.

Well, the next morning, he gave me a call and introduced himself.

At first I though he was joking because he said, This is Elton Dorval calling."

At first I thought it was a joke. I had never heard the name Elton or Dorval before and I thought it was one of my fun loving friends trying to play a prank on me.

So, I so uncouthly said, "Elton who?"

But he was patient with me!

Elton went on to tell me about being in the same book store and what he observed and that he loved art and cartooning.

And from there we—we talked for quite a bit about both and thought we had enough in common to share some of our experiences and mutual interest.

Elton invited me to his home and I went on a Monday night.

We hit it off from the start. Our visit was great;

A friendship was born!

It grew from there to almost every Monday night for well past thirty years.

We got to know each others family well.

We found we enjoyed a lot of the same things.

He taught me to paint with an air brush.

We listened to each other's old time radio and shared our recorded music.

We shared so many things.

At one point, we spent several years pursuing a mutual dream.

Our decision was to start a comic strip.

It wasn't just a casual attempt.

We did a lot of research and study.

Our first major decision was to not do an adventure strip even though we both really enjoyed them and would have loved to create one. We wanted to have our strip in the newspapers and we thought that the adventure strips did not have as good of a chance to make it there. So we went with the odds.

Cartoon strip it would be!

First, we each identified our favorite comic characters and listed what we thought made them special. Why did they succeed? We then set about discussing possible characters that would have some of these qualities.

We invested considerable time then in developing our stable of characters and in determining the relationships of one character in the strip to another and how they would interact with each other.

We both spent time with the design of the characters.

As we got near to the point of actually starting our first panels, I was committed to extensive traveling for the company. I asked Elton if he would feel comfortable doing the drawing of the early panels if I concentrated on developing the comic strip gags we would use.

He agreed.

And so, on my next trip abroad—to Lagos, Nigeria; Cyprus; Athens, Greece; Nairobi, Kenya; and South Africa with another dear friend, Al Hornish—I developed a number of pages of gag ideas while on the airplane and in the hotels later in the evening after the business meetings for the day and Al and I disappeared to our respective rooms. I even thought of a few of the ideas while Al and I were guests of the Cyprus General Manager at the U.S. Embassy.

I was excited about some of them.

I thought we were getting close to bringing our comic strip to fruition.

When I returned from my trip, Elton and I sat down together.

I was more than kind of excited. I really thought there were some fairly good ideas in my compilation.

Then, I confidently showed him the list!

I watched with great anticipation as he read gag after gag and page after page.

There were no smiles from Elton.

There was no ha, ha—no facial reactions, no nodding of the head, absolutely no acknowledgement of any kind.

Here I was so sure that I had close to a hundred workable gags for our strip—and that some of them were really pretty good!

No response from Elton—not even a smile!

Well, my first reaction was a silent one—I couldn't believe it.

We had the characters developed!

We knew how we want them to work together!

Yet—it was now readily apparent that either we both had a far different idea of what it took for humor in our strip.

Almost a hundred gags—and no smile—meant maybe our individual senses of humor did not mesh!

The truth was that we both liked a lot of the same strips in existence at the time. Yet, there were some places where our preferences were different. I began to think, during those next few minutes, that the gap was a much larger one than I realized.

I liked some of he more sophisticated type humor strips such as Frank and Ernest where they did such a successful play on words. I liked Far Side because of the true imagination that was a bit off the wall. I liked Doonesbury.

These were Elton's favorites.

However, we both liked Beetle Bailey, Peanuts, Blondie, Family Circus and so many others.

I just sat there for a moment in silence.

So did he!

Then he spoke, "I don't get it!"

"Get what?" I asked.

I do have to admit—that for a few minutes—I thought that this particular venture of ours might come to a screeching halt if we couldn't agree on what constituted good gags for our strip.

However, the result was that we sat down, as good friends do!

We talked at length about what a good gag was for a comic strip.

We analyzed the gap was between my particular sense of humor and Elton's idea of humor was for the comic strip.

There was good input!

There was a healthy exchange of ideas.

And guess what?

We ended up with a much stronger product that would later be published as the strip Happast VII.

It took three years to get there, but we did it—and it worked because we did it together!

We go it published locally and it ran for a year and we had ideas piled up for another number of months.

Then, just as we were ready to go national with our strip, Elton suffered a great personal loss. His wife Barb died suddenly from fever resulting from an inoculation she received in preparation for a trip they were about to take to Africa.

Quite naturally—we decided to put the strip on hold. Things were not humorous for Elton for quite a while.

Much later, when the time was appropriate, we both sat down and looked at what it would take to get it going nationally and we researched it carefully.

Our findings were that the strip could take fifty to sixty hours a week to maintain as we viewed it. We had learned a lot from the time we first began.

We both had even greater time commitments to our primary job with a great employer. I had a major project under way that would take three years of around the clock effort and for which I would receive a major award from the company.

Elton was planning to remarry. He was fortunate to later meet another wonderful person—Josie. They fell in love and did marry. We still spend a lot of time at each other's homes and our friendship hasn't missed a beat.

There was no room to commit so many extra hours at this juncture and give full justice at our professional careers in our primary occupations—even with Milton Caniff in the wings willing to back us.

Plus there were so many other interests that we had including many that we shared in common that could fit into the time windows we did have together.

So we mutually agreed to retire the strip. We had a lot of fun with it.

We treasured the time we had developing, producing and having the strip published.

We do continue to share other creative ventures and are both members of the Wisconsin Water Color Society.

It was great fun and a time to treasure.

We also really loved sports and fishing.

A very special and fond memory is the first time Elton took me out onto Lake Michigan in his fishing boat.

It was a good sized boat and he had me drive it over the slight waves of the lake's inviting blue waters while. Meanwhile, my sons Don and Greg had a field day catching huge Coho Salmon under Elton's tutelage. The great thrill of watching the excitement in the eyes of our sons Don and Greg can't be surpassed—as their eyes lit up with each big finned glistening beauty that they caught. They were huge and I'm sure that their memories may make them seem even bigger.

I would be remiss, while talking about cartooning, to not mention that there was another potential collaborative effort with a good friend at cartooning together.

My good friend Tom Newman was quite the clever person was a very interesting sense of humor.

One day after hours, he was in my office and we were blue skying about a number of things. I don't remember who came up with the idea first, but somehow we talked about creating a book of cartoons of humor in the work place.

We both had seen so much as professionals working in the Human Resource field that we began to rattle off potential joke after joke. We both had so many contacts and experiences shared from our counterparts at a number of Fortune 500 companies and others.

We even did about ten cartoons together before the demands of our careers took us away from it. This was well ahead of the now famous strips about humor in the work place. However, for some reason, Elton and I ere the ones that found the time together to take the next steps.

How far back was all of this cartooning adventure?

Well, one of our lead characters was "Caesar Carterous" when we started the development of our strip. And, by the time we actually launched it, we had to change his name to "Caesar Reaganous"!

There is an irony here with the name change of Caesar.

Some time after, I became quite ill and for the first time in my career missed a number of months of work. I was in and out of hospitals with infections that stem back to my Ankylosing Spondilitis.

Sam Johnson, the owner of the company for which I worked, also happened to be Chairman of the Board of the Mayo Clinic in Minnesota. He ended up sending me there to try to help me. I ended up being there at the same time Ronald Reagan was there following his fall from his horse in California—and we did get to exchange a brief hello. This added a little more meaning to the fun we were having at his expense in our comic strip.

Had we continued our comic strip, each of the succeeding Presidents would have become Caesars with whom we could poke a little fun at. For me, this would finally have been an avenue to put some of my Political Science major to good but humorous use.

I will never forget the ashes our comic strip almost came to when I first made that list of gags, but most of all—I will never forget the fun we had creating our strip and finally getting it published. It ran for a year.

I will never forget that the Michael Angelo of cartoonists, Milton Caniff had promised Elton that he would help us take the strip national. He liked it!

The cartoon strip is now stored on a book shelf—but the fun of our venture remains.

We sure had a lot of fun with it before we put it there. I do think we could really have gone national with it with Caniff to open the doors for us!

So what did we do when we got together after that?

Instead we've concentrated our innovative energies on creating watercolors, our mutual first love, and other art forms—and me on an occasional book and writing music with Jim Holt.

It is funny how one gets inspiration or gets started down different roads.

I would be remiss without mentioning one of my classmates at Saint Adalbert's grade school in South Milwaukee, Don Swendrowski. It was he who inspired me to start cartooning without even knowing it. I had always loved comic books and the Sunday comic pages in the newspapers. I also had been drawing what ever came to mind since I was a young child. However, one day Don brought a pencil drawing of a Disney character to class, I think it was sixth grade and I think it was either Disney's famous mouse or his famous duck. I as so inspired by his sketch that I started drawing them myself. So, one never knows how what they do might trigger or motivate another. I don't think I ever told him until the fifty year class reunion from South Milwaukee High School!

YOU CAN NEVER TELL WHAT ENCOURAGEMENT CAN DO

My art career really had several stops and starts. I won several awards in high school with my ceramics and with my watercolors.

Then came the army and starting my family!

I fit in work with watercolors and managed to have my work featured in a number of art shows.

I also was privileged to learn the art of Seri graphing from a fine master teacher named Dick Jensen. It developed to the point where I was getting a lot of attention for my work. Later my family would be invited to Wustum Art Museum in Racine to help me run the serigraphs using the Art Museum's facility and equipment to generate the serigraphs. It truly became a family project each time I ran serigraphs.

Some raised and lowered the frame for the screen.

Others poured the inks on the screen.

We took turns operating the squeegee to force the ink through the screen and onto the paper.

We also put a new sheet of paper onto the frame for the screen for each print.

Another would take the finished paper with wet ink and hang it to dry.

As the years went on we would paint watercolors together.

Again, my work drew favorable attention.

Then things changed.

I had to travel quite a bit and my job required more and more time as did the time I needed for my family as they grew and had important needs in their lives.

There was a period of about six years where there was no painting at all.

I did try to keep up with some form of taking a lot of photographs when I traveled and also while home.

As I neared early retirement for health reasons, I tried to paint watercolors again

I remember it well!

I painted three of them!

They were horrible!

I was ready to throw them out, when my son Don came over for a visit. He asked me if I had started painting again. So, I him down to the basement and showed him my three not so good paintings and told him that maybe it had been too long since I used to paint.

"Dad" he said. "Dad, don't give up! I know you can do it! I've never seen you quit anything before!"

So, I tried to listen and promised not to give up!

I heard more encouragement from Cheri and Dan.

Then Don and Mardy arraigned a retirement gift for me. They arraigned for Don and I to go to Minneapolis, Minnesota to a watercolor workshop. It just so happened that the workshop was conducted by the all time favorite watercolor instructor for Don and Greg and Cheri and I. We had been using his art instruction books for years. I was very excited about finally getting to meet him—Zoltan Szabo!

ZOLTAN AND MORE

It wasn't as if we hadn't studied with some great artists before, but this to us was the ultimate. Don graduated from the Milwaukee Institute of Art and Design.

So, here we were in Minneapolis to meet the artist we had so admired since we first took Don to an art store and found his first book on a shelf in 1971, "Landscape Painting in Watercolor" at an art store in Milwaukee near what was to become a home of the Milwaukee Institute of Art and Design. I fell in love with it and showed it to Don. So did this young artist. .

We could see that art burned in Don's heart from the time he was small. Don liked to draw and paint everything, but as a young artist he reminded me a lot of my former classmate Wiley Miller with his deep love for painting animals and birds. The covers that Wiley painted for Fishing Facts Magazine over the years were classic works. Don reached that level early in his art career after graduating from the Milwaukee Institute of Art and Design when he would be invited to feature his paintings in the same shows as Robert Bateman. Since then, Don has branched out to so many things from nature and has really excelled.

Zoltan eventually had the most published how to art books in the U.S.A. He was a real master of color and the characteristics of the various pigments. During his time at art school in Hungry, he said he would study by day and make his own pigments at night as a part of his education. It was no wonder he knew what each color could do when you took it out of the tube. And—he would teach us.

He also had a unique paint brush that he developed with slanted bristles that allowed one to do unique things. It was particularly helpful with a technique that artists call lost and found edges.

All of us have adopted his brushes as an important part of our arsenal of tools for painting water colors.

However, most of all he was a fabulous painter.

The unexpected happened,

The beauty of it was that we became best friends in the process and we would be so for the rest of Zoltan Szabo's life.

Greg would later go with us to another of Zoltan's workshops. He had the same fire in his heart as did Cheri.

Our work really hit new heights after his workshops and our works achieved new levels of recognition.

Zolltan had a great way of critiquing which is a very helpful thing for any artist to receive. It teaches one to be non defensive.

The less defensive one becomes—the faster the learning process.

He gave us so much encouragement and really took us all under wing to get us to a new high level.

To this day, I give much of the credit for being the artist I am to Zoltan. I think that my children would echo the same sentiment. He thought we had talent, but he made us oh so much better. I can never thank him enough and so I give him credit for that here.

However, the real gift was that Zoltan adopted us and our children as part of his family and we adopted him and his business manager Willa as a part of ours.

It became a very strong relationship including visiting each other's homes across the country and all of the ways that good friends maintain contact.

We had lots of conversations by phone over the years and wrote emails back and forth about so many things. And when we could, we visited with each other in each other's homes or met him reroute as he traveled from workshop to workshop.

One of our many great treasures from him is a video Zoltan produced in the basement studio at his home. It was made as he painted an original casein painting—with Greg and I in his studio. A unique plus for us is that the video captured us in the background conversing with each other as he explained what he was doing and why. That was truly special. We still have the video and still have the painting.

Years later Greg and I would go to Scotland to paint on location with him. There we truly sharpened our skills at painting on location. The love fire for art burned brightly in Greg's heart as well.

One of my fondest memories of the trip in addition to being there with Zoltan and Mardy and Greg, was getting up early with Greg and hiking down to the sea shore before sunrise. Then the real challenge and thrill was to capture the sunrise in watercolors as the sunrise really seemed to race along with the speed of light. It was also unique because the salt water air from the sea kept the watercolor paper moist longer than normal. We each painted some of our favorite paintings at that site on those mornings.

The greatest gift of all, however, was the gift of friendship that would grow deep and special.

Zoltan had the most dramatic life story about studying art in Hungry, the country where he was born. His life was so captivating!

He actually began by sharing a fascinating story about his personal experience with a lady named Therese of Konisreich from Germany and his doubts about her stigmata and how he came to actually witness it as a teenager.

He went into so much detail about his encounter that we could almost feel we were there with him.

We then asked him more about his youth. Although we didn't expect it, he graciously unfolded his life story to us.

It was fascinating!

He and his father served in the same army and the same unit caught between the Nazi military machine and the advancing Russian army from the East.

The story is truly amazing of the jeopardy he faced and of his escape eventually to Canada and then to the U. S., where he became a citizen—just before his death!

A major reason he had to flee for his life was his support of a Cardinal who opposed the Russian take over of Hungry. Zoltan served mass for him. During a demonstration against the takeover, Russian tanks rolled in and rolled over a young mom. Zoltan rushed out and saved her baby.

During that night, one of his best boyhood friends came and told him to run as fast as he could without even stopping to see his family. Zoltan was told by his friend that the friend had to take a job working for the police to support his wife and family.

The friend also said he had an order to pick up Zoltan and put him in prison.

The friend told Zoltan that he would put the order at the bottom of his stack of those he was to pick up that night. He told Zoltan he would be back to Zoltan's room in a few hours. He also told him not to stop and to run as fast as he could to escape. Zoltan stopped at an aunt's home for money and ran as fast as he could.

The rest of the story is even more fascinating and I have the original copy of it as he put in down on paper for Greg and Mardy and I. When our good friend passed away, I sent it to Willa McNeil to pass on to his family.

As I understand it, part or all of it has since been published one place or another. I think it would make a fabulous movie to use his story as the opening and then add the rest of his fascinating life to it.

Another day during our visit, and over a glass of wine at his home in North Carolina, we told him how much we appreciated his sharing his life's story. We told Zoltan that his story should not be forgotten. Zoltan was about the same age at that time as I am at this writing.

He asked if we would like it if he wrote it up for us.

And, so he did.

He wrote it up for our family and sent it to me.

It was a real treasure for us and we kept it as we promised.

Then, when he passed away, we sent it to Willa McNeil for his family for their archives. As I understand it, it was then made public as part of the tribute and memory of our dear friend and really a part of our family for as close as we became. He often told us that.

Don, Greg, Mardy and I were privileged to be with him in North Carolina during his last days. Here we were to be there with him during his last days—and only as Zoltan would do, he asked to meet with each of us separately. When he did, he did what the best teacher I ever met did. He gave us each pointers about how to fine tune our painting techniques. And we each did. And it worked for each of us.

Among our great memories is that Don has an original by Zoltan in his living room that was a gift when he won a national best of show award at a prestigious California competition. Greg treasures the original Casein painting that Zoltan did for us in his study during a visit—to teach us his love for this new technique. Mardy and I treasure two original paintings that were featured on the cover of a very special book by him. He told me about the book as he was writing it. He wanted to leave some of his favorite techniques to the world before he left. And that he did.

His spirit and his teachings do live on in the art that we do to this day.

MORE ENCOURAGEMENT

There was a lot of encouragement from my children along the way.

Greg was studying communications and art at the University of Wisconsin in Milwaukee, Wisconsin.

He was also on an internship at a major company in Milwaukee and since I had just retired he asked me to go back to school with him while he was there. And so I did and studied under another master—Larry Rathsack.

The encouragement from our sons pushed my art capabilities to new heights and to membership in the Wisconsin Watercolor Society.

Years later, Jeff was coming off of just publishing his first novel. One Sunday he came to visit and said, "Dad why don't you try to publish all of those stories you wrote for us over the years?"

We had quite a discussion about his thoughts and reasoning.

Jeff prevailed and the result was my first formally published non business book.

Another example of teacher turning into a friendship for me was Berta Sherwood. To me, she will always be the grand lady of art for Racine, Wisconsin. I first met her through a workshop she was teaching at Wustum Art Museum in Wisconsin. It lasted about three months. I'll never forget how I asked her about how to mat and frame paintings. Instead of just answering my question, she invited me to her home where she took me totally through the A,B,C's of everything a young artist should know. Years later she would invite me to join a small group of artists that she selected to meet each week for the better part of a day in her home to exchange ideas and to create paintings together. She was another of the beautiful people who encouraged me.

My first session in Berta's home, I realized it turned out to be a very select group of prominent area artists including my good friend Elton. Two others were Jean Thielen and Joyce Odom—also good friends to this day. We met every week for many years. And persons enjoying a common interest turned into wonderful friendships.

This was a very special group of talented people and they ended up teaching each other and helping each other to new heights. Berta was so good at encouragement.

While I value the teachings she gave to me as an artist, I can not begin to measure the depth of the friendship that she gave to me and to the gift of other friendships that developed between the other artists in the group.

One of the truly fun things that came from her invitation to friendship was watching all of the talented people in the group grow to newer and higher levels. Like all good friends who go on from this world, I miss her a lot.

Berta would also partner with me to help do something new at Wustum Museum in Racine. When I suggested bringing famous art instructors from across the country to Racine, Berta partnered with me to make it happen.

The result was that the first artist we brought to Racine to Wustum Museum was Zoltan Szabo. And for me, there I was surrounded by two of my favorite art teachers and two of my best friends. We would end up bringing many more great artist instructors to Racine—working as friends and as a team.

She did ask me to do one of the hardest things I have ever had to do for a friend. As she was dying she called me to the hospital. She asked me to be her messenger and take notes on directions she would like to see taken at the local art museum in Racine. I think I sat for two hours by her bedside as she struggled to get her wishes out and for me to record them. What I took from that is just what I saw coming from Zoltan at the same stage of his life. Here was another great teacher—

literally being a teacher to the end—wanting to pass on their most important thoughts about their gift!

Sequence wise, Berta passed away some years before Zoltan. Both were great personal losses to me. But the gifts of self they gave will never be forgotten.

Another artist who inspired me was Bob Johansen. I loved his treatment of anything he touched with his paint brush. So, I attended one of his workshops and borrowed from him. Sequence wise I initially studied from Berta, then Bob and then Zoltan. Bob and I became friends and he even rode on a commuter bus with our sons Don and Jeff while Don was attending Milwaukee Institute of Art and Design and Jeff was studying Journalism at the University of Wisconsin Milwaukee. They also became friends. I offered to make a video for Bob to sell of him doing one of his paintings. Cancer caught him way to young and we never did get that project off of the ground, but his influence and inspiration will always be with me. As fate would have it we would meet his daughter Ann some years later for the first time and we have a special spot for her in our hearts. To me, Bob was absolutely one of the finest artists ever to come from Racine. When I was younger, seeing the beautiful treatment he gave to lighthouses and watching him paint—certainly had to be a spark to me in the development of my love for painting them in my own unique way.

Another fine friend is Lyle Peters who has always been encouraging to me and for Greg.

While on the subject of encouragement from people, it is critical that I mention the daily encouragement from Mardy! She encouraged all of my creative efforts and my professional career. She helped me to do all of these things despite my disability from the car accident.

There are other outstanding artists like Tony Van Hasselt who have helped shape my artists tool box. Greg and I even had a hand in encouraging one of his videos on his unique techniques for putting human beings in paintings. Tony is another fabulous artist and was one of Berta Sherwood's favorites too.

I know one thing for certain! God put Zoltan, Berta, Bob, Lyle, Mardy and all of the wonderful people there who have been part of my life and they were there for me in so many ways! This includes all of my children who have been there for me so many times in so many ways.

I am often asked how many paintings I think I have done over the years. I really don' know the answer. With the help of my family, we probably created over sixty different serigraphs over the years. That is a lot of family teamwork because we worked together in one way or another to print these.

I painted some oil paintings and a few acrylics over the years and I don't know how many watercolors there were.

I have kept one sort of record though.

Since my first workshop with Zoltan about sixteen years ago, I have had over two hundred and fifty pieces in print—most of them from paintings since that workshop. To me that is more of a measure of just how much wonderful encouragement and support I've received over the years.

Even more so, it certainly underscores the goodness of the gifts from the Greatest Artist of them All—the Creator of all artists!

MENTORS

Those who help us along the way, parents, siblings, uncles, aunts, grandparents, etc are really mentors. Some mentor us by example. Some mentor us by going out of their way to show us and to teach us by various means.

While I've mentioned some of the very special people who helped my creative growth—there were definitely some who were key mentors in other areas.

Tony Koenings was the executive who recruited me out of my role as Cost Accountant for the company and enticed me to come to Human Resources. He taught me so much about the great values that were tradition with Johnson Wax, the great company for which I was privileged to work. We shared much the same value system. It was Tony who taught me that a Human Resource professional should be the one who puts the interests of the employee first and foremost in their dealings. It was Tony who first introduced me to a famous quote by one of the owner CEOs of the company that discussed what it really was that counted to those responsible for running a company. It went something like—people are first and foremost, the only thing. All of the rest is shadow.

I saw this later evolve over the years with management to—putting both—looking out for the employees and the interests of management on an even plane. Then I saw it develop in many, many companies to be that Management's interests were to be addressed first and foremost. It was quite a metamorphosis to witness evolve in the corporate world.

Fortunately, the company I worked for let us always keep the interests of the employee very high!

Unfortunately, while not true for the company I worked for, I also saw many in the broad corporate world seemingly ignore or back away—consciously or unconsciously—from moral accountability and responsibility as the bottom line seemed to over rule the corporate conscience for many organizations across the country and the world. Some of it was done in the name of being competitive. Some of it was done in the name of higher bonuses and/or other forms of incentives or reward. I believe for some it has been happening without realizing the human or moral impact of their decisions or actions.

Fortunately for me and other executives of the company for which I worked, Sam Johnson always kept the interest of the employees high on his priority list and held those of us who had something to do with it—decidedly accountable. Whenever we presented something to him, he would always ask, "How will this affect the employees?". He would not accept a negative answer to it. I was to hear this question many times over the years!

Another mentor who did so much to help me grow as an executive was Roger Mulhollen—a Senior V.P. of Human Resources when I worked for him. He taught me how to handle myself as an executive, what was expected from me at that level and how to be successful in that environment. Then he gave me the freedom to do the things I was capable of doing and supportive all of the way. He was a great one to work for and I will never forget him. Equally important, as I will address a little more later, he was aware of my disability and the difficulties it posed for me and he allowed me the flexibility to work through and around them. He also allowed me plenty of room to exercise my creativity in a corporate role at a high level.

It was under his tutelage that I learned to be comfortable in a unique role of working directly and regularly with the CEO and owner of the company, Sam Johnson. It was in that capacity that I worked for Sam— with all of his direct reports in the U. S. and abroad—and then with their direct reports.

I met with his management committee frequently and had direct contact with members of his board of directors and interface with members of the Boards of Directors on which Sam served.

I always felt that Roger added the polish that people like me and Jack McMahon and Tom Newman needed to work at that level—more about them later. He helped us to reach new heights.

We all gained recognition nationally and, in some cases, internationally because of the national and global experts he allowed us to contact and work with and develop relationships with to mutually exchange ideas. He allowed us to become experts in our own unique areas of accountability through these types of exposures. We were the beneficiaries of his mentoring and his selflessness.

Roger never seemed to want anything personally in return. He just wanted his executives to be the best that they could be. I always felt he was the most unselfish top executive for whom I ever worked. I was so fortunate that he was there when the opportunity fist came for me to work directly for him.

The best mentors are special people who are willing to go beyond what they have to do and do what they do because they really want to! They are great teachers and they are great at knowing when to hold the reins and when to let the race horse run!

One of the interesting challenges he threw my way early in my Human Resource career was to take a key role in the annual employee communications meetings. These were very important to the company. Employees were addressed in groups of about three hundred employees or less in all of the company's U.S. locations until every employee attended a session. The typical program consisted of a state of the business audio visual presentation, a follow-up live presentation by the company's President and then it was my turn. Sitting in the front row at each session, in front of all of the employees, was the Company's owner and CEO. The President and all of the Executive Vice Presidents.

My role was normally a presentation of some sort about Human Resource issues that were germane at the time—followed by me fielding, live, any questions the employees may have from the audience. There were no questions that were off base. The catch was to answer them directly, answer them well and be true to the policies and guidelines of the company plus the traditions established by four generations of family owners for the company and their commitment to concern for its employees. It was a task left to me for many years and what a terrific growth opportunity and experience base for the future. But, Roger mentored me for it in the early stages and then trusted me with it. This was his style!

He'd teach early on, let you go and do it and then get out of the way except to fine tune with appropriate coaching along the way if he thought he could help! However, usually, he looked for good people, helped to get them established and then got out of the way. He was also our best cheerleader! And when performing at a high level in an organization, it is good to have someone who was there to let you pick their minds. He was proud of his students when they were on their own and flying high on their own. Roger, for me, was always like touching base with the old master who imparted his wisdom to you early on and then was always there for you if you needed him. I can't say enough good about him!

I had several mentors who were very good friends of mine and peers in the corporate world who shared their expertise with me and I, likewise, tried to share mine with them. They too helped me grow.

Tom Neuman was the company's Training Director and as good as they come. He was always sending me clippings, magazines, emails or the titles of books that he thought might help. I often wondered where he found the time to do all of that because I know he helped so many others too. Tom was named National and International Training Director by his peers across the nation.

Jack McMahon was our Corporate Director of Management Succession. He was a wizard at what it took to be a successful executive and a manager at a high level and he too shared with me the wealth of insight he had. Jack was named the Management Succession Director of the Decade in the U.S. by his peers. Although we both had our own management consulting firm, we often worked together as a team for the CEOs and company owners with whom we consulted. We had a lot of fun doing this in concert. One of the unusual things about consulting at this level is that we often found ourselves in the position of becoming confidant to these gifted high level professionals. The higher a person is in an organization, the harder it often is to know how unfiltered the feedback is that they get from those around them and so they too need someone with whom to talk things over and get another's view point or input and sometimes coaching.

Years before, we might have been uncomfortable with this role, but in actuality, when one consults with high level executives a unique phenomenon takes place. Many of those jobs are lonesome jobs in a sense. They are usually the tops in the organization that they head. And as such, it could in a sense be lonesome because they can not always be sure of how screened or unscreened the information they receive is in fact. There are also those things they just can not talk over with most if any in their organization for a variety of reasons.

If a consultant delivers successfully and their counsel works, it is only natural to get closer and closer to a confidant arrangement as time goes on. Because of our unique roles with the Chairman of the company we worked for so many years, we worked as internal consultants to so many executives allowing us to hone our skills. Plus, at Johnson Wax, we were encouraged to seek out the world's best experts in those areas where we needed to focus our attention.

That gave us such great access to so many fabulous minds in so many areas. Sam Johnson was so great at encouraging both of us to get the counsel of the best. As a result you learn and learn and learn. Working for a great company like that with the credentials and reputation it had been great in another sense. It created a unique access to the heads of other companies where some of our top executives served as directors on their Boards of Directors—to add our opinions to questions that came up.

The sharing done with each other made us all that much better. Jealousy was never an issue.

Jack used to say if you want to learn how to do something, seek out the best person you can find in that arena and try to get close to them in some way and learn from them. I was lucky to have these four gentlemen around me at critical junctures in my professional career.

For Mardell, her mom Vivian was such a great mentor to each of her daughters and to her daughter in law. She certainly encouraged and shared her love for prayer. She also instilled a love for crafts of all kinds and taught them what she knew every Monday evening in sessions at her home for ever so many years. And they all grew and all became quite accomplished at the skills she would bring to the table. Vivian was so unique with her talents. Her hand work was so beautiful. Vivian also had a strong interest in performing theater when she was younger including performing on stage. I do think she is a part of the creative stream that our children find in their blood! Mardy, in turn, passed these passions and skills on to her children and now on to her grandchildren.

For me, my mom was a great mentor—as she was for all of my brothers and sisters in terms of dealing with adversity and the importance of faith. She certainly surmounted the former while at the same time being a true role model to us—leading us through difficult times. And, she certainly held fast to the latter. Tough as it got at times, I never saw her give up hope! She was our rock!

Mentoring with Dad was quite different. He took me with him so often when he would meet with his customers as a painting contractor. I got to watch, close up, how he planned, how he solved problems, how he used interpersonal skills, how he went about negotiating, how he supervised and dealt with his employees, how he handled customer relations and how he resolved issues. That was super training for a youngster! I didn't realize it until some years later.

Mentors are very special persons. Not everyone is willing to give of themselves and of their time to do so. They are priceless!

It is good to give—from what we receive!

I, in turn, got to mentor some extraordinary people like Ray Johnson and Wes Coleman, Paul Saffer—now special friends, who—in turn— have touched the lives of so many others. And there have been others along the way. This again is a part of giving of the gifts one is given.

Like pebbles in the proverbial pond, as Tom Newman often said, we can all impact others with the special unique some things we have to offer.

GOD GREW OUR FAMILY IN SPECIAL WAYS—VERY SPECIAL!

Our family comes from all over the world. God definitely had to have His hand fully in its coming together for us!

Two grandchildren come from Taiwan.

One comes from the Honduras.

One comes to us from China via South Korea.

And they all know about the special daughter, Mandy, who came into our lives nine years ago from China and how she became a part of our family. She is now an integral part of their lives too.

I believe with all of my heart that family is—whoever you so commit to with your own heart so that they fully belong there forever—and, that they commit the same to you in return.

Like a Cinderella story come true, we went to Mandy's wedding in Switzerland only a few years ago and met her personally for the first time and her wonderful husband Sebastian Chablis who has now become another son to us. It is, truly better than any fairy tale because it is a true story—a true story from the heart.

All of them also know how Mandy expanded our family further yet by introducing us to three other members of her family! Through her excellent skills, as a translator—she helped us to get to know them so well! In fact we then fell in love with each other too and they all have become a part of our family through commitment from our mutual hearts—and we part of theirs! She is also well schooled with computers.

At Mandy's wedding we met and also fell in love with her mom Jing Yi and her dad Jiade! We all became part of each other's family with her dad and mom calling my wife Mardy and me his brother and sister. Then we—in turn—now call them the same—from our hearts.

While there, we also met her younger sister Ting who is now also our daughter. The story is a long one indeed—of how we met through a mutual friend who was living in China for a few years! He introduced us via the internet and encouraged us to write to each other! Eight years later got to meet and greet and hug each other and to seal the bonds of family even more then before!

Mandy's dad Yu Jiade is a marvelous Christian artist from China. Her sister Ting is also a fabulous artist!

Our children know that we fit together like a hand and a glove with our love for art and music and our strong mutual love for God.

They will know how Mandy has a beautiful singing voice as does her sister and how they collectively join their voices with their mom and dad to sing together—much like my family did as a child and much like my family does today.

They will know of our mutual love for God!

They will also know the value of speaking more than one language and how Mandy's tremendous and diverse skills at translating many languages were a key to this all happening.

Certainly—no one can deny the hand of God in all of this. Who else could bring two families together from so far away as Racine, Wisconsin and the heart of China and have them fall in love with each other and become one family? And, who else, but God could give them so much in common from so far away that they fit together like they were meant to be that way from their very beginning?

Ours is a truly international family with members today directly from China, Switzerland, the Honduras, Korea and Taiwan. Our ancestries date back to so many countries for past generations that it underscores that at the bottom of it all—we are all people of our Creator's Love and connected to each other as God's children! We are all the product of God's love and, even though it isn't obvious to some folks, He intends for us to love each other and the full beauty each of us adds to the world through our being here—if we want to let God's light shine through us.

What binds us together? Love! We all truly do love each other very much! What a gift from God!

MORE ABOUT ART

I've shared some very personal memories of some of the special artists in my life. Now—a few more words about art.

Art is a very individual thing in terms of what each person likes.

Each piece that is created invokes different feelings in different folks.

The beauty of it is that the artist can express what captures their interest and imagination and those things that come from deep within in such a wide variety of ways.

One of the added thrills is when you find someone who enjoys it too. You can get together at any location and each can create what moves you.

You can share techniques and ideas.

You are always learning because you never know all there is to know and the options available are ever evolving.

For our family, it is just an added dimension when two or more of us can get together at each others homes and on location.

Our works are displayed at many shows and galleries and on TV together. Often there are three or more of us represented at these events. It has also been special to watch our works go from being part of shows—to being featured, but more about that later.

And, with God's blessings, our works have risen to the featured art at shows at galleries. One gallery even dedicated a full two years to featuring us as their prime artists—and as a family of artists.

For us the fun is in the creating, sharing and displaying together; however the best part of it all is the together.

And now we are seeing the fascination of the grandchildren with this as an avenue to enjoy.

So, friends, children, grandchildren—God's gift—what gifts to enjoy! And, as our family has grown to Switzerland and to China—the sharing is ever richer!

The other element is how one's work is received by others. Some artists don't care about this aspect.

Yet, I feel there can be a special dimension.

For me, a work of art is not completed until it is viewed and—even more so—it is received by someone. That is a necessary element to communication, if that in fact is what art is. The artist sends, the viewer receives and a whole range of dynamics is possible in between.

The reactions to a piece of art are so individual and so different.

Sometimes that interaction and reaction is so special—it takes the artist to another level of enjoyment.

There is, however, one particularly unusual set of reactions that I personally experienced involved a young couple coming into my art booth at a show to view my work some years ago.

They were so happy!

You looked at their faces and couldn't miss it.

The young couple gleefully announced how they had just become engaged.

They held on to each other—smiling from ear to ear.

The young lady was drawn to one of my paintings—and the young man—to another.

She looked at him with all aglow and asked him to buy the piece as a remembrance of their engagement. I thought it was a sure thing.

Well, it wasn't.

He stuck to his guns about his strong liking for the other piece.

Back and forth!

Back and forth!

Louder and louder!

Louder and louder!

And then it happened!

He stomped out one side of both!

She stormed out the other fast enough that her long hair flying!

I never did learn the outcome and have often wondered!

Art, for me, does have so many parts!

However, the most important part of art for me—is that the best part comes from the heart!

There are a lot of artists in the family today. Our sons Don and Greg each added paintings to the cover of my book "The Green Turkey" to join a painting by me. Greg illustrated the cover for Jeff's book "In Flying Colors – Volume II". Jeff asked me to illustrate the cover for his book "In Flying Colors – Volume I". Yet, there are other fine artists. Dan loves to draw comic characters and excels at jewelry making. Cheri loves to paint. My brothers Jerry and Jim and my sister Jan all love to paint and draw. A sketch of George created when my brother Jerry was ten years old is found earlier in this book.

Our home is wonderfully decorated with paintings and drawings by Mandy and Tintin and their dad. I can't begin to say enough about just how much each of them mean to me.

Their love for creativity has always been a part of their lives too. It showed up in so many ways. While in their younger and earlier professional careers they also loved to test the waters and entered various competitions.

Jeff would win photo and writing contests in high school. He would later go on to become an award winning Journalist early in his career both in sports and non sports reporting including Best in the State of Wisconsin for coverage of a fishing event, an award for a story about dog sledding while a reporter in Wyoming, and the JC Penny Missouri contest as the best in the whole country for Lifestyle Section Features for piece on sunbathing. He actually started earlier with an award at an 8th grade science fair. Jeff would be a writer for newspapers in Racine and Milwaukee, Wisconsin as well as Jackson Hole, Wyoming.

Don won various contest with his art throughout grade school, would illustrate the cover for his high school's year book his senior year and then go on to win awards early in his career. He would win awards at many shows and was awarded the "Judge's Favorite Choice Award" in La Jolla Village's National Art Competition in California back in 1977 and it would be displayed in the show's Top 100 Artists Exhibit that year. Don is a manager of an art Department for The Bradford Exchange.

Cheri and I would both have our works featured in separate shows that displayed at the same time at Wustum Museum when she was younger. Cheri shared her creative endeavors with children in her Day Care Center.

Dan would enter other types of competitions including winning first with the soap box racing cars he would build. He would make one for me in later years as a remembrance. He would also provide art work of comic book characters to decorate the walls and halls of the school his children attended. Dan works with computer graphics.

All four of these would enter an art contest with over 3000 entrants one year and either win or place in their division.

Greg came along last age wise. He would also win various art contests along the way while he was in grade school including a First Place in an area wide "Lighthouse" illustration contest when he was nine years old in a class with youngsters one and two years older than him, First Prize in a Centennial Art Contest when he was eleven, and other contests including a Golden Key Award in High School.

Greg also did the total art work for the High School year books both his sophomore and senior years including the covers. Then he would go on to have his writing and his art featured in major events while attending the University of Wisconsin in Milwaukee.

He would do commercial ads that would appear in Milwaukee's major newspapers and a program for a major play on Milwaukee's East Side. He also created a radio commercial.

Each of the children put so much effort into developing their respective creative talents.

However what makes Greg's achievements amazing to those who really know the full story is that he did these things while being disabled. He managed to somehow fit these efforts in over time despite the personal challenges, and they have been significant, that he was dealing with involving his health. He had full responsibility for the full creation, writing, photography and editing work in creation of a multipage special event feature would go on to win a national award for Northwestern Mutual Life during an internship with them while he battled his disability trying to make his way through college.

What made his accomplishments at these early ages so amazing, to those who really know him, was the ongoing battle with his disability and his efforts to achieve despite the personal challenges to him. So, in his case, it is just so hard to imagine for many—what it took for him to accomplish what he did.

The nature and the challenges of his health would continue to impact him so much more and more as time went on! Yet, despite that, I can never forget what it took for him to try so very hard and to achieve what he did. Speaking of inspiration—Mardy and I saw it from him every day.

In so many ways he reminds me of my brother Jim with his courage, faith, his heart and perseverance despite the health challenges they both have faced and of my Aunt Gertrude of another generation in my family. For all three, I saw that God was put first, that hope was special, that giving up didn't have a place on their palette of life and that they knew that they were not alone.

Continuing in the spirit of being more open with truly sharing in the hope of maybe helping others, I share here that I understand their journey somewhat too in many ways. However, the nature of the limitations for me has been far, far less.

One specific example was having to make decisions such as should I continue my medication for Ankylosing Spondilitis (which the doctors declared a necessity for me) to slow it and its effects down—a staple in my medicine cabinet for about forty years. Or as a key medical specialist directed me about a year ago—to consider seriously—if I was willing to stop taking it to help save my kidneys which have weakened over the years with this line of medicines.

I can't let these things stop me as long as it is humanly possible because God is there for me. I have been off of these medicines for a year to date now, and this book is among my attempts to keep on trying and keep on using what is still humanly possible for me. Literally speaking, I hope to get my posterior up off the ground from the challenge posed, dust that challenge off and keep going. I hope to continue to try to continue to create new paintings in the same vein. I hope to continue to create because that is a gift He has let flourish and nourishes within the realm of my body. In the process, I believe He has helped shaped me anew on my journey.

Each of us has had our works featured individually. However, as I've noted a few times, we have frequently also had our works displayed as a family on a number of occasions in a number of venues, exhibits, T.V. and galleries. Those, for me, were the most meaningful—because it was as family.

Our home is also full of very many pieces of different kinds of crafts by Mardell. She changes the décor for every season of the year with pieces she has created—making our home always looking new and alive for the different seasons of the year. When I see the many creations from my family, how can I help but to know that God is good!

There were so many things our family enjoyed doing. Among them were the great basketball games that were played in our driveway. First there were the games our five children had against each other. The four brothers made sure that their sister Cheri could shoot too. When she did win a game of horse on the driveway, the size of the smile on her face was immeasurable.

One of my favorite memories was the year that Dan coached Greg's eighth grade basketball team and Greg was named to the All Star team and Dan was named coach of the year.

Things continued to escalate on the driveway pavement.

There were the intense games Dan would have with his friends. The irony is that is friends at this stage were boys from the rival school which Dan and his grade school team would duel with each year for the city championship.

Then the games advanced more yet—when Greg brought several of his friends to join the mix. These were no mere basketball players. One of my favorites was Wagner Lester who was the basketball player of the year in Wisconsin. Another was Jim McIlvaine who was also an all state player and would go on to star at my alma mater, Marquette University and then play in the NBA. What I really enjoyed though, was when the sun went down, the boys would all come in and stay up until the wee hours of the night playing strategy games such as Risk and then graduate to computer games when they got to be in vogue.

(Note: The art work on the next three pages gives a very short tour of some of the family artists. In order—are my brother Jim's drawing on the top of the very next page and our daughter Cheri's drawing on the bottom of the same page. The page after features a painting by our son Greg "A Rose for You". The third page shows one of our son Don's paintings—that of a black panther. My brother and our two sons have very extensive collections of their works. Cheri, the new comer in recent years is showing her deep love for art too!)

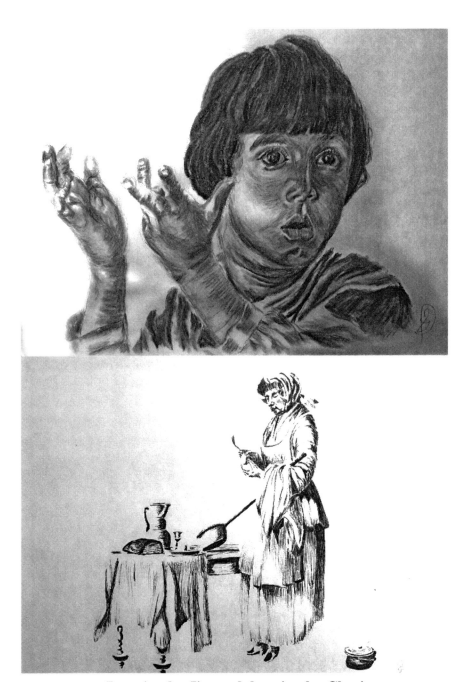

Drawing by Jim and drawing by Cheri

Roses for you by Greg

Panther by Don

A FEW MORE THOUGHTS ABOUT
BEING CHALLENGED HEALTHWISE

While I've mentioned my Ankylosing Spondilitis (AS), I haven't said much about how it came to be.

Most of our grandchildren know that I am physically disabled stemming from a mid afternoon car accident when I was twenty-nine.

Until recently, I don't think too many people knew despite the things I have been able to do.

Our Ford Fairlaine was an unfortunate target.

It was the victim of being in the wrong place at the wrong time when I was twenty nine years old.

We were at a stand still at a traffic signal with cars ahead of us and no where to go.

We were hit by an intoxicated driver in a full acceleration mode. She was going very, very fast as she approached all of the cars that were standing still waiting for the traffic light to change.

Then she hit the accelerator and went even faster when she rammed into us—sending me to the hospital. My son Jeff was hurt a little also and he was with me in the rescue squad when I lost consciousness.

They weren't sure which way things would go for me for a time. When I returned home, it was a while before I could return to work. I had such limited range of motion and limited mobility for a long time.

Thanks to two friends I made it to work because they picked me up and took me home for two years before I could drive again.

My condition—resulting from the accident—is, as I mentioned earlier, called ankylosing spondilitis or AS. It is a bit scary sounding if you were to read about it in a medical dictionary or on line. It was all of that when my doctor first explained it to Mardell and to me.

I am sharing just a little more of the specifics here about this in hopes that maybe it may help promote more open-mindedness for some people in positions to do so about those with disabilities. Specifically there may well be possibilities for some with disabilities to contribute if given the chance and if the individual is able to try.

I would hope that some—in a position to make a difference—will look beyond what the eye can see.

My wish is that maybe more folks may just be a little less leery about trying to make it possible for those with disabilities to do the things that they are able to do and to improve their chances to achieve their dreams and improve their lives and the lives of their families.

So here goes. Without going into a lot of detail here, among other things, AS generates a fair amount of pain and restricted movement of some joints and other moving parts of the body. It is an ongoing process by which joints and other moving body parts solidify and can restrict movement. It is progressive. Yet, it is not always that easily visible to others—unless they pay extra close attention.

Because it is not readily visible externally, most people don't know I have this condition. However, from time to time, some external symptoms give it away a little. For me, a slight limp from time to time is the most external frequent sign until I needed double knee replacement.

Another more significant challenge—that I could often readily mask—is a serious struggle with loss of energy at times. Only those really close to me could know how much of a challenge this can be for me. My secretaries Alice and Ruth were such great helps here in knowing where I was when I wasn't at my desk when I normally would be.

There was one particular external sign that did cause more good folks to take notice! It was when I had to begin wearing braces on my arms because I was losing more of the flexibility in my hands and arms and the pain levels reached new thresholds. This is not a particularly easy thing for an artist at this point.

For a while, this caused some of the truly fine people—and I mean this sincerely—that I worked with, concerns. Some stepped forward to ask me if I really had to wear the braces at work.

They were genuine in their worry and meant well.

They were concerned that some might think I could no longer perform at the very high level people were used to seeing from me.

Ankylosing Spondilitis has many calling cards, but God has helped me throughout my life with them. Fortunately, I was able to continue to be gainfully employed at a significantly high management level despite the challenges AS would pose for me.

In fact, nothing more had changed then a normal progression of the AS for me. I was able to prove that there was no reason for that concern by continuing to be a key part of the management team. It wasn't my hands of my legs that I needed. It was my mind—and it seemed to work just fine. In fact, all of my performance reviews were with "Outstanding" performance" ratings. Plus, I was known as a very effective communicator. The parts I needed to excel at my job were working more than well while those that were slipping had no real impact on what I could do. My one on one meetings with top management including the Chairman of the Company were frequent and very successful. My presentations to the Top Management Committees were often. I represented the company to many important organizations. I was the featured person for a major part of many of the mass employee communications meetings. A little more about these things will come later.

Roger Mulhollen—Senior Vice President of Human Resources, one of the finest persons I ever worked for, knew about it. As mentioned earlier, he was also one of the finest mentors during my career.

Roger addressed my energy drains by making it possible for my periodic visits to the nurse's office for a short nap to refresh from time to time. He did it in such a way—to be seamless and invisible to everyone else but to the few that needed to know. He knew it and together with the medical people at the company protected my secret throughout his tenure with the company. He helped me in other ways and yet, held me fully accountable. In fact, when I took the job reporting to him, he told me it was so sensitive, I couldn't afford to make a mistake. I tried to do that.

He said he expected the best from me.

I tried to do that.

And lots of good things happened for me.

I certainly give him most of the credit for facilitating the opportunity for me to overcome the restrictions of the AS on the job and to allow me to do what I had to so that my professional career could take wing as a high level executive. I was even allowed a special music set up in the office for when I needed to relax.

He helped me in another special way by helping me to keep my disability a secret between him and me. I believe that kept most from seeing a disability as a limiting factor. I never felt that all the years I worked with Roger—because it wasn't.

Roger supported me. He helped me to fly to high levels despite my disability.

I tried to be the best I could be—in return.

He allowed me to use the gifts God gave to me.

It didn't stop me from my travels around the U.S. and the world. For that I give tribute to God as my copilot. One such trip was to Africa shortly after a hospital stay. There was a need. I wanted to go. Roger supported me. So did my family. The doctor gave me good instructions and the right preparation for the trip. The General Manager on the African end even provided me with a place to rest and refresh during the day.

The mission was successfully accomplished—despite restrictions, limitations and all.

Long hours and performing at a high level consistently—with the challenges of AS—is really hard to describe. All I can say is that the challenges were very real and there—daily—and sometimes severe. But, I do feel not many really knew except for those who needed to know.

Working at this pace at this high level did take a toll. Based on advice from my doctor, I retired from the company at age fifty five and a half. I gave the Chairman three years notice when the doctor first laid it on the line. I had a very important job and I knew it would take some time to get someone else up to speed. My responsibilities were global in nature for this multinational company.

However, I told him before I told anyone else because, although I was reporting to a Senior V.P. at the time on the company organization chart—I also had a private role reporting directly to the Chairman. That role had to do with anything he wanted to talk about relative to his top executives around the world including their performance and the amount of their salaries, etc. He used to tease me every now and then, because I was the one that recommended his compensation to the Board of Directors each year and I helped him to write his own performance review for the Board. He took this all very seriously even though he was an Owner/Chairman. So, I was asked to be objective in my views of his performance before he wrote it up and I proofed his drafts when he finished. He had an agreement with me that while he was living I wouldn't tell anyone about the meetings we had in private. The V.P. I reported to, knew I met with him alone most times, but never asked why. I think there was a clear understanding. My cohort and friend Jack McMahon had the same arrangement, but I don't know of anyone else who did.

Because he had so much confidence in me I just had to tell him long before anyone else so he had time to do whatever he thought was necessary to do.

The Chairman of the company called me to his office several times to try to talk me out of it. He did wonder at first why three years advance notice, but when I explained, he understood and wished me well.

I believe me, me, me is never the right answer to the good things achieved in one's life. I believe it is we, we, we—that is—God and the people he puts into our lives that help us in life. Plus there are the gifts He gives us to develop and for us—to do with them what we can to put them to good use—to the extent that we can.

There are a string of others who made my achieving more doable for me despite my disability.

Adding a few of the many people on the list of the people who help form the "We" in my life are two super secretaries I had during this time.

I have to give a lot of acknowledgment to my secretary for so many years, Alice Garukian! Alice is a perfect example of what I mean! She was absolutely the greatest! She helped me in special ways on the job, when necessary, so that I could perform at a high level as an executive. She was so special and so fully aware of my disability with its twists and turns and—like Roger—made my efforts to overcome so much more possible. All I can say is that God made it possible everyday. Alice was flawless and special. She was like one of the family. My children and Mardell all knew Alice and she knew them.

She was a sensational secretary and is a very special person. Her family too—was very special to me. I knew all about her children and I had known her fine gentleman of a husband Mike for many years before. Again, more of the special people God put into my life.

Then when Alice retired to be a grandmother and spend time with her grandchildren, He sent me another special person to help me as my secretary—Ruth Albee Smith. The list goes on and on. I need to underscore all of my family members and personal friends along the way.

Both Alice and Ruth were fantastic at giving the best possible support I could hope for and—as an important quality for me—they knew my family and my family knew them. This was important when I was traveling—particularly overseas.

Even as I write this page, Mardell is sitting next to me making a plastic canvas piece of art—small purses that contain small note pads. And what does she do? She occasionally looks up and encourages me.

An invisibility to the eyes of others—is a characteristic of many disabilities! So many disabilities are not always perceptible or readily apparent by external appearances alone. And, even more so, few really actually know how the challenges really affect a person or what is going on inside the person affected because it can't be seen! Some times that is convenient. Sometimes it makes matters difficult.

They also may not fully understand what is truly required of persons with disabilities who do to try to function in a world of persons who do not have them.

We all relate to so many things based on our own personal experiences and exposure to the world around us! It is a lot like the old saying that if you haven't walked a mile in someone's shoes—it is indeed difficult to actually, truly perceive what it is like!

While my grandchildren know some of the things I can't do—they certainly know of many of the things that God has helped me to do instead!

A big door was closed for me—but my, oh my—He sure opened a bunch of wonderful windows in my life beginning with my family and friends!

God certainly helped me to make the transitions from what I could do before the car accident—to finding ways to maximize those gifts that I still had—some of which may have been somewhat more dormant before the accident.

He certainly helped in my transition, fueled my will power, helped me up when I was down and definitely helped me to see those new windows that He opened! He certainly filled my life!

A LITTLE MORE THOUGHT
ABOUT BEING CHALLENGED

It's been said that each person is the sum total of each person they meet and that they are a blend of their experiences and the impact and reactions to them along the way.

Having said that—I would like to lift the curtain—and—share a little more about the word disability in my life.

However, it is important to stress that what happens in the life of one disabled person and what they are able to do and not do is not and should not be assumed to be the same as for another. Disabilities are so different and how one is able to respond is so different. And, the support systems are so different! And for some, the disabilities are far more limiting than they have been for me.

The following are my thoughts as experienced through my prism and through my own unique set of circumstances.

A good starting point is that just because some disabilities aren't visible—doesn't mean they aren't debilitating. There are so many factors including energy, physical limitations, emotional strength, durability, support, spiritual wellbeing, hope, etc., etc. etc.

Although you can't see the impact a disability is having on a person, that doesn't mean the impact isn't real or that it isn't a bona fide challenge to deal with for that person. Often the magnitude can be far greater than others realize—even enormous!

On the other hand, I would like to say that some—definitely not all—people are fortunate to be able to accomplish so many things despite the challenges! For these it can happen if the hurdles are accessible—and—one doesn't let the hurdles get in the way. It is important to note that—sometimes these hurdles are remarkably high and difficult!

Sometimes, for some, it is possible that, if you are willing to do whatever it takes—you may just be able to find a way, with God's help, to meet certain goals you may set.

Other disabilities, no matter how hard one tries, may prevent one from meeting some expectations of their own or of others!

From first hand experiences with others, I know personally that with disabilities, it is also import to note—that no matter how hard one might try—some just may not be able to achieve certain goals that they have set or expectations that others have set for them.

The catch is to climb the mountain of feeling positive about one's self—no matter what!

This can sometimes be an extremly tough mountain to climb!

No one person can measure that mountain for another!

I do believe that God wants each and everyone to try to climb the mountains in our lives the best that we can. The best that we can—is the key—and don't worry about the rest!

It is not appropriate to assume that we know what another is going through, but only to be open to trying to truly listen and to try to understand!

Listening is such a big key—with and open mind.

Assuming can be very hurtful. Trying to understand the best one can is another. One should not assume they know how someone's disability is affecting them.

Without experiencing what another is going through, we can not fully appreciate their challenges.

Our reference base is not their reference base.

However, we do share the love of the same God in common! And one person is just as loved by God as another no matter what including their color, their education, their skills, their achievements, their contributions.

All He asks is our honest love in return and trying to do His will. I think that is what makes "Thy will be done" such an important part of the Our Father that His son taught us first hand!

SOMETIMES THINGS
COME IN BUNCHES

Sometimes we deal with things that happen one at a time. And sometimes one at a time can seem overwhelming!

Sometimes they can come in bunches!

Last summer is a good example of that for us. Last summer, in early June, our son Greg was helping Mardy with gardening.

Suddenly, Greg came running into the house calling out, "Dad, dad, come quick—mom fell! She's hurt!

Mardy was in an awkward heap on the ground and in lots of pain. She suddenly fell for no apparent reason. Greg and I raced behind the rescue squad and met up with them at the hospital. She had broken some ribs. That was far better news than the broken neck they feared.

It took months of diagnostic follow up testing and several specialists—following more falls and—, on one occasion—more broken ribs to finally diagnose what was happening. Until the diagnosis and a successful treatment regimen were determined, it was a frightening time for those who love her. Uncertainty is always difficult about things that are potentially very serious.

Within a very short time of Mardy's fall, her brother Don's daughter in law was hit by a drunk driver while riding her bike. It was a hit and run incident—followed by a flight for life trip by helicopter—followed by a long and painful recovery period. Shortly after that her brother Don's house caught fire and he barely escaped. He and Mary Ann, his wife, went through a very difficult time from then until February 1st of the following year before their home was rehabilitated and they could move back in. We were there last night, as I am working on this book—as a matter of fact—to join them in their first night in their restored home.

These things never happen in a vacuum either. There was so much else going on. I was working hard at helping my son rehabbing a home that he purchased and there were a variety of other major things going on. Other things in life don't always stop despite the far more serious matters that may happen in our lives.

While there was much that was very, very worry-some and of significant magnitude, in short order, there was a place to turn. One could turn to God. And I know we all did exactly that.

Mardy is doing just fine with her medical course of action. Don and Mary Ann's daughter in law is recovering and their home is just wonderful now after the restoration.

While all of this was happening in short order, there was much to pray for. And, as it is all working out, there is more to pray for again—in thanksgiving.

WHAT ABOUT GOD
IN THESE SITUATIONS

Loving God is possible for each and everyone!

From this love comes strength and hope!

And, offering our dealings with the hurdles in one's life—to Him—is an option that most can follow. This is true even if it means truly accepting the size of the cross!

Isn't this one of the most difficult—yet—greatest goods anyone can do?

I think that God really hopes we will find the means to feel this way!

I believe He really wants us to trust in Him—to do our parts the best that we can but then truly trust in Him!

Those impacting the lives of the disabled—,can help if they are up to it!

This requires understanding of the necessity for patience—while the person facing the challenge is addressing their particular mountain.

It is also helpful—to the extent that one is truly able—to try to understand and accept and support those who are disabled. My wife Mardell has definitely done this for me and so have my children! They have been magnificent!

It is perfectly OK to change course—and to look for what it is that God has in mind—even though it may not be something we readily see at the moment or don't know how it is possible to accept.

Again, it is important to acknowledge that it is God who knows what He wants from us given our own particular set of circumstances.

At the same time it is most critical to remain hopeful and in love with the God who will help us on that journey, no matter when or where or how!

Perseverance can help us to prevail!

At the very least, however, if one keeps trying—and one truly trusts in our dear God,—that person will get to wherever it is that God wants them to go under their particular situation!

I feel that some of the real keys are—understanding where one is at—what is really possible—giving it our best with what we have—and giving ourselves to and trusting in God!

A truly essential step is honest acceptance of where one is—without giving up on God and on what we have!

Not giving up on one's self is an essential piece of the platform from which can build! Holding hands with God is another! Me and God is a whole lot more than me alone!

The best combination for happiness is doing our best, as positively as we can, while simultaneously letting God do the rest.

God truly understands us! It is really important to understand here that He really loves us! Even when it may get difficult—it is important to remember that one will "never walk alone".

Easier said than done; however, the less we worry about things we can not change or impact and the more we trust God—the easier our journey becomes.

I think a good way to view life is as a team sport—God and me—and those special individuals He adds to the mix for us!

I've learned that mountain climbers—do not climb mountains solo!

He has helped me so much over so many roads that I could never have traveled on my own!

WE ARE NOT ALONE

When the challenges of life are deepest and when one can feel the loneliest—that is when it is important to remember that we are not alone. "Not alone"? Yes—not alone! Oh, we may feel like it at times! And then we do think that!

Yet, I know that He has been there for us through encephalitis, through disabilities, through oh so many challenges. I just know that when I could feel most alone and most uncertain, that I can be confident, that if I looked for Him—I would find Him!

I also have found that even while I was looking for Him, the truth of the matter is that I was never alone!

He was there all the time!

It may have taken a while at times to realize it or to feel it—but He is there—always was—always will be.

If we stop, if we pray and most importantly—if we trust—we will find Him!

He never has to look for us!

Once, when Mardy was working so hard to find her way back from the devastating impact her encephalitis had on her, we took our children for a walk in the snow to one of our favorite places, a park called Petrifying Springs.

There, she and I and our children walked through the snow across a bridge and back. As we turned around to look back at the bridge and the footprints of our journey across the bridge and back, Mardy held my arm a little tighter.

"Honey," she said, "When I feel better, someday I hope you will make a painting for me of this bridge—just the way it is now!"

I turned around and looked back and saw the multiple sets of footprints and I think I may have seen what she saw when she asked me. There were so many thoughts as I did so. One of them was of a small wallet sized card my mother Eleanor once gave to me—right around this time—containing the verse "Footprints in the Sand". I still have it.

And, so, my camera captured it.

And some years later I did get to paint it.

The print from this painting is one of my favorites for so many reasons now.

I also wrote a poem for it and include it here to share some of what was in my heart at these reflections. I also included it in my book "The Green Turkey and other Holiday Classics:"

SUNSHINE ON MY BRIDGE

No matter where I search,
No matter where I go,
Someone's always with me—
Someone that I know.

Brooks and streams,
Wide rivers to forge—
Some way for me,
To transcend—each gorge.

Sometimes, I know—
As I fear starting across,
That just standing there—
Is the far greater loss!

~continued~

Shadowed velvet outlines,
Very clearly show—
Footsteps laced in patterns
Across the silver snow!

His sunshine finds and warms me—
Like none I've ever known!
As I travel each bridge—
I go—not alone!

I think it is obvious that I make no secret about how important God is in my life.

I have needed Him much and He has always been there.

I try to remember that it is His will and not mine that is the ultimate guiding factor in all things.

One thing I like to do that is not unique to me is to like some time to pray and some time to meditate.

There are so many wonderful references available about approaches to meditating. Mardell's cousin and dear friend of mine, Sister Kathleen Bohn of the Racine Dominicans, has been very helpful to me in this area. One of methods I like is the quiet time while meditating contemplatively—a time free of to try to totally clear one's mind totally of all thoughts—a silent time that is open to let one's heart open to God's word. When one's mind is totally clear it is a lot like remaining totally silent and giving a friend total air time to say something to you.

Another method is that while reflecting on some aspect of Jesus' life—trying to put one's self there as much as possible.

I.e.—if thinking of the crucifixion—to stretch out one's arms and hold them there extended for the duration of the reflection.

A second example would be that when thinking about the birth of our Lord and the tiny holy babe—to hold one's arms as though cradling a baby and thinking of what the experience would be of hold the Holy Infant there at the stable during the extent of one's reflection—or to hold one's hand over one's heart as though lovingly cradling the infant Jesus in their heart.

Yet another would be trying to imagine the feeling of a crown of thorns actually situated around one's own head while thinking of that part of His agony and suffering—to try to envision how Jesus may have felt or what He experienced.

The more one can put one's whole self into a prayer or meditation, the more opportunity one creates to possibly enrich their experience!

God hears our prayers no matter what acceptable style or method we choose.

An explanation of prayer that has been around for a long time is that praying to God is really having a very comfortable, honest, open heart to heart conversation with your best friend—because that is what He is—the very best of best friends!

There is another short story I would be remiss not sharing here since it has an unusual tie to my painting "Sunshine on my Bridge".

There have been so many galleries and businesses that have featured my paintings over the years. One of them, earlier in my art career, was a Jewelry shop in Racine called Starburst Jewelers.

They featured a number of my original watercolors for three months.

At the end of that period, I needed to take them back down to use for another scheduled exhibit.

When I showed up to take the paintings to the next showing, the owner of the Jewelry Shop told me he just loved one of my paintings particularly much and would like to purchase it. "Sunshine of my Bridge" happened to be the one.

My immediate answer was a gentle no—because of the meaning it held for me.

He persisted and said it had particular meaning to him to and he again asked me if I would sell it.

Parting with a painting is often hard to do for an artist.

There are some paintings in particular to which the artist develops strong ties. Mardell and I certainly had ours to this one. So I told him why I couldn't part with it.

Despite my explanation, he asked me one more time if I wouldn't part with it. He asked me to go home and tell my wife about his strong desire to purchase it.

Well, I said that I would, but cautioned him not to expect an affirmative answer.

Mardy surprised me a little when I told her about what transpired.

She said that if the painting meant that much to the Jewelry Shop owner, maybe there is a way we both could be happy to part with the painting.

Then she told me about a ring she saw in a jewelry case in the store when she came to view the exhibit of my works.

She said she fell in love with it, but it was so expensive!

Original paintings of mine had been climbing in value at that time and a trade in monetary terms would be even up.

I asked her to think about it for a few days. And—she did.

Then one day she brought the subject up again.

She said she had given a lot of thought to the Jeweler's request.

She went on to say that if the painting really meant that much to him, she would be willing to part with it in an even up trade. That way she would think of the painting whenever she wore the ring.

Then she smiled and, I think trying to make it easier for me too, she went on to say that she could wear the ring but couldn't wear the painting.

So the trade was consummated!

The Jeweler was happy!

And—Mardy still wears her ring!

The print in my stable of prints of my original paintings, which is one of about two hundred and fifty different prints of different paintings today, is one of my favorites.

There is a lot of symbolism here for me of the gifts of both giving—and—receiving.

THE LADY OF MY LIFE

None of the good things in my married life would have been possible without my wife Mardell. We share our families, our friends, our pastimes, our pets, our hobbies including the many crafts at which she excels.

Her support and the support of my children in so many ways through the years are treasured gifts.

There is a story connected to my meeting Mardell, that I would be remiss if I didn't tell you about it—while I was living in the land of George and Sandy and Tiger and Goose.

School was expensive—and coming from a poor family meant stretching one's dollars as far as one can.

Each year I would buy a used car hoping it would last me until the school year ended. There was a friend of a friend who always fixed them up.

Back then, I paid only somewhere between $200 to $300 for them Admittedly, they weren't much to look at.

I tried to make my money stretch farther at the end of my freshman year at Marquette University and did not buy another car that summer.

Well, the idea wasn't a good one initially. The car I had broke down in October! It was just a few weeks into the school year and so I had to hitchhike—not a good idea today.

A classmate of mine from school, Dick Mattis—Mardell's cousin, was the driver for a car pool from Racine. I didn't know him well and never knew that Dick drove right past my house every day.

One day, while I was hitch hiking, he recognized and stopped to give me a ride. He had three passengers in the car. I then became a permanent member of the carpool for the remainder of my time at Marquette.

What is significant about it is that Mardell's brother Don was also a passenger in the car pool. The dress code for the people in our car pool was casual.

Every morning, on school days, we would get picked up in front of our homes.

The drill in the evening called for us to all meet in the student library and for the driver, to stop and pick us up to take us home.

One particular day two of the passengers did not come up to school. It also—just so happened—that Don was more dressed up than usual for a presentation he made in the School of Engineering.

I also had to dress up more than usual! I wore a blazer with a white shirt and neck tie for a speech I had to give that day.

I also wore eye glasses for the first time that day.

Well, needless to say, when Dick came to the library to find us, he didn't recognize either one of us and left for Racine alone.

Don and I waited for an hour past our scheduled pick up time—which wasn't all that fixed—and didn't know Dick had come and gone.

So, when Dick didn't show, Don invited me to ride home to Racine on the North Shore train with him and said he would get his dad to drive me back up to Racine. Marquette was about twenty miles to the north of where I lived and Racine was about thirty five miles to the south.

It sounded good to me. It certainly was a better idea than hitchhiking in the dark. So I went to Racine with Don on the train.

Mardell was a senior in high school and usually worked nights at Zahn's Department Store in Racine. But that night she had off. And guess what? We met!

It just so happened she was doing a paper on Francis Thompson's "Hound Of Heaven' and I had just finished studying it at school. The entire piece was in my English Literature book and is still an all time favorite of mine.

So, I did the proper thing. I loaned my book to her.

It just so happened that she wrote a very nice thank you note that she included with the book when her brother returned it to me via the car pool.

Her brother Don became our mail person for the next three years and later my brother-in-law.

I think a few of these kinds of things are enough to indicate that God helps matters along when He thinks it is necessary.

No one has a bigger heart than the wonderful young lady who became my bride!

One of her beautiful qualities is her sense of humor. I love a good sense of humor! She needs one to put up with me at times because I am a bit of a joker and I take after my dad at sometimes being a tease. Sometimes dad would go too far with the teasing and mom would let him know about it. My teasing is a bit different than his and very much on the light side, but occasionally I get a little carried away with my family and very close friends. Mardy has always known when to let me know to rein it in a bit. She knows I mean to harm when I tease, but that I like to only to have a little innocent with those I know well. I expect and enjoy the same in return. One has to remember that I am a person who likes to create humor in cartoons that I draw. I think my siblings and I all grew up having fun with each other—and I stress the "with" part of this statement. Occasionally, though, the girl of my life lets me know if I get close to going a bit too far.

(Note: The photos on the next page are of Mardy and I.)

Young Ed

Young Mardy

Composite of Ed and Mardy

TWINS

Mardy is a twin! That created an interesting encounter for me!

As you may recall, I first met Mardy when her brother brought me home on the train. Being November when Don and I took the train to Racine, one would think that I would be quick to respond to Mardell's note.

However, I couldn't!

The straight forward reason is that I was hitchhiking because my car wasn't working. I needed every dollar I made to cover the various costs of going to Marquette.

By late spring, however, my funds were in a better place.

We had that first date.

It was to be a special one because I was taking her to downtown Milwaukee.

I dressed to the hilt!

However, I was so surprised when I pulled up Mardy's home and there she was.—sitting sideways on a step on the front porch—dressed in blue jeans!

Oh well, I thought as I made my way from the curb to the porch, maybe I miscommunicated.

The attractive young lady just looked at me and smiled.

"Hi," she called out!

I tried to be casual as I approached the stair on which she was sitting.

She just continued to smile.

Then—she broke the silence.

"You must be Ed! I'm Mardell's twin sister Margie.

I have to say I was surprised at just how much they really did look alike to me on that occasion.

Remember I hadn't seen Mardy since November.

"She is inside, just about ready!"

And she was.

And she was just as pretty as I remembered her to be.

And we talked and talked all the way to Milwaukee and all of the way back to her home. That was a sure fore sign that something was brewing in just the right way. And that was always the way it was with the two of us. It was easy for me to see her as my best friend.

We once went to an outdoor theater on highway 41 in Oak Creek to see a movie called "This Could be the Night"! We never saw the movie because again, we talked and talked and talked.

So, to me that seemed like the appropriate setting to propose to her several years later when I had a diamond ring, for her, in my pocket.

So, we went!

I gave her the ring!

She accepted!

Once more—we didn't see the movie!

We eventually did get to see it in its entirety—when it came to television some years later—in our first home!

Another insight to the girl of my dreams—she has always been so supportive—no matter what. That includes the long hours required by my profession, the time I spent traveling around the world and away from her and our children for my career, the funding for my creative ventures, my disability and the things it has not allowed me to do, whatever—she has always been there for me. She has always been encouraging and she really has always been my very special life partner.

A simple example that may give some insight to her occurred— when I was discharged from the military—just months before our first wedding anniversary. It was a hectic with starting a new job, finding an apartment, getting it furnished and all of the customary things including all of the usual start up costs that new marrieds do have.

So, our budget offered little wiggle room for our first wedding anniversary.

I saved my lunch money and purchased one rose to give to Mardell.

So, that first anniversary included candle light, a rose and a special meal that she made for us!

I hoped she would know what it really symbolized.

She did!

She was so sweet about it, that she received two flowers for our second wedding anniversary and three for our third, etc, etc.

A FLOWER A DAY

There were other far more exquisite tokens of love and affection occasionally along the way too. But the flowers for each anniversary were by far the most significant and became more and more important to both of us as the years have gone by. I think, for us, it has symbolized that the most important gift we have to offer each other is just that—each other!

As of this writing, the flowers for Mardy each February over time—have now exceeded seventeen hundred—a number that surprised both of us. However, for me, it symbolizes—in a small—way just how important she has been in my life over years of marriage to date. This February, the count in her flower arrangement has grown to forty nine

THE ROUTE TAKEN

Another example of God helping matters along—is that I was the very first one from either side of my mom or dad's immediate family to go on to a university. There was no one there to be my guide.

So, when I registered at Marquette University I really didn't have a good idea of what I was getting into.

My counselor was a member of the Political Science Department. Totally unaware, I told him I would like to go to law school to enter politics. He guided me toward a Political Science Major and a Philosophy minor. I also had a major in ROTC because it helped pay my tuition. I'm sure, like most college students, one met a lot of special folks along the way.

One of them, Dick Hessing and I got to know each other in ROTC. We became very close friends. His family worked against Hitler during World War II in his native Germany before coming to the United States.

As I remember it, his family paid the ultimate price when his sister lost her life during an air raid as they raced to a shelter.

Another memory of Marquette was having Bob Harlen, most recently of the Green Bay Packers as one of my classmates. Bob, Dick and I were on the same drill team and got to perform at Marquette's football games and basketball games at half time.

As I mentioned, one of my mom's more distant relatives was a Circuit Court Judge in Milwaukee. During my junior year he found out I was thinking about politics and called me and invited me to lunch. He told me he thought I would be far better off as a lawyer and enumerated a number of reasons for redirecting me.

Somehow that just did not seem what I wanted to do for a career.

The bottom line was that changing direction here would mean graduating without a solid major to use to earn a living.

Yet, all was not lost.

I had learned in my days in the country to never give up.

I would do what ever was necessary to change direction.

When I finished my undergrad degree and then tour of duty as an officer with the Army—I received a letter of commendation for leadership from my Battalion Commander. It proved to be quite nice.

When I applied for a job with the company that was to be my home away from home for thirty-four years, they were impressed with the letter from the military. So they gave me an unusual offer—despite my majors. I do have to feel that God again had His hand in this.

They were going to test a number of college graduates—it turned out to be a large number, for a brand new position in the company called Financial Division Trainee.

They never had a position like that.

But they wanted to create an opening for someone they hoped would be bright and they could shape to be a key to their organization for the future after the molding was done.

The only requirement was that a person had a degree, showed potential and finished with one of the two highest scores on the test.

I was fortunate to have the highest score. That plus their liking of the letter from the military about leadership helped them to reach a positive decision in my favor!

So, they gave me one of the two open positions.

I had to promise to go back to college nights to pick up the required business courses, which I did evenings for the next seven years. I did this while in the Army Reserves, Mardell and I were starting our family and I was working full time.

Yet none of this would have been possible with out Mardy's support and love!

It was always there!

But, again, I had learned during the lean years to never stop praying and to never stop trying.

I was fortunate to rise quickly to a corporate executive post and to get special awards from the company including a major one from their Board of Directors.

However, again, I must add, that I learned all that we do is not of our own merit, but rather gifts from God that we are meant to use well and to share with others. Efforts can come from within.

The gifts we have to work with, however, come from the One who created us.

CRADLE TO WHEREVER

There are a few interesting sidelights about Johnson Wax, the company I was privileged to work for.

First of all, I could never have asked to work for a more wonderful CEO that Sam Johnson. He cared so much about his employees—in the tradition of his father and grandfathers. That made it a real pleasure for me because it allowed me to be consistent with my own values during my career in Human Resources.

Secondly, I sometimes tell friends how my ties to the company were unusual. It begins with the fact that Mardy's dad grew up in the top floor of a tavern owned by his dad and that was located on the exact spot that Johnson Wax would later build and office building. I would later have my office in that building when I served as Worldwide Corporate Director of Compensation, Benefits and Planning for the company.

Further, Mardy and I had our wedding reception in the company cafeteria which was a wonderful place for a reception. Mardy was working there as a data input operator in the computer area when we were married and was eligible to use the cafeteria. Ironically, the food service function would later be one of the departments that reported to me at one juncture during my career.

Then, all five of our children were born in Saint Mary's hospital in Racine. The hospital was located across from the Frank Lloyd Wright building.

The irony is that Johnson Wax would later purchase the hospital building when the hospital was moved to another location. It was then converted to a research building for Johnson Wax.

FRIENDS AND FAMILY

Friends are so special. For me, there are the friends I played sports with, fished with, socialized with, created with, worked with, and the various kinds of "withs" in my life!

There are the friends from school over the years.

I think that is what makes family moves a bit more difficult for the children in the family.

I know that I truly missed my classmates from Saint Adalbert's grade school when I suddenly had to transfer to another school after completing six grades there and already into the first month of seventh grade. I never really got to say my goodbyes because of how sudden the change of schools was. These ties can be strong. I still correspond with some of them.

The only one that I was able to keep in touch with during the first few years after our move was Johnny R as I used to call him. He was a year ahead of me at Saint Adalbert's.

John lived a few houses away from my grandmother Anna's on the corners of Nickelson Road and Rawson Avenue in South Milwaukee—where my dad would pick us up after work on school days.

John used to ride his old Ace bike all the way out to where I lived in Oak Creek during the summers and dad would tie his bike to his model A Ford and drive him home when he wanted to go back.

He particularly liked to fish in the Root River.

Often he would stay over night at our home and I would stay overnight at his.

His mom was the nicest person. It was John who introduced me to football. I would play it with he and some of his classmates on a vacant lot near my grandmother's without any pads. I still remember John saying that if you want to play football you have to learn to tackle and to try to tackle low. So they put me in the center of the defensive line the first time I played. And, then, the biggest guy in their class, I think his name was Tony, came running at me as hard as he could with his knees pumping high. I hit him hard and his driving knees returned the favor knocking the wind right out of me.

I learned how to take the hit and get right back up and go at it again.

There were lots of good friends in high school. For example, Craddock Duren and I—were a couldn't miss to become friends.

He sat directly behind me in all of the classes where we were seated alphabetically.

We both had brothers named Jim and they had both become friends.

We would eventually get together again years later after he got out of the Navy and I got out of the Army as officers. He was cardiologist at that point. His wife was a doctor too, but the kind that examines persons who don't make it.

When Craddock came to our home in Racine, he joked about his job—that it was as to be the heart doctor and hers was to catch the mistakes he made.

The funny thing was that as Craddock and I were walking around the yard chatting and catching up on old times—he told me how he and his wife did not eat pork and he mentioned other things. He said it was because of his bias as a heart doctor.

The other humorous thing is that—unbeknownst to Craddock—Mardy had a pork roast in the oven!

But we got through it just fine and laughed a good laugh!

There was the whole gang that I played baseball and football with at the various country schools in Oak Creek.

There were the kids from art class.

There were so many more.

There were friends like the first friends Mardy and I made in Racine after I came home from the military—Jackie and Bill Shepler.

Bill and I met while serving in the Army Reserves. We went back and forth carrying our babies to each other's homes and eventually becoming Godparents for one of each others children.

Some friendships take us to deeper ties than one might have dreamed possible when the relationships began. A classic is being asked to be Godparents for each other's children. For example, Bill Shepler and I met through our time serving together in the army reserves. He and Jackie and Mardy and I became very close as did our families. We became Godparents for their son Scott and they became Godparents for our son Dan.

You have special love for and memories of friends like that which will never go away.

We also became Godparents for Jim and Lorie Holt's son Elliot.

Love is the one word that I think describes where some relationships can grow to become!

I told one of my grandchildren once, that love is something that can show up at any time in one's life. It definitely isn't only blood related.

Man meets woman and each can give their hearts to each other even though they never knew each other before.

The same can be true for each child that enters our lives—no matter how they get there!

It can be true for those friendships that reach deeper than other friendships.

I started this out by talking about missing classmates.

I think that missing someone—or someones—could possibly be a sign of good news in a way. It could serve as a good measure of just how much you miss each other when you do not get to see each other for whatever reason.

When there is some form of separation and we really miss someone that has been in our lives—it may really be an indication of the special gifts they are to us when God puts them into our lives. It may also give pause to think to enjoy each of them while we are privileged to have them there.

This certainly applies to family—big time.

If friends are so special on the scale of things—it is hard to measure the special meaning family can have in one's life.

Some persons that we meet become part of the family because there is a mutual acceptance of each other from the heart that develops.

An example of what I mean would be taking in a child who has no where to go and you become so close that your hearts become wed to each other.

Another could be elderly neighbors might feel about a younger person or family next door that looks after them.

Another might be someone that your family takes to heart for a variety of reasons—so that they are just one of the crowd that may form your family. They fit in and they belong and you all belong to them in their hearts too. Love knows no divide.

When people think of earning their way to heaven, some think of doing the big things.

A pretty perceptive person said something years ago that I think rings so true. Thomas Moore once said, "The ordinary acts we practice everyday at home are of more importance to the soul than their simplicity might suggest." I believe that applies to friends as well.

And—it certainly applies to strangers or any one in need.

For example, we have very good friends who are in their later seventies and early eighties who participate in meals on wheels.

The good they do is so marvelous.

And yet, the common courtesies they afford us as friends like the calls to see if you are OK when you are not feeling well or the hugs they give when you need one or the biting of the tongue when you are having a bad day are very special.

Picking up something for someone who drops it on the floor, running out to get the mail for them, holding the door, doing one of the simple chores they would normally do, helping with homework, playing a game when there doesn't seen to be time, joining them in an activity when there doesn't seem to be space in your day for it, making their favorite meal or treat for them, just being there for them, etc., etc. fit into this category.

The list is endless.

Thinking of others is the key.

Being more Christ like is the best key.

Patience, listening even when it is hard or maybe boring, trying to understand, prayers or reading scriptures together as family, a smile when needed, a hug when unexpected, a lift of any kind that might help the day, a phone call or a visit, a card, understanding, being there when it isn't expected but needed, choosing to turn on their favorite TV show instead of yours, a cup of coffee or tea together, a phone call, and e mail, a hug and on and on and on.

When this is going on, ties are tightened that are bound to make us miss one another.

Even when this "isn't going on", we all do miss the "not going on".

Therese of Lisieux, France focused on the little things and wrote about them in her book "Story of a Soul".

Big things we do are super, but the little things we do for others are the glue that holds us even closer to God. That is when we try—in our own way—, to step into and follow the famous "footprints in the sand"! I firmly believe that those footprints lead us on the right journey throughout our lives.

My mom once gave me a small card with the footprints poem. I keep it near my computer and it is there as I type this page.

TEACHING

There have been so many good teachers along the way!

Besides those in the classrooms and workshops of all kinds, there is an almost uncountable list including parents, grandparents, brothers and sisters, uncles and aunts, friends, good supervisors, leaders of all kinds. There are just so many who teach us!

Then, there are those we don't know personally—but who teach us directly and indirectly by setting good examples in ways that we can't help but notice! Some can be very public figures and some are those we learn about only via the many communications tools available to us because of what they did in the privacy of their lives and how they did it.

They can be so special in terms of how they affect us.

For me, I received an unexpected experience of being asked by my teacher at Oakwood Road School to help teach reading to those in the younger grades. I don't think that I fully realized the impact of it at the time or the foundation of confidence and the seed it planted to teach that it was planting in me.

I believe it is important to give back.

I had a chance to seriously begin to hone these skills as an officer in the army—particularly as an officer in an advanced basic training unit and later as an instructor in the Army reserves for the Corps of Engineers.

When my children started asking me to make guest appearances at their schools to do presentations about art, I didn't hesitate. It went from making presentations to actually giving art lessons to their schools each year, grade by grade. I loved it!

Mardell was a great supporter of these visits to the schools and, for years, I spent some of my vacation days doing just that.

Eventually, this lead to being artist in residence at Whittier School in Milwaukee for grades one through six—with a little time spent with the kindergarten crowd. The irony is that I feel I came away from the experience being the one who learned the most from the enthusiasm of the students.

This would also carry over into many of the other things that I was fortunate to do in my life!

I mentioned that I would also get to lecture and teach over the years at high schools, colleges and universities about human resource and management subjects, planning and management. I would also conduct seminars and be a guest speaker at business and professional association meetings across the country and around the world including national sessions.

I would also get to work with some of the world's finest consultants and with professors from some of the great universities including Harvard, Cornell and the University of Southern California.

I even got to MC a one hour TV program interviewing prominent artists.

All of this came a long ways from the boy who got to help to teach first, second and third grade. I still give my one room school teacher credit for the confidence I learned here.

Again, more gifts from God in areas that I never ever dreamed of as a boy let alone get the opportunity to do—particularly when our family went through the toughest of times!

INSPIRATIONS FOR ME

It wasn't just the impact of my wonderful Aunt Gertrude during my youth that left her mark on me.

There is also the major inspiration of me by my brother Jim and his wife Bonnie and their examples of dealing with his MS!

MS came to visit him after he had started a wonderful family with two boys and had a good job

Jim's strength, determination, focus and undying love for God through it all clearly showed me an approach to meeting unexpected and unwanted changes in one's life and how to come out of it growing and perhaps giving more in different ways than you did before the adverse event happened.

Jim's support from his wife Bonnie and Mardell's support for me has been so very critical to both of us.

Also, aunt Ruth, my mom's youngest sister, was more like an older sister to me.

I did not comprehend fully the magnitude of the gift she was really giving during all the times that I stayed at her home, she made some of my favorite foods and we just enjoyed the gift of each other's company.

As one grows older I think we just begin to understand how much we should cherish the gifts God sends us in the form of special people in our lives.

God took her to heaven at age forty-four from MS, but the love and many gifts she gave to me will never be lost and I try to make sure they live on in me and in how I try to be there for others.

Two more major heroes in my life are my wife Mardell and our son Greg.

Mardell contracted encephalitis during her pregnancy with Greg. The trauma for both of them was so significant!

And yet, I witnessed Mardell's valiant long struggle to come back for something so debilitating and for Greg to stay so positive in his approach to the effects this has had on his health.

All, I can tell you is that every day living with them and watching them struggle to recover and make life meaningful was so much of an inspiration to me.

I can not say enough about either of them or their positive impact on me.

No one really knew just how difficult their respective challenges have been—not even those close to them.

I have watched them up close and tried to be there for them as much as I can!

I am truly very proud of both of them.

What both of them championed through—has made my disability pale by comparison.

So, God gave me living examples of how to deal with what some would consider adversity and turn that into a source of strength and will power.

This part of my life's journey has truly helped to reveal the goodness and love of God! Even when skies seemed so totally overcast, when one struggled to look past the haze—He was clearly always there. He forever has been. He, for eternity, will be.

MIRROR IN THE WOODS

Reflections of the past when we were young, never quite fade away.

From time to time I still drive by the old homestead in Oak Creek. It is now a park way as is the former farm to the north of where we lived and the house and farm buildings across the highway from where we lived.

I've stopped a few times too and strolled through the field and into the woods.

My children have made this trek with me a few times.

And they have gone down to the Root River and I've showed them the spots where Jim and I fished and where Jan and Jerry and Judy would sometimes join us.

One of those memory stirring stops came when my brother Jerry made a visit from his home in Arizona.

He came in spring and wanted to see if we could find the pond in the middle of our seven plus acres of woodland. That was the right season to try it because that is when all of the melted snow would raise the pond, in the middle of the woods, to a higher level than normal.

And there it was—the beautiful pond!

Like a unique mirror, it reflected back to both of us and to times past with each other.

There we were again, in our memories with dad sawing and chopping parts of downed trees for fire wood after work some evenings by moonlight, with Jim and Judy and Jan picking berries or playing hide and seek or playing cowboys or any of the other games we could conjure up in our imaginations and sometimes just sitting there on a log or a stump taking in all that it had to offer!.

There would also be memories of George flying overhead as we traipsed through the fields to get there or Sandy trailing along at our heels.

Jerry left his camera home in Arizona and borrowed mine.

He took a photo of the pond.

I still have a copy of it in my art studio and it does bring back lots of memories of family and of times long ago!

GUIDING LIGHT

There is one constant for me that serves as a guiding light—for all that has gone past me and all that lies ahead.

I have often tried to answer two key questions. Why did God put me here—and what does he want from me?

The later question is easier to answer—yet so much harder to live. He wants us to follow the way of His Son!

We can spend our life time doing that and learning about how to follow Him better.

If Jesus is chosen as our personal lighthouse and if we try to follow His Beacon, He does show us His way.

His Beam guides us through the maze of persons, circumstances and experiences that impact our lives.

His Light gives us direction even on the cloudiest and foggiest of days.

Otherwise, life can be a lot like not knowing where you are going on a journey and then being surprised that you are ending up somewhere else!

The symbolism of Him as a lighthouse in our life—lighting our way and showing us direction—is a very strong one and is definitely an influence in my love for photographing or creating paintings of lighthouses. One of my lighthouse paintings, "Windpoint Sunset", will be in this years s Wisconsin Watercolor Society Show!

I wrote several poems hinting at this symbolism without saying it in so many words. Each of them was written after the enjoyment of painting a watercolor by the same title and later then having prints made from them.

These verses are found in my book "The Green Turkey", but I think fit here to share a little of this.

When one sees a lighthouse and in the natural settings they are placed, it is not much of a stretch of the imagination to ponder the creativity of the One who made all of the majesty we experience there and the many free gifts that are there for us to enjoy such as the sunsets, the sunrises, the birds in the air, etc. etc.

For me it is also a reminder of the free gifts He has in so many places and so many ways for us to enjoy.

The first two compositions reflect on a Racine lighthouse that is truly a beautiful landmark. Whenever I see it I can't help but think about Who it symbolizes to me:

WIND POINT SUNRISE

Pebbles and stones,
Rocks and sand—
Far out into the lake
Like a pointing hand!

Tower of white
Searching the sky!
Beaming bright light
Probing far—
From on high!

Ancient shoreline,
White caps waking,
Cresting waves,
Splattering—breaking!

~continued~

Gulls wings stretching,
Screeching, calling,
Gliding, drifting
Snow is falling.

Afghan of white—
    Covering all,
Satin colors
Softly sprawl!

Hues aglow
Flavor the scene.
The rising sun
Sighs—serene!

WIND POINT SUNSET

Soft shades luminating in the West,
Behind a pillar white,
Setting off a special glow
As though some gallant knight!

Trees surrounding everywhere,
Like so many sentinels profound—
Vigilantly, silently holding sacred
To their ground.

Agile seagulls flying, soaring,
Searching, scooting randomly, off and back—
Circling round and round—
Screeching, calling, submitting their own—
Uniquely special sound!

~continued~

Shimmering snow upon the earth,
And glistening elsewhere too,
Projects the beauty of it all
To folks like me and you!

A foghorn intones its pitch,
Like a seaman's deeply lonesome wale,
Calling out to his daughter—
Drifting far out from the shore,
Floating—skipping—sailing across,
Seemingly endless spacious water!

Setting out here at the Point,
A very special view,
Cast against eve's early sky,
Stands a guardian true.

Sun, its glow surely waning,
Bowing for it's curtain call—
Slipping slowly from our sight;
Throwing shadows everywhere,
Giant fading ember, glowing less—
Now, no longer bright!

Looking up—from the lake,
The vision holds one fast,
Casting spells, a lifetime full—
Memories promising, forever—
They will last!

Wind Point Lighthouse standing tall,
Readily answering with your special beam,
Peering—searching out with radiant light;
To each one's soul caught up out there,
Spellbound—hopelessly captivated—
In your magic of the night.

Another is from a painting of one of my favorite spots to travel with my family. I can often visualize my children, all as so much younger then, wading from the shore line in Door County Wisconsin—out to the shore of the island where this extraordinary lighthouse stands.

Yet, again, whenever I see it, I can not help but think of the imagery of God as a lighthouse with His beacon calling to us—even from our darkest moments.

CANA ISLAND MORNING

The East side of the Door
In Wisconsin's Northern County,
Holds forth its court
With nature's loquacious splendor
And a most fascinating bounty.

Treasured there
On an isle unique,
Towers a servant tall,
Patiently quiet—
Never to speak!

Princess of the Point,
Surveyor of the tides,
Greeter of the gulls,
Elegantly shy—
She graciously hides!

Concealed from shore,
Albeit, from the water—not,
Searches her majestic Whiteness
In secret vigilance,
At this secluded spot!

~continued~

Building of brick,
Warm and yellow,
Like surreal music.
Escaping, ascending—
From some artist's Cello!

Rocks poised below,
Surrounding her base—
Randomly, scattered and clustered,
Adding luster and beauty
To her radiant face!

High above,
So near eve's celestial sky,
Appealing, enchanting—reclusive light;
Like a Cyclops peering through—
Its lonely, intriguing, solitary eye!

Ships searching for shore,
Shore sending to ships,
Beams dancing out—
In short flirting blips!

Seasons slip by,
Like star dust—they splinter,
Dazzling—radiantly, she dresses
For a stay by the Winter!

Inviting—"Come—come!
Come visit and see!"
Silently she beckons,
"Wade 'cross these waters to me!"

The last few lines touch on God's beckoning to us.

My son Jeff feels the imagery in the same sort of direction and ponders this in a poem he once wrote for volume one his recent book—"In Flying Colors".

We both wrote our verses quite independently.

Because we were both so busy at the time—I didn't see his poem until he showed it to me for his book.

A painting of a lighthouse, from my heart, appears on the cover of his book at Jeff's request to give particular emphasis along this line. Inviting another family member to contribute to a creative effort just continued the link between various family members and their creative efforts.

As I've mentioned, he also included prints of paintings by his brothers Don and Greg and his sister Cheri in this book.

While he saw the prints of my watercolor paintings of lighthouses on which my poems are based, he did not see my poems about them until we sat down to talk about this book.

Jeff's poem directly encompasses and is much more direct with some of his reflections on this imagery.

So, it is only appropriate, then, that his poem by the same name appears in mine.

And he has graciously agreed to allow me to include it here.

LIGHTHOUSE
by Jeffrey K. Danowski

Ghost ships—sailing in the night
Seagulls screeching—on a never-ending flight
Harmonizing with the ocean-surf lullaby
Kaleidoscope patterns dancing across a watercolor sky
Ghost ships—silhouettes on prism horizons
Sailing away from Titanic icebergs and tropical storms

~continued~

To a safe harbor—shelters warm
Lighthouses—towering over oceans and lakes
Guiding us home—no matter which course life takes
Through rough waters to friendly shores
May our treasures be many—behind each of life's doors
Lighthouse—keep me off the wrong course and on the right
With your eternal luminous light
Astray in the wilderness—lost in the woods
Thanks to family and friends for helping me the best they could
Then a music box-memory plays a familiar song
Leading me to the place where I belong
Suddenly familiar—the prism horizons appear
Leaving my trouble behind me—no longer alone
I'm headed for a safe harbor—the place I call home
Lighthouses—towering over jagged mountains and rough terrain
You are my sunshine even if it should rain
Through rough waters to friendly shores
May our treasures be many
Behind each of life's doors
Lighthouse—keep me off the wrong course—and on the right
With your eternal luminous light
When the moon and stars disappear from the sky
And you're alone in the darkness—wondering why
Take a second look across the Milky Way
And thank God for your tomorrows—today
Paradise lies beyond the prism horizons
Forget your troubles and things you don't understand
And rest peacefully in the palm of God's hand
He can right a sinking ship
Or guide a ship that's hard to steer
Even if we lose our compass
Just remember God is always near
He is the lighthouse that illuminates the galaxy

~*continued*~

Lighting the path to paradise for you and me
He'll guide us through rough waters to friendly shores
Our eternal treasure—the key to heaven's doors
Lighthouse—sharing love and kindness
Will help keep you in my sight
Drawing me closer to the home
Of that eternal luminous light
Lighthouse—burning from within
Like no light I've ever known
I long for safe harbor
I know you'll lead me home

The answer to why God put us here also seems to have two distinct parts.

We know He put us here to know love and serve Him in this life so we can be with Him in the next.

But the "How" part of achieving these things—can get clouded and seem to be less clearly defined sometimes.

Our understanding may even change from time to time for each person individually.

There are times, places and situations where we can have an impact!

Sometimes we impact others without ever realizing it by our acts of omission or commission.

Often we have little idea of just how significant or lasting these impacts are and can be—however apparent—or subtle the situations or needs or the well being of others may be!

BACK TO THE KALEIDOSCOPES

I am just a person just like all others.

Who I am and what I did—I did through the goodness of God—and with the support of Mardell and of my children—all five of them and now the six, seventh and eighth with Mandy, Seb and Ting—through our years of becoming one family! God helped me to do this despite my being disabled. How can I ever thank Him enough?

All this said, it is probably even less than likely that our grandchildren can imagine that I too was once a teenager. I certainly was and probably still am at heart.

I would like to share some of what has been in my kaleidoscope with them!

IMAGES

For me, the kaleidoscope keeps turning with some images fading somewhat and others coming into sharper focus but none ever dimming in my heart. I have truly been blessed!

I keep seeing—reflected in the mirrors of eras past and to come—living, loving images of times, of the many wonderful people and of the added gifts of dogs and cats and a crow!

I have not been able to run as I did years ago through the fields with my dog at my heels or my crow over head because of my disability, but my heart still races with them.

Thank you for flying back in time with me and drifting back in memory over the wings of George!

It has been a while since George glided over head and landed on my shoulder, or Tiger crawled under the grates or Sandy had her puppies or Goose led the charge against the intruders!

Yet—how can I ever forget!

(Note: The photo on the next page is our family photo from December 2007.)

Family Portrait, December 2007

KALEIDOSCOPE II

There is one more thought I would like to underscore! I've tried to share some of that throughout my book! The point is that—the people in our lives are important. Thus—the person we are in the lives of others—is also important! Here is one such example of this!

When our Mardell gave birth to our youngest son Greg, it was truly joyous because the doctor did not give either of them much of a chance of surviving her encephalitis while carrying Greg!

But they both did!

Even then, the journey was a long one. I am very proud of how Mardell fought her way back and of how each of our children gave their all to help her along the way.

But there was outside help too!

The one person who really really understood what was going on after Greg's birth was Mardy's dad Norbert! He was there everyday babysitting so I could go to work. I think that in many ways he was a second dad to our son. They grew to be very close! Norbert was there to help me to help Mardy, but he did also become a special figure in Greg's life.

I think that Greg saw him as a second dad!

When Norbert passed away, Greg had a difficult time at his funeral. Difficult as it was, Greg was not able to cry and let it out!

Some years later, when Greg had to write a paper for school, he chose to write about his grandfather. To share a little of how much others in our lives can mean to us, I share that piece here with you with my son's permission:

Red Knights and Black Dragons
(A Small Boy and His Grandfather)

By Greg Danowski

My grandfather, as I remember him, was of 100% German origin. That means a great explosive temper, a precision craftsman and a serious analytical and practical thinker. But, to me, a boy of five, he had a heart of gold. His sense of humor ran like an underground stream, only to pop out now in luminous pools that would make elves merry. My grandfather's silver white hair blended with the balding top of his head. His square, solemn face was stern, but a sparkle was always in his eye and reflected the wit in his heart. On rare moments, a grin slipped by his straight mouth, reminding me of how much he loved me.

They say my first word was for him…"Grandpa," even my first steps. He went to the hospital when I was just about ready to walk. I guess I was a stubborn kid and refused to walk until I again saw him after he was better. I do not remember these events. I know them only as they were recounted to me. I believe them to be true; I loved him and worshipped him as one does a saint in prayer.

I remember best our time spent over the checkerboard. They are etched like acid into a glass plate. Each memory plays beautiful pictures over and over every time they come to mind.

Our games were laid down with care in a friendly war with two winners every time. The "Board" was worn and old, but very dear to me. A cardboard piece, that once folded for storage, now was split in two along the crease. The two halves needed to be placed together so the red and black arena on which I was taught could be played upon. The checkers themselves were not plastic like new versions. They were smooth, time worn, pieces of wood containing wisdom that became apparent with each move. I remember the pieces were stored in a Planters peanuts can. They fit perfectly. I could never think of a better, more personal container for them.

After sorting out the pieces and arraigning the board, a race took place, mainly by me, to see if I could set up faster than him. We would play two or three games—never more. It seemed the right amount. My grandfather always seemed to know when enough of anything was reached.

Grandpa, sitting like a gray, noble, gentle fox, would almost always take black and I red. Red checker always move first. Like an eager knight rushing into the fray, I would move my piece diagonally. Being only five, I was an impatient kid. Checkers taught me many lessons including patience, a thing my grandfather had much of with me. Even though he had an explosive temper, his patience was long. Usually I would lose...and lose...and lose. Grandpa taught that lesson well. No matter how many times I lost, I always came back with a strong hope of winning. Often I moved myself into the worst possible position. Then with his sparkling hidden grin, Grandpa triple jumped my fancied red knights like some black beast, a winged dragon engulfing an army. Occasionally he let me win. I knew that he did, but it made me try all the harder to learn more.

Checkers was my first real game, which I learned at about four. Ironically, as I grow older, live seems more like the lessons and patterns I was taught on that beaten old and torn checker board. My Grandfather taught me that life was not black and white. At first, checkers may seem that way. Looking deeper I was shown that losing was winning too, a concept difficult to understand by many or most. There may be a winner and a loser, but the shades of emotions, the way we accept the result, makes it a lot more complex. And of course, one game was not the end, only the beginning—a series of games to be won or lost with pride, love and hope. Grandpa didn't say all these things outright. His eyes, smile and short sage advice every now and then made a young boy learn more than any lectures in philosophy ever will.

When I was eight years old, my grandfather, after a lifetime of illness and health problems, of which I was unaware, grew seriously ill. Doctors said he would not make his Golden Wedding Anniversary only a few weeks away in September. Christmas would be impossible. Even a few days or hours were as far as the doctors would allow his life sentence. He struggled and fought; Grandpa's winged dragons still flew. He made it to his anniversary party, Christmas and then my birthday on January 30.

Six months later, in July of my ninth year, he died. I saw him, a few days before his death, on the couch where we often say and played checkers. He lay there unable to get up or see much of anything clearly. He thought a T-shirt I had worn was a picture I drew. I only smiled and thanked him for the compliment he gave. The day he died I was not with him. I did however, feel a sense of peace and presence that day, only to be told later he had passed away. Perhaps it was my grandfather or the wisdom he held in his eyes I had felt.

I said before that Grandpa won most every game and those he lost I knew he did so on purpose. I also mentioned how I looked forward to the day victory would shine on my banner and my red knights would conquer his black dragons. All that time of trying to win and prevail at checkers…I realize now and perhaps I realized then, that I had won. I had won his love, his knowledge and his perseverance against all odds. That is a greater victory than anyone can ask.

I did not cry at his funeral. I don't know why. I think he was still with me and always be. My tears fall now, not for loss—for love. I have spent a brief moment of time with a man who will always be at my heart. While not enough time, more than most who have not known him, breathed him and loved him. I am told that Grandpa often said he saw in me something great. I only hope I have the courage to see the same thing he did—that my Red Knights may someday be as great as those Black Dragons.

I've tried to share the impact of persons on the lives of others. We all impact those around us one way or another. And, in many cases, we have choices about how we do that. That is what makes each of us unique.

When people do good things, it is often natural to overlook the true humanity of the person!

And, so, I would be remiss if I didn't touch on the real humanism of Norbert because, like all of the people in this book, he was a very real person with a very real personality and qualities. One of the things I liked most about my father in law was his enjoyment of good jokes and he liked to have fun.

On occasion we would get to go to a Milwaukee Brewers baseball game together even though he really was a big Chicago Cubs fan as was I as a boy because their was no major league baseball in Milwaukee at the time. We were both fans of the old time Cubs like Andy Pafko and Hank Sauer.

We also saw more than one Green Bay Packers game using tickets I got from my friend Charlie Tommet each year. One such Packer game was played in Milwaukee when it was near freezing and the rain just fell in buckets driven by the wind. But, he didn't mind. He just brought along a plastic drop cloth for us to huddle under as we watched their star running back Travis Williams break off some beautiful long runs.

But the most fun I had with him was fishing. We would go fishing for those delicious perch off of the North Pier in Racine. He would use trolley lines, but I liked to use the traditional cane fishing poles that my dad taught me to use as a boy. We both liked the quiet and peacefulness of Lake Michigan on a warm day and we certainly loved the fish.

My favorite memory of him though was fishing with him and Mardy's cousin Bill Bohn on the Willow Flowage in upper Wisconsin. It was so beautiful and wild like there. It was easy to get lost if you didn't know your way around. There were sunken logs every where. And underneath the water—there is where the treasure was. Those waters were full of Northern Pike, Walleye Pike, Crappies, Perch, and huge muskies. So every time one got a bite—your imagination could go wild with thoughts of just what was tugging at the end of your line.

What made this particular story a favorite of mine is that both Bill and Norb had a very active sense of humor! Norb's was more subdued, but it certainly was there and he loved to laugh. Bill's was not subdued in the least.

Well, early one morning, we set out in a boat onto the flowage.

This time Bill looked at Norb with this grin on his face and said "Norb, the only fish we keep today are the walleyes.

Both Norb and I thought he was kidding!

And, as luck would have it, Norb caught the first fish!

It wasn't a walleye!

Instead it was a very nice sized Northern Pike.

Norb handed it to Bill to put on the stringer hanging over the side of the boat.

Then it happened!

I thought for sure Norb was going to want to kill Bill!

Why?

Because Bill promptly took the Northern and flung it over his shoulder—back into the flowage!

I thought Norb was going to jump in after it—he was so surprised!

"Norb, I said Walleyes only" echoed Bill's voice loudly across the waters!

It stayed quiet for quite a while in the boat as Bill sat there with a grin on his face.

Then everything seemed to go into a deep freeze.

No matter where Bill took us to try to catch fish, we never even got a single bite or hit.

Finally, Bill decided to take us trolling at a place called Two Islands in the flowage.

We began trolling back and forth—back and forth.

Suddenly Norb called out, "I've got a big one!'

He started reeling it in.

Before anyone could say anything, Norb called out again, "Wow, it feels like a whale just hit the line again while I've got the first fish on!

And he struggled reeling!

And the fishing rod bent wildly!

Bill tease, but not to loudly, "It had better be a walleye Norb!"

Just as suddenly Norb called out, "I lost it! My line—it went slack!"

He looked so disappointed!

"It's back!" he called out again.

And he reeled and reeled!

But the tip of his fishing rod wasn't bending like before.

When it got to the boat and Bill landed it in the net, we all stared in surprise!

Norb had landed a very good sized walleye!

But—the real eye catcher was the fact that there were teeth marks from the middle of the walleye to its tail!

The answer was obvious!

A big Muskie had hit his walleye as Norb was reeling it in! And, then, just as suddenly—let it go again.

All of our imaginations went wild thinking about just how big that muskie was. Every time we looked down at the large scarred walleye in the boat the muskie in our minds seemed to grow bigger and bigger!

It was a great memory for Norb and one we will never forget.

What makes this memory special for me is that it was the last time we would every fish together. Norb's last wish for me was to take our boys back up to Bill's to catch some of those fish, but—as he put it— enjoy the beautiful wilds together where the eagles soared and fished the same waters.

Norb was also very gifted with his hands, machining and making things out of wood. All of us still have some of the treasures he has made. And, if one knows our family well, they would know that some of his love for these things also flows through their veins including his son Don's and his grandson in return. His daughters Bobbi and Mardy also like to work with wood and saws, etc. and so do our sons.

But, most of all, I will always remember the eagle of a man Norb was and how he soared as he helped his daughter Mardy and I through a very difficult time and became so close to Greg in the process.

This is what God does when he puts special people into our lives. Each of us in our own unique way has the potential to be special in some way in the lives of those around us—just by being open to His wishes. Maybe only in small ways, or with a smile when it is needed or an ear when someone needs to be heard—or with other gifts of sharing the gifts God has given to us—but there are ways if we are open to them!

One more though about grandfathers and fathers: Speaking of fishermen, my dad was certainly that. We did so much of it together—

Lake Michigan, the Wolf River at Winneconne and the Bark River! We had many a memorable experience together fishing these waters!

As much as he was an avid fisherman, dad was also an incessant reader. He was constantly reading for enjoyment. However, he also was self taught about many things through books. If he had to do plumbing, he read about it. If he had to do electrical wiring or masonry, he read about it. There were always "how-to" books lying about.

I often witnessed what happened when problems occurred with situations or tasks a hand—and—when these resources weren't around and solutions were not readily available or affordable to him,

So often, at these times, I saw him innovate and Gerry rig—coming up with unique solutions to resolve and remedy the situations. He was creative and an innovator and I often wondered what he would have accomplished had he been able to finish his formal education.

Despite not getting beyond the seventh grade. because of the hard economic times in our country when he was a boy, dad had the courage—after his retirement at the age of sixty nine—to go back to school.

He took up typing and researched English grammar on his own and then made a concerted effort to fulfill a long time dream—write the All American novel. His dream sat on the back shelf for all that while—when he did all of the things he had to do during his pre-retirement years.

Once he started, he worked so hard at his manual typewriter—burning through the dictionary and the thesaurus and finishing his book—but not getting to take it to that next step.

So, I don't think he would mind if I also dedicate this book of mine in an unusual manner. The "unusual" comes about with the thought that, perhaps in some way, my book could substitute as—that next step for his book!

So—here it is—"to my dad with love".

Over and over, I watched his sheer determination and rising up over and over again to meet the most serious types of challenges—often against very difficult odds.

Did he show me what hard work and effort is all about and how to face obstacles in life? The answer has to be a very definite—yes!

Did he inspire me to go on to write my books? The answer is undeniable!

He and mom, each in their own way, definitely helped shaped who I am today!

Both grandfathers loved fishing. And, since we just splashed through the waters of time with Mardell's dad Norbert, it is probably a good time to visit the waters of Jeff's memory about another grandpa.

Jeff wrote this the day after the passing of this grandpa—my dad—Ed:

Fisherman
by Jeff Danowski

A long time ago
Way back when
Lived a peaceful man
Who promised to come again
Lord Jesus, gentle Fisherman
He caters to bobbing souls
Going down for the last time
He caters to evil ones
Leading lives of crime
Those living in sunshine
And those stranded in the rain
Those filled with happiness
And those in sorrow and pain
He lures them with kindness and love
To God's kingdom in Heaven above

~continued~

Sometimes we stumble
And sometimes we fall
Sometimes we fail
To answer his call
Through it all
We must never forget
The Bible says if we keep trying
The Lord Fisherman
Will be there with his net
For he's a man of love
A man of peace
A man of kindness
A man of hope
When we're in troubled waters
He'll never hesitate
To throw us a rope
Gentle Fisherman
Luring us with kindness and love
Ever closer to God's kingdom
In Heaven above

Not so long ago
I remember when
I met a peaceful man
He was there for me time and again
Grandpa, gentle fisherman
Perched on the rocks
Of a stormy north pier
Never showing signs of fear
He sat proudly
Patiently
Helping bobbing souls

~continued~

Hour after hour
Time after time
At the day's end
While counting his catch
The joyful tone in his voice rang out
Like a pleasant chime
His favorite lures
Kindness and love
Just like the Great Fisherman above
When someone would stumble
Or someone would fall
Through it all
He would never forget
He was a fisherman
And throw out his net
A man of love
A man of hope
A peaceful man always there
To throw out a saving rope

The final cast has flown from his pole
I know he's found
The Great Fishing Hole
His lures kindness and love
Have led him to Heaven above

Over and over
I think time and again
About the greatest people I know
All fishermen
Luring God's children
With kindness and love
To the Great Fishing Hole
Heaven above

~continued~

Like my parents
And grandparents
I'm doing what I can
I know I'm not perfect
But with lures of kindness and love
I'll be like the Great Fisherman
With those lures of kindness and love
Someday I'll join
The Great Fishermen above

(From Jeff's latest book "In Flying Colors")

KALEIDOSCOPE III

GEORGE

Creatures large
And creatures small—
God it is
Who made them all!

There is a favorite
In my heart!
His coat of feathers
Was just the start!

A persona special
With humor galore
Was his trade mark—
Smiles left for ever more!

Flying high,
Soaring low—
Landing on my shoulder
For all to know!

~continued~

Letting me discern
He was a part—
Of our country family
From the start!

A dog—
A cat—
And a goose—
To bat!

A special spot
There will always be
For my friend the crow
And what he meant to me!

My wish is that everyone gets to know some of God's non human creatures and the gifts they have to offer and what we can give in return.

George 2

KALEIDOSCOPE IV

Jeff included the following two verses in his newest book "In Flying Colors"—an anthology of poems he created over the years.

When Jeff and I were discussing the final editing of this book—he made a special request—asking me to also include them both here. He felt they might provide a little perspective from eyes other than mine.

So, to honor my son's request, here are his verses:

The Artist
by Jeff Danowski

Some of them are businessmen
Some of them are city workers
Some of them are factory workers
Some are writers
Some are painters
And some are carpenters

But no matter what their profession
Our fathers
All have something in common
They're all artists

~continued~

As they try to raise us
And share with us
Experiences we need
To lead happy lives

The environment we grew up in
Or are growing up in
Is the canvas
Our fathers were given to work with
It's also one of the things
That makes us all unique
And in our own special ways

From life's palette
Our fathers begin their Masterpieces
With the essentials

First a stroke of sunshine
To dry up life's sorrows

Then a painted smile
So that we might find
Happiness in our lives

Add a touch of encouragement

A touch of forgiveness

A little sensitivity

A little humor

A little discipline

~continued~

Surrounded
By a lot of love

Though things
Don't always turn out picture-perfect
There's comfort for me in knowing
My father has tried to do his best
To give me what he thinks I need
So someday
I'll be able to create and paint
A masterpiece as great as his

This next verse from Jeff adds another perspective:

Brush & Pen
by Jeff Danowski

It's a crazy world
I cannot understand
But I met a man
With a brush in his hand
He made things clearer
And painted a picture for me
My life is full of color now
Not just black and white
It's still a crazy world
But now I can see

This world is full of people
I cannot understand
When along came a man

~continued~

With a pen in his hand
He jotted down some notes
And spelled it all out for me
He said
Don't try to understand the people
Love them
And watch them smile
As you set their spirits free

His words
Have the beauty of 1,000 pictures
His paintings touch my heart and soul
He'd give the shirt off his back
To keep me on the right track
We disagree now and then
But I love that man
With the brush and pen
I love that man
Who taught me to use
The brush and pen

In a hurting world
Where things hardly go as planned
I also met a woman
Who carries a brush in her hand
She's always there
To paint a smile on my face
She's turned my memories of home
Into treasures time cannot erase
Then she took a pen in her hand
And jotted some notes for me
She wrote
In this crazy world

~continued~

That's often hard to understand
Remember,
Yours are not the only
Footprints in the sand
God is there to guide you
With his loving hand

Her words
Have the beauty of 1,000 pictures
The smiles she paints
Warm my heart and soul
Even though we disagree now and then
I'll forever love that woman
Who holds the brush and pen
I love that woman
Who taught me to use
The brush and pen

Then—Jeff encouraged me to go a little deeper yet with some of my thoughts and so did Greg!

Even though, much earlier, I tried to share some things—they both pushed me to go a bit further.

So, at their request, I will try to reach a little deeper!

Here, then, is a little snippet—of some intrinsic thoughts from the heart—of the now seasoned version of the boy who loved George!

Were someone to ask me if something stands out in helping me to make choices and decisions—I think the best one word answer is that one should seek the two big **"Ts"**—**"Truth"** and total **"Trust"**.

Taking the time, making the effort and maintaining the interest to **search for the truth** can produce solid foundations from which one can build, confirm, redirect, modify or change the course that one has in mind—or help to find the one answer for which one may be searching. The search for truth can take many routes.

The application of this principal applies to so many things. For example, I found that an interesting thing to do when studying one's religion—is to look for the truth by going way back in time to the very early church and really study what was being said at the time—by whom and why. It takes time and commitment. Many very learned folks have benefited from this experience.

One of my favorite searchers for truth is Thomas Aquinas—particularly how he captures and unfolds it in his philosophical works.

In matters of true importance, truth and nothing but the truth is a good friend.

Truth is the one "Beacon" – that if followed by us mere mortals—can help shed light on the right path to life's choices and decisions!

As mere as we may be, we need to remember that we are not "mere" in the eyes of God!

That leads directly into the second "T".

As important as the search for truth is—even more so is total **trust in the right something**. By that I mean a total trust in God. If one can achieve this—there is nothing that one can not begin to deal with and we will ultimately end up in the right place.

If one can trust that God knows best and will care for us and get us to His ultimate promise for us, then it makes it possible to put our focus where it belongs and to follow the beacon that He sent to us—through His Son—to show us the way.

If we trust in His Divine Mercy, we know He has our best interest at Heart and is always forgiving no matter what!

He sacrificed so much to show us how much He wants us to trust Him.

He is always loving.

And—if God can love us that much, than there is nothing that we should fear if we commit to Him and place our total Trust in Him.

He will—as one of my favorite Hymns says—take us up on Eagle's wings.

Oh, we need to do our part the best that we can, but if we truly Trust in Him—we have made the wisest choice we can possibly make.

One of the great impediments I see for so many persons is that they step away from the Truth and the Trust in God, because of the human frailties and vulnerabilities of some of those who accept the mantle of administering within the earthly structure of the heavenly guidance He set in place for us to find our way. The pursuit of the real Truth, in this case, can help to see through that and beyond that and not take our eyes off of the ultimate prize!

For example, if one knows that one is in the right store for the right really special deal of a lifetime, and happens to get a bad clerk, one can see beyond the clerk and stay in the store and not miss taking advantage of that deal of a lifetime.

The truth is not the clerk.

The truth is the right store and the deal of a lifetime. And the trust is then in the Owner of the store. We need to get past the impediments to the truth and there can be many during the journey.

Another example, at great risk of sounding like a soap box, would be the lyrics for some of today's music. It is to me, one of the best examples I can think of today!

First, I should say that my family and I have always loved music in all of its forms over the years.

So many have played instruments and been in bands over the years and even written original music including me—I have an appreciation for all kinds.

The world is full of good and great music and continues to be. I've enjoyed it in so many forms including from my visits to Africa, Europe and other parts of the world.

However—some of today's lyrics and unbelievable. They no more represent the Truth than any of the other distractions in today's world. These lyrics are somewhat sugar coated by masking them in the sounds of music that are up to date and appealing for each of the newer generations.

It hurts for me to see the shock value and the false and misleading premises and promises of those words are knowingly used to lure the young, in their formative stages.

The sad part is that it is done to lure them to the stores to spend their cash—not to give them a look at the truth. The real truth here lies with why the greedy purveyors of music containing these lyrics are constantly pushing the non truths out there onto the young and vulnerable. The answer is simple and their motivation deliberate—to make a profit regardless of the personal cost to the young and the innocent. To me—they are nothing more than predators of the young and bear the brunt of the dulling of consciences and misdirecting the values of so many of the true treasures of our world—the young.

The end does not justify the means and bad lyrics are not justified because they generate profits for some.

Our freedom of speech is so misused forming the shield for the purveyors to hide behind while the mercilessly get away with it.

Instead of the truth, these lyrics continue to present false pictures of what truth is and leads the young away from the truth. Sadly, it is at a time when the young are most vulnerable and trying to reach for their place in the world of the grown ups. It is like approaching that proverbial sharp curve in life—.and it is here that it is one of the most dangerous times for them to miss the truth.

I so believe that mistakes made following the false beacons of some of these lyrics can cost the young for the rest of their lives if they buy into them.

False lyrics are a gigantic Pied Piper that is alive and well in today's world—and—we haven't found the will or the way to put it away.

Yet music is so good and such a special gift. The search for truth can help to separate the beautiful from the destructive.

A major assist in the pursuit of the truth is achieved when placing one's trust in the One who set the path. The next step requires a bit more from us—following His path!

Without belaboring examples of the importance of truth—another is how politicians tell us what they think we want to hear based on polls taken daily. Here again, it would be so good to hear the truth so that we can vote for the true options—not what gets politicians elected. So many politicians don't really tell us what they really stand for. So we, the citizens, vote for the image that politicians paint of themselves—much of it based on polling. It would be nice if we knew who they really were and what they really stood for and where they would really lead us—the truth.

Once upon a time, news reporting was very different than today. It used to be that there was a strong effort to try to report the facts and substantiate them before rolling the presses. I don't think and many others don't think that is so true any more.

Many news papers have obvious biases and it shows in their coverage and editorials.

Another potential non truth vehicle is propaganda. It can be used by taking non- truths and non-facts and part facts to create a picture that someone or someones put out through various media forms to shape the opinions of others in one way or another—usually with a purpose of some sort in mind.

How significant is this?

Well, historically, it has been used effectively to shape and mislead the peoples of nations—i.e. Germany in the 1930's with particular focus on shaping the minds of their youth. One of the tricks used was to repeat untruths over and over and over again! Unfortunately it has been a lesson well learned by some to mislead the masses. A lie told often enough—can seem like the truth if persons are not careful.

With today's twenty four hour news stations and channels on radio and TV, by flipping channels it is easy to see the biases that one or the other have built into the communications teams they have assembled. It is no longer just news reporting, it has become more bias supporting in so many cases. The questions than needs to be asked for each—should focus on—for what purpose?

The answers can go a long way to help get at the truth—and I believe—determine the directions today of nations, the world and history.

With satellite TV the biases can now be taken world wide instantly and can shape a world opinion of one nation or another and of its peoples. Since the biases of the different networks and TV news channels are so different, a search for the truth would ask which one or ones are presenting the correct picture? Which ones are presenting the truth?

When I used to consult and coach CEOs—I would teach them to view each idea presented to them—no matter how good it sounded with a very fundamental question that could go a long way toward giving a green light or a red light to what was being presented. The coaching went something like this for the decision maker or makers.

"The question I have for you Mr. or Ms. presenter, is—"for the idea or action you are proposing, I need to know—you are suggesting doing what you propose *in order to accomplish What?* " This is often a difficult question to address, but it can help sort out the difference between those projects and or activities that are *want to do projects* from *need to do projects*. This can go a long way toward making a more sound decision. There may well be nothing wrong with "Want to do" projects"—but the decision makers should have a chance to know the difference between *want to* and *need to*! This helps to put the emphasis on the true reasons for doing something and the allocation of resources and effort.

So there are major reasons for and challenges to seeking the truth today. They are important ones with today's mass communications capabilities and resources.

And, in a fast moving and interrelated world—it is important to try to seek the truth for so many reasons and at so many levels!

So, there you have a glimpse of my favorite two "T"s. My trust is in the real Truth who has shown us the Way with His heart and with His very life, with His arms opened wide, for us!

There is one more ingredient in this mix that I think is very important—the big **"L"**!

That is—to be open to **God's Love**. If we can open the eyes of our hearts we can find it.

His is there always.

He never goes away.

It is not just a case of saying, "Ok—show it to me."

"Show me Your Love!"

If we truly commit to and reach for it with our hearts we can find it and also find our love for Him growing more and more openly. It is a case of being open to it's being there unselfishly for us to wrap around ourselves.

The most beautiful music we can make here—is the music of a two-way street—God's love is there for us always and it becomes a remarkable symphony when we try our best to return it.

A side benefit for us and those around us is that the two-way street then becomes like a stunningly beautiful flower in full bloom with all that it offers. And the ancillary benefit may be that it just may touch the hearts and the lives of others we encounter in our daily lives.

Therese of Lissieux is connected in writings to roses from her pursuit of God's love and she beautifully underscores it in her book "The Story of a Soul" where she talks about the benefit of the little things we do in our lives and how we can direct and dedicate these.

If you should wish to try remembering these three things, try thinking of **TTL—*"Through The Lens"* of life's real kaleido-scope**—and everything you see can be viewed in a new light and with more beautiful design, clarity and purpose.

Good purpose is certainly worth living for and pursuing with all of the commitment one can gather.

It is worth trying to climb mountains for, endure what one must endure and dust one's self off over and over again after each fall and to get up for and try, try again.

I believe our task is to continually try the best we can to take whatever we may have left in our fuel tank—however much or little that may be—and lay it on the line—the best that one can—for God. What one may have left may be very little or very significant, but the reward—regardless—is the true gold at the end of life's rainbow.

One more principle that I believe is critical in this world. The need to forgive—truly forgive from one's heart and move on is so paramount in today's world. This goes for the little things that irritate or hurt to the big things. Hanging on to old hurts or differences or injustices only keeps people from doing what Jesus did from the cross—He forgave everyone—everything! I think that was an example He wants us to follow. It doesn't mean being tied to one or ones who hurt us or may have wronged us, but it does mean forgiving, truly forgiving and moving on!

A MOST IMPORTANT DEDICATION

I conclude with a final and most important dedication of this book—to the Devine Mercy of the God who makes the most wonderful things possible!

And—I remember Him in my favorite prayer every day at three in the afternoon—"Jesus I Trust in You"!

I also dedicate my work to His most Sacred Heart plus a dedication of my entire family and our friends for all generations to the protection of the Immaculate Heart of Mary.

She is our heavenly Mother—just as He gave her to us—from His outstretched hands and from His heart while on His cross!

AS AN ASIDE FROM THE STORY— A FEW THOUGHTS FOR BUDDING ARTISTS

Since the subject of art and artists in the family comes up often in this book, I would like to share some thoughts for those who are growing or wanting to grow with creating paintings or perhaps taking their works to new levels.

It seems most persons want to get better at those things that they love to do!

One of the conversations that others frequently initiate at art shows, and other places, is about the "how to" part of art.

A good many folks ask how they can learn to improve their painting techniques or how to help their children advance with their drawings or paintings.

Some get more specific and ask how to paint the way I do—or my children do. I think that if I counted these conversations over time, the number would be quite high.

There are lots of things one can learn by trial and error.

And—that is just fine

However, it can also be expensive in terms of art materials utilized without getting close to the results one really wants—let alone the investment of time while experimenting.

It also doesn't minimize the possible disappointment if the hoped for product level is not what one wants it to be. And, sometimes that can be a turnoff for those who might otherwise continue in their pursuit of this creative outlet.

Since life is about sharing the gifts God gives to us, there are a few hints that I have tried to share with others over time—if they expressed an interest. And, should you or someone you know be at an early stage with exploring art, I would now like to share them here in the hope that they might be helpful.

Short of going to art school, here are a few things that might be beneficial as an assist to a novice artist's learning curve—some of which were initially pointed out to me by others years ago

First of all, the love for drawing or painting can show up at any point in one's life. Eventually, one can get to the stage where they want to begin or try to get better.

Then they want to know if there is help available to achieve that.

There was a time when I, like so many others I know, used to get a bit flustered doing the best I could and then still not being able to achieve what some of the really good artists do.

Well, there are a lot of things, some of the quite basic, that one needs to know but may not even realize are important.

Helpful tips about the materials they use might be of help.

Focusing on watercolors for example, there are different types of paper available with different potential results and different ways to prepare it before applying a paint brush.

There are different kinds of brushes and ways to use them.

There all kinds of little tricks that can be used to achieve the result one wants.

And there is one that is particularly frustrating when a budding artist first finds out about it. To get the best results, it is helpful to understand that there are different grades of watercolors. The better grades are often used to help achieve the best results. Student grade paints do not have the same properties. Learning the properties of the various colors and brands of the various colors is an important element for taking ones work to a higher level. Zoltan was a master of understand this and explaining this. For example, some pigments are more grainy and can be used for specific purposes like painting the grainy sand on a sea shore. Some are staining and hold fast where they are placed. Others are non staining offering a number of wonderful possibilities. It can get even more complicated. Sometimes the same color, named on a tube, can be staining for one manufacturer and non staining for another manufacturer. This should not deter one because you can find this out by experimenting; however, occasionally one can find a "how to" art book that goes into the specifics.

Then there are a number of principles of design that are ever so helpful, once mastered, in achieving the results one wants. Several of the artists, I learned from, were from the school of a New York art instructor of years ago named Ed Whitney. To me, art teachers like Tony Van Hasselt and Tony Couch seemed to sprout from this sort of foundation.

A lot of folks never even know that there are workshops being conducted all over the country and the world by some of the really good artists of our times. This is a good thing to do—if one can—because, in addition to demonstrating how these artists achieve what they accomplish, they often critique the works—daily—of the participants in their workshops. This is where a lot of real growth can take place for some.

Sometimes the periodical art magazines—one finds on the shelves of book stores—list a number of these workshops in the back of the publication. Now and then, they even do a special feature article focusing on the workshops that are available, when and where they are conducted and the price.

In Racine we are fortunate to have a facility called Wustum Museum where a variety of talented art instructors and skilled artists conduct workshops on a regular basis. Many communities have such facilities.

Another source for improvement in drawing and painting would be the art books and magazines found at many bookstores. Some of these stores even have sections dedicated to this. There are often beginner's books there as well as for advanced learning—this includes great books for the young artist in families. I encourage these as great gifts for birthdays and Christmas. I even have a few dog eared ones of my own from many years ago.

A last thought before leaving this subject is that many of the top flight art workshop instructors now have "how to" videos that lead you through the artist doing a painting demonstration for you. Some of them are better than others. But, short of going to a workshop it can be a good way to see—for one's self—how they achieve the results they achieve.

Plus, a person can go back and go over and over and over portions of the video to help study the techniques they use—so that they can sink in. These videos are available for different painting mediums.

Again, some art magazines, will advertise some of these videos and some art stores make them available and sometimes the libraries carry some for taking out.

I share these thoughts for anyone out there that may try to advance in their efforts at creating paintings, but are unfamiliar with these avenues.

There are some artists who might reach high levels without the help of good instruction or instructors along the way.

However, if you or someone you know wonders about how to get to that next level, my hope is that some of these thoughts might be helpful to you.

Sometimes it can be a choice between the school of hard knocks and the school of hard study.

Just as learning a foreign language takes lots of time and skill practice—so does art.

The key thought I would like to leave for the budding artists reading my book, is that it takes a lot of learning the tricks of the trade, however achieved, and lots of overs to achieve consistently at a high level.

The more tools and tricks one has in their tool box—the more successful each well or loosely thought out painting can be and the more fun one can have when they experiment with their creativity!

The most important thing is not to be intimidated, but to get into the water.

Little that is really good, in the way of accomplishment comes without some effort. There are at least five ingredients to creative success—four of which are desire, learning, commitment and practice.

Don't forget a most important ingredient—having fun on your journey!

In my case, I try to add one more important thing for me. I try to start each creative venture by offering it as a prayer to the One who provides the gift and is the source of all of creation.

ABOUT THE BACK COVER

Since some of the focus has been about art and my love for it and the out of doors and winged creatures, I've tried to include a little of the past impacting my art of the present. So, I've selected five paintings, for the back cover, that were completed over the past sixteen years to share a peek at that. In order, they appear—from top of the page to the bottom:

"Blue Jay Morning" is an inspiration from a love of birds of the wild and those that visit our back yard—as Blue Jays do. They are so royal and majestic looking, particularly when they are perched against an early falling snow in Wisconsin.

"The Roost" came about as a direct reminder of George and his games with the chickens in our backyard when I was a teenager. It is also a reminder to me of the many times I raided the nests in the coop for eggs each day as a boy and of the chicks from the selected eggs that we used to incubate and hatch. The actual direct inspiration occurred while touring a historic site of old barns with Mardy and our son Greg and visiting one such chicken coop. The sunlight streaking through the window aroused memories of days of yore!

"Kay's Geese" are also a direct tie to my youth and Goose our watchdog of sorts. I've always had a fondness for geese and ducks and swans dating back to that time. These happened to be two geese that I saw wondering down a slope and toward a pond one afternoon during a visit at an old farm site that would become the home of Mardy's cousin Sister Kathleen. I couldn't resist the shadows that seemed to be at play over the coats of feathers that the geese wore.

"Family Swim" also has a tie back to unusual one of my foursome of pets when I was a boy. I do love to watch geese fly and to swim, unlike Goose. Goose never could fly and we didn't have a place for him to swim.

One day when our children were younger, we all took cameras in hand and wondered down to Hanche Pond—a beautiful small sized body of water—walking distance from our current home. We were all out on a photo taking safari!

Mardy our five children at the time and I wondered out of the car and around the edge of the pond. Each one was intent on capturing some of the beauty before our eyes. Suddenly I noticed this mother and father goose and five goslings moving down a slope and slipping into the water for a swim. The parallels between their seven-some and our seven-some couldn't be missed. Snap when the shutter on my camera. And—later—my paint brush went to work with watercolors. The title was a no brainer and a natural!

"Country Colors" It would be impossible for me to capture the impact of country living on me from just a few paintings. Aside from the beauty of rolling fields, unfettered tree lines, places for nature's creatures to roam, there are a few things that can take a step in that direction.

For me and others, larger buildings gracing country sky lines are more than just barns. They are treasures disappearing from our skylines.

Influences resonate for me—from daily walks through the field to get our daily gallon of milk from the farm next door—and—the times I would spend in their barn talking with my friends while they worked. They are present from times in and about the haylofts of the barns of my Aunt Bernice—or—from the barns peering back through our car windows when dad took us out for rides in the country—or from those my bike passed while exploring or on the way to the homes of my friends—or—those Mardy and our children saw during our drives through Wisconsin country sides and across the U.S. on our family vacations and travels.

Most of all, there is the natural intrigue and beauty conjured by unforgettable images of barn structures aging and rising against sunrises and sunsets, snow falls, harvest times and offerings of the various seasons. Further, their unique histories could offer natural drama through possible stories that their silhouettes may hide—or may forever remain untold.

For me, they also mark the transition of a city boy who moved and became a country boy and is the product of both!

MORE

Many emotions have stirred and directed the movement of my paint brush as it explored the colors, the contrasts, the shapes, the symbolism, the inspiration, the depth, the design, etc. of so many creations, settings, moods, dynamics and influences. Birds or barns are not the only themes that take hold of me! Although I do have to admit to falling in love with subject matter that presents itself in out of doors settings, reflects the moods of nature, and/or the beauty of the scenery and settings presented to us for pondering by the Master Painter.

These thoughts carried over to lyrics I wrote for Greg's eighth grade graduating class at the request of Greg and his classmates in 1985. They were then skillfully put to music by my good friend Jim Holt and sung at their graduation mass by them and then recorded for their posterity. At their request, I also created a serigraph to accompany the song. I still hum it to myself once in a while and it stirs up a lot of old and very good memory dust! This may be a good way to bring my sharing via this book to a close:

At a Glance—
About the Author—Edwin K. Danowski

Formation and Development as an Author/Writer: Ed has been writing for many years. His background is so varied and broad, ranging from highly technical to the most fanciful of works—that it amazes those familiar with the spectrum of his works.

Over the years, he wrote many stories and poems for his children and family. A genuine feeling of warmth and love permeates his work. At the encouragement of others to share with the world, he complied those related in one way or another to holidays and gathered them into his new 283 page book – released late last year—"The Green Turkey and other Holiday Classics"!

He acquired the title of "The Artist Poet"—because of the sensitive and accompanying poetry he sometimes writes to accompany some of his well known watercolors.

Ed also got to write for The Artist's Magazine with its global circulation.

And now—he has completed this true and fascinating story about four pets early in his life and what happened to them and his life's fascinating journey as the years progressed—"A Dog, A Cat, and a Crow"!

Diverse Underpinning: Ed's background is like a many sided coin. Here is a quick look at some of the turns

As a high level corporate executive during thirty three years at one of America's top one hundred companies for which to work, he was instrumental in the written, audio and visual employee communications both nationally and internationally. He went on speaking and question/answer tours for the company regarding company programs each year for many years. His accountabilities were worldwide and took him to many corners of the globe.

While at this company—he was responsible for many innovative changes. The company's Board of Directors recognized him with a special award for his unique contributions. While there he was also responsible for the business book "How to Talk to an Actuary" that was sold to corporations throughout the U.S. .

He then provided the leadership in founding an innovative major health care company that provided a new direction in addressing health care problems and was appointed Operations Vice President of the resulting company, by a number of leading businesses and government in the region and then guiding its successful launch.

Afterwards Ed headed his own top management consulting firm for CEOs of companies across the United States for many years. During this period, he authored a number of self published successful business books on various aspects of management for use by his clients and is in the process of completing a new book for publication that focuses on the art of successful planning and its missing link as well as truly effective communications between employees and management.

Formation and Development as an award winning artist: Back into the creative realm, like most artists, Ed's interest blossomed as a youngster. A premier artist, his awards began coming early in sixth grade and during the four years he studied art in high school. He would later study art at the University of Wisconsin Milwaukee studying watercolors under Master Instructor Larry Rathsack. He also studied with many prominent artists over the years, particularly with his long time close friend and mentor, one of the worlds's most published watercolor instructors and artists, **Zoltan Szabo.**

Art Achievements and Showings:

Over the years, Ed's works have been on display and in juried shows in many galleries, businesses and in private collections around the world. Ed is a member of the **Wisconsin Watercolor Society**.

Cartoonist: It wasn't just the paint brush or the written word that captured his imagination! He ventured into an area that he felt allowed him to combine both visual and written communication—cartooning!

Ed created and had cartoons published over the years including for a student newspaper while at Marquette University.

Then, he and long time friend and fellow artist Elton Dorval, co-created and published the cartoon strip Happast VII.

Photographer: He love photography and is an award winning photographer.

Song Writer: Ed has composed music with special friend Jim Holt with Ed concentrating on the lyrics. This includes numerous church songs which have been sung by church choirs.

Inventor of Games: Somehow, he also found time to invent a number of games selling three including "Tee Time", "Brontosaurus Hunt" and "Fling".

Other contributions to the field of art and beyond: Ed has also been contributing to the art world in a variety of ways behind the scenes and publicly for many of his seventy one years. This includes narrating TV art auctions for Wisconsin artists at Racine's Wustum Museum, serving as Master of Ceremonies on a two and one half-hour television special featuring some of Wisconsin's other most prominent artists, serving on the Board for Wustum Museum in Racine, serving as Artist in Residence at the Whittier School in Milwaukee.

Among other things, Ed is also known for his work and assistance to provide comfort and support, by dedicating three specially created pieces of his art and donating prints of them to the families of the victims of 9/11 in New York, the Pentagon and Pennsylvania. He received recognition from President Bush!

Over the years, he has, consulted on occasion with local, state and national government leaders on subjects where he has expertise. This began with his very first venture in this area many years ago—advising Wisconsin Governor's Council on Aging under the direction of acting Governor Martin Schreiber!

Ed lectured and taught at business schools and universities, was a featured speaker at local and national conferences, meetings of business and professional organizations and huddled with many world experts on various business related issues over the years including at some of the country's major universities.!

He also served on various boards and as an officer for many professional, charitable, civic and church organizations over the years.

Motivation: Art and writing, to Ed, are very meaningful and rewarding ways to do just that! "It offers such special & unique ways to share your inner most feelings! "Watercolors and creative writing own part of my heart! I believe that God gives each of us special gifts and talents and that it is our unique obligation—not to keep them—but to develop them to the maximum and to do His will by using them well and—most importantly—sharing them with others! A light under a basket whether it is a smile or a hug, an "I love you" or a painting is a treasure lost to the world for however long it is hidden!" "Before starting each creative effort, it is offered to God in praise and thanksgiving for His gifts that make it possible!"

A Family Sharing: Those that know Ed and his family know creativity seems to run in their veins and in more than one discipline.

Many years ago, the inspirational Madonna Martin, of the Racine Dominicans, began an innovative program to foster and grow and find the possible directions for creativity within a family of creative people. The family of Ed and, his wife, Mardell and another family were selected as the pilot group and worked with Madonna at her inspirational center called Kere Place.

Today, two of their five children work in the art and graphics field including one as an Art Department Manager for a major creative products firm. All of them are creative in their own right and two of them are award winning and published writers. The artwork of Ed and three of his children have appeared in various art shows together.

Art work by Ed and his sons Greg and Don appear on the cover of Ed's book—"The Green Turkey and other Holiday Classics" which was published in 2007!

His son Jeff published has several published books including "The Teddy Bear Necklace and "In Flying Colors", published in 2007, as a two volume set—Ed's art work appears on the cover of one book and his son Greg's art work also appears on the cover of the second book. Additionally paintings by his daughter Cheri, sons Greg and Don as well as some by Ed are featured inside of "In Flying Colors"!

For this family—creativity is definitely a part of their lives! So much so—it has been the subject of various newspaper articles and the subject of a one hour special television presentation about his family.

For Ed, his art, his music, his books and his other writings are a skillful way of sharing the inspiration he feels deep down inside. And, in this true story, "A Dog, A Cat, and A Crow", one will find out so much more about that and what may have fanned the flames of creativity and causes them to burn with such intensity!

YOUNGER CHILDREN'S VERSION

INTRODUCTION

This version is for the young and the young at heart!

As you get ready to read, please know that this story is true. It is about four lovable creatures that form a very unlikely family, but family they became. This is the story about them and their life's separate—yet, together journeys!

LOOK UP

Soft, black velvet wings opened easily. The crow flew in circles and started to come down. Gently, he landed on the boy's shoulder. He put his beak next to the boy's ear. He whispered! The boy listened!

This special bird did this over and over again. He and the boy had become very close friends!

This is where this story begins—in a place called Oak Creed.

The young boy grew up in this town, just south of the city of Milwaukee in the state of Wisconsin. He had a lot of fun!

He could run in the fields with his brothers Jim and Jerry and his sisters Jan and Judy.

The fields were very big and there was a lot of room to run and play!

Trees grew all around the edge of the fields!

A river ran nearby!

ONE SPECIAL MORNING

Early in the morning the young boy named Ed went for a walk. It was very early!

He heard a very soft noise! It wasn't loud! It was very quiet!

At first, he did not see anything!

Then—under a bush, he saw a tiny little puppy! She was all alone and she was very cold!

Her fur was a pretty color, just like a chocolate cake.

Small white spots and pretty yellow spots colored her face like special touches of frosting!

She also had a soft white star shaped spot on her chest!

The young boy picked her up—slowly—gently!

She was trembling!

So—the young lad patted her fur!

Gently he rubbed her forehead between her ears to make her feel better.

He also patted the center of her very small nose.

He wanted to let her know that he liked her very much!

She liked that!

She also liked him and licked his hand with her tiny tongue!

The tiny little dog had no home!

So, the boy carried the tiny puppy home.

He was so happy when his mom said they could keep it.

The tiny puppy became part of the boy's family.

They called her Sandy!

CARDBOARD BOXES

Jan found a box for Sandy to sleep in.

Judy found some soft old towels and folded them carefully to make a bed.

Then, Jerry carried little Sandy down to the basement.

That is where she would sleep!

Yet, she wouldn't sleep down there alone for long!

A few days later, Jerry found another tiny creature without a home.

It was lost too!

It wasn't a puppy!

It was a very pretty and cuddly little kitten!

His fur was very soft and yellow orange!

He had lots of darker colored stripes—and they made him look like a tiny tiger!

That's what they called him—Tiger!

Tiger had a special spot to sleep!

He loved to sleep between the tiny puppy's legs.

He would curl up, close his eyes and rest!

He felt very safe there!

Sandy and Tiger became very good friends!

HOLD THE PHONE

One day, the young boy's friend, Russ, called him on the phone.

"Guess what I found," his friend asked!

"I found a tiny baby crow in a nest!"

"There is no one to care for it!"

Russ asked, "How would you like to feed it—and raise it as your own pet?"

The young boy did not hesitate!

He quickly said, "Yes!"

Young Ed was so excited!

Now they had three young pets—a baby dog, a baby cat and a baby crow!

The tiny young crow was a black beauty! He really was! They called him—George!

He had very tiny thin legs, a small pointed black beak and flashing dark eyes!

He even looked like he had a smile on his face!

Because little George was so very very small, they had to feed him with an eye dropper!

Jim and Judy carried the little crow down to the basement—so he could sleep with the other two pets.

Guess where he liked to sleep?

George liked to fall asleep sitting on the back—of Sandy the puppy!

So that's how they would sleep—all stacked up like and ice cream sundae!

Tiger would curl up between Sandy's legs like the banana in banana split!

George would perch on her back and sleep just like the cherry sitting on top of the ice cream sundae!

Young Sandy didn't mind at all!

The three liked each other very much!

THREE IS COMPANY,
FOUR IS A CROWD!

Well as if there wasn't enough excitement, one day soon, something else happened that was really fun!

Ed's dad came into the house one day and called, "Surprise!"

He added, "Come into the kitchen! Come here! See what I've got!"

All five children stood around a small shoe box he placed on the kitchen table!

Dad opened the lid!

He reached inside!

Out came the surprise!

There—cuddled in his hand—was a young gosling!

He was as cute as any young chick or young duckling. But, he was neither! He was a young goose!

He made a soft squeaking sound—almost like a peep, peep, peep! He looked so cuddly!

Well, you might ask, how did they sleep?

Of course, young Sandy, Tiger and George continued to sleep in one box—all curled up together!

The young goose did not quite seem to like the arrangement!

But—he readily slept in another box right next to them in the basement!

It wasn't a case that the imaginations in this family wore out!

It is just that they did not think a fancy name fit this new little creature!

Everyone just called him—Goose!

GROWING UP AND CLIMBING UP

One day the fuzzy little, busy little, stripped little kitten tried to climb the stairs.

And—Tiger did!

Sandy did not know how yet.

Neither did George or Goose!

The mom and dad in this family eventually moved them all upstairs.

The five children made a special spot for them to sleep.

Mom feed the baby animals and birds milk and crushed corn, bits of bread crumbs, water, and other good things they liked to eat.

But, each animal—had a little different taste.

So each animal—liked a little different food!

The children spent a lot of time playing with their new pets. Because their pets were so small, the children were very careful with them!

GROWING UP

It didn't seem to take long for these four little creatures to grow up!

George loved to have his feathers stroked gently. He also learned to fly at an early age!

Goose never did learn to fly like George!

Sometimes Goose would fly a little, but he could travel only short distances. Goose couldn't fly very high!

He liked walking on the ground almost all of the time. That is what tame geese do!

Sandy and Tiger both liked to sleep in front of the fire place.

The young dog and cat liked to play games with the children. They liked to sleep a lot. They liked to eat. They also spent a lot of time— with each other!

These two furry and two feathered pets all grew even more during the winter months!

They spent most of their time indoors. They also became very good friends!

When spring came, the two animals and the two birds spent a lot of time out of doors. In some ways—they didn't change much.

They still all liked to play! Each had their own way of playing.

Tiger and Sandy would let us know when they wanted to come into the house!

They also let us know when they wanted to go out again!

They always came in or out through the back door!

George didn't seem to like being outside at first. He seemed to think he should be in the house all of the time!

Sometimes he would fly up and land on the kitchen's window sill. "Caw! Caw!" he would cry!

He would sit there for the longest time. Then he would do this over and over again!

Slowly, he got used to being out of doors more.

Crows love to fly! So did George! After a while—he would sometimes soar overhead! Then sometimes, he would land nearby for a visit! Sometimes he would visit Tiger or Sandy of Goose. He seemed to deliberately keep in touch with each of them!

Other times—he would visit the young boy and his brothers and sisters. Sometimes he would find them working or playing in the farm fields! Sometimes, he would find them in the yard.

Suddenly, George would fly toward them from somewhere in total surprise to them.

Then—he would land on the ground and slowly walk over to them with a kind of swagger! He would make crow sounds! George wanted to visit! He wanted to play!

Every day, the family would let him back in the house. George would sleep in the house at night with Sandy and Tiger. They stayed good friends! They also continued to sleep like an ice cream sundae— much to the surprise of everyone.

George had some favorite things to do when he was home!

He liked to strut across the mantel on the fireplace.

He also liked to look in the long mirror that hung there! His reflection would seem to look back a him whenever he looked in the mirror. This would fascinate George! Every way George would turn, his reflection in the mirror would turn exactly the same way George would turn. The reflection would do everything George would do. George loved to be in front of the mirror!

George looked like a dancer at times the way he walked. It almost looked liked a waddle, but not quite. The children called his walk—a strut!

Sometimes George would fly over to the couch or a chair and— then—hop on someone's shoulder!

He loved to get his beak close to someone's ear. Then he would make sounds almost like he was talking to them. They were funny sounds! They were like whispers!

George also liked to sit on someone's knee or wrist. He was ever so gentle with his pointy claws.

Sometimes, he would sit on someone's shoulder and watch T.V. with them.

He also liked to watch while the children and the adults in the family played games—or—the children played with their toys!

Sometimes he would get right down on the floor and want to play right along with them.

The five children—and their mom and dad—treated George just like one of the family!

He was!

He really and truly was—as much as any creature of the wild could possibly be!

UP—AND—UPSTAIRS

George had another favorite part of the house!

He loved to go upstairs to one of the bedrooms.

Ed shared his bedroom with his brother Jim. That is where George liked to go the most!

Jim played guitar. He also sang songs when he played! Ed would try to sing along with him. Sometimes their dad and brother Jerry would join them in the room and they would all sing together. Their family loved to sing!

George loved to watch them. He would listen very hard. He would turn his head to the side, as thought that helped him to hear better.

Sometimes he would sit there for a really long time.

Sometimes, he would make sounds as if he was trying to sing along too! He truly thought he was one of the humans!

Then, one day, a startling thing happened!

Some of the children were playing baseball in the yard.

George was gone about three days this time! He had not been home for a while!

Suddenly, a large flock of black crows flew overhead. All of a sudden, they landed on the trees in the small orchard near the house.

They were so many that the branches of every tree seemed very full!

The children did not know what to think!

They started calling. "George! George!" Again, they called. "George! George!"

Suddenly, one of the crows flew up into the air from one of the tree branches!

He circled up and over the children's heads twice!

Slowly he landed on the young boy's shoulder!

Ed was really surprised! He was also very happy!

George stayed for the longest time. He flew from one child to another. He took time to whisper and caw to each of them!

He put his beak against one of their ears and rested it there almost like shaking hands to say hello!

Then, suddenly, George surprised everyone again! He flew straight up into the air!

The other crows followed him as they flew up into the air too!

George called, "Caw, caw!" Then they all flew away as suddenly as they came!

The surprises for the day weren't over yet! It was as if George was beginning to find out that he had two families—the human one with his pet friends—and his crow family!

Early that night, something else special happened! There was a peck, peck, pecking at the upstairs window! It was someone tap, tap, tapping with a small coin on the glass!

Ed ran to the window and opened it!

There was George waiting to come in!
I was the first time that George ever asked to come in like that!

It was really a surprise—a pleasant surprise!

When the window was opened, George hopped in!

He made all kinds of sounds from his throat as though he wanted the boys to sing with him!

He turned his head one way—and—then another!

Sometimes he strutted back and forth across the top of the desk as though it was a stage!

George made lots of sounds as if he had lots to say!

After a while, he spread his wings and hopped to the floor.

Then, he waddled over to the door.

George wanted to go downstairs! He did not hop down the stairs this time. Instead, he spread his wings and glided down over the staircase—made a sharp right turn and flew over to the living room mantle!

He seemed so excited at his new found ability to come and go where he wanted to be at the moment!

He visited with everyone!

George set a new habit for himself.

From that time on, on a fairly regular basis, a flock of crows would fly overhead. Ed would call our, "George!"

The other crows would continue to fly wherever they were going!

But, not George!

He would circle down from the flock and land on the shoulders of one of the children. That was always so exciting!

He also made lots of visits—to the upstairs bedroom—by tap, tap, tapping on the glass!

HOW ABOUT THOSE CHICKENS

George was full of tricks. He was just beginning to show a few of them!

He was becoming a big tease!

It was very hard to keep from laughing at the things he would do—and—he seemed to want to make you laugh!

One of his favorite things was to play a game with the chickens on the small garden farm!

Along with the grain that the family fed to the chickens every day, they also fed old scraps of bread.

They would first break each slice of bread into pieces!

Then they would scatter the pieces on the ground for the chickens to eat.

One day Jan was out feeding these scraps of bread to the chickens.

Suddenly, George appeared from nowhere!

He was good at that by now!

He watched the chickens go after the bread crumbs for a while.

He seemed to notice how they would run after a scrap piece.

When most of the scraps were gone, the chickens would start to tug at the remaining scrap pieces with each other! The chicken that was the quickest would win out and get the last remaining scrap!

All of that would change with George when he was around! That was when he would have fun with a game he made up on his own!

He would often sit on the roof or a shed and watch the chickens scurry after the scraps.

Then when all of those chickens would rush for those last few pieces of scraps—the game was on!

Show time!

When there was just one single morsel left, George dove for it!

He would pick it up in his beak—then fly a short distance away from the chickens.

Next—he would drop it to the ground and watch the race!

The chickens would scurry as fast as they could for that one last single crumb!

Just before the chickens got there—George would fly up and dart at that same scrap!

His timing was so good—he always got there before the chickens!

He would then fly away with it and drop it another time.

Again the chickens would race after this last remaining crumb of bread.

Again—George would fly at it and pick it up and drop it again—a short ways away. This would go on over and over again—until George tired of the game for the day and the chickens had had their share of exercise!

It was like a race for the chickens!

For George—it was like—I'll bet you can't catch me!

Then—George sat there as if he were laughing at his own funny joke! Everyone who saw it laughed too—very hard!

One time he tried his trick on Goose! But Goose didn't want to play. Goose also let George know he didn't want to be teased!

George understood!

TEASE, TEASE

George was just getting started!

He just kept inventing new games! It is hard to remember them all—there were so many!

Another time he teased the father of the family!

The dad was building a chimney. He bent over and took a small package from his pocket. Then he put it on the ground next to him!

There was a swish and a blur! George swooped down out of nowhere! He was really good at coming out of nowhere these days!

He settled on the ground—near the dad!

Then—as quick as a blink—George darted toward the dad's small package! The teasing crow grabbed it was his beak like a thief!

Then off he flew—just like with the chickens.

George dropped the packaged only a short way away!

Can you guess what happened next?
Just like the chickens, the father ran after the package!

And, again, just like the chickens, George got there first!

Then, again, just like the chickens—George picked it up and flew away with it, but only far enough so the father could not get there too quickly.

The dad tried three times to get his package back!

He just was not fast enough to catch the crafty bird!

George flew up to the roof with the package – and caw—cawed!

George may have been laughing, but the dad did not think it was funny any more!

George was really smart. He knew it!

George dropped the package right away so the dad could pick it up!

Then, like only good friends do—they looked at each other—dad on the ground and George on the roof where it was safe!

The dad laughed!

George seemed to laugh right back!

He apparently thought he was safe after the dad's laugh. George lifted from the roof and circled a few times. Then he gently landed on the father's shoulder.

The dad sat down with George still sitting there. It must have been fifteen minutes or so before either one moved! It just seemed like they carried on a conversation with the dad talking to George—and George with his beak by the dad's ear.

What makes this part of this true adventure even more fun—is that the dad also had a reputation as a big tease!

TEASING SOME MORE

One day George decided it was time to tease the mother too!

Monday was always washing the clothes day if the weather was nice.

Clothes driers did not exist in those days.

And, since it was sunny out, the mom decided to wash some of the clothes and hang them outside to dry.

A long piece of white rope was stretched between some poles which were a fair distance apart. This was so that when the clothes were hung over them, the bottom of the clothing would be at least several feet above the ground and be able to dry for the air out of doors.

The clothes were held in place by wooden clothes pins. The clothes pins were slipped were slipped over the clothes to hold them on the line by pinching them like two wooden fingers!

So, the mom washed the white sheets and other white things.

Suddenly it started to rain!

The ground became very wet. There were puddles everywhere and lots of mud.

The mom was pretty patient! She left the wet things sitting in a wash basket.

Then, when it stopped raining, she went outside to hang the wet clothes on the line to dry.

She had just finished hanging the last nice white bed sheet on the line—and turned and went back into the house!

All of a sudden—you guessed it!

There was this tell tale Caw Caw of George ringing through the outside air!

It was unmistakably his call!

It was as if George was teasing the mother as loud as he could! She was inside the house! He was outside of the house!

The mom ran to the kitchen window!

Then without putting on the boots she wore when she hung the clothes out to dry—she raced out the kitchen door!

"Scram!—Scoot!—Noooooooooo! George.—stop it!"

Her voice called out!

It was too late!

There he was!

George was picking off the clothes pins with his beak. He dropped them down into the mud below—one by one!

One by one the white bed sheet and the other white clothes fell down into the mud!

What a mess!

The mom was not very happy about this at all!

She called Ed. "This is your bird," she said—as she looked right at the boy! "Its your crow! Its only fair that you help me get the mud out of these clothes!"

And the boy did!

He loved his mom!

And, she loved him too!

Luckily the mom had a sense of humor. A week or so after it was all over she laughed about it and told the story many, many times over the years! Every time she told it she laughed heartily—and so did every one else!

George had a lot of other tricks too!

He would move pencils around—and other small objects when he was in the house!

Then George started to collect things that were shinny and then hide them somewhere!

No one dared to leave coins lay around or paper clips!

One time—a ten dollar bill even disappeared from the kitchen—and was never found!

Regardless of how he loved to tease—George never seemed to try this with Sandy or Tiger!

George never quite tired of sitting on Sandy's back. Every now and then, when he stayed over night, you'd find him resting on the back of his favorite perch!

Sandy never seemed to mind!

Sandy never grew tired of George of Tiger!

Neither did his family of people!

SANDY

One day Sandy surprised everyone at the family's home!

Early one morning, she had seven of the tiniest, cuddliest little puppies!

Together, they had fourteen sparkling eyes that couldn't see yet

They had twenty-eight slender legs that wiggled almost as fast as their tiny slender tails!

Their little tongues wanted to lick every person around!

The family was so very happy!

So was Sandy!

Sandy looked up at the family as if to say, "How is that?

Ed had a little secret he whispered to Sandy when her puppies were born!

He named one of the cute little ones—**"George"**!

CPSIA information can be obtained at www.ICGtesting.com
Printed in the USA
LVOW05s0921110514

385281LV00002B/596/P